Running City Hall

Running City Hall

Municipal Administration in America

DAVID L. MARTIN

THE UNIVERSITY OF ALABAMA PRESS
University, Alabama

Library of Congress Cataloging in Publication Data

Martin, David L.
    Running city hall.

    Includes bibliographies and index.
    1. Municipal government—United States. I. Title.
JS331.M287   352'.00724'0973   81-14646
ISBN 0-8173-0154-2   AACR2
ISBN 0-8173-0155-0 (pbk.)

To the memories of

my grandfather, a city councilman,

and my father, a fireman, who first

introduced me to the machinations

at city hall

Contents

Contents

Contents

Running City Hall

1: The City in American History

The city is a political organization for local self-government. The word "municipal" is derived from a Latin word designating certain towns which were given special privileges by the Roman Empire. Today a municipality is an incorporated entity with its own separate government, as opposed to unincorporated communities or settlements under a larger political jurisdiction such as a county or state. Some incorporated municipalities may be classified as cities, towns, or villages, depending on the size, but all have their own government.

Colonial Cities

In the United States, many municipalities existed before statehood or even the nation. In fact, the first American political organization for self-government, the Mayflower Compact, was made by the Pilgrims before they got off the ship:

> Having undertaken for the glory of God . . . and the honor of our King and Country, a voyage to plant the first colony in the northern parts of Virginia, we do . . . solemnly and mutually in the presence of God and of one another, . . . combine ourselves together into a civil body politic, for our better ordering and preservation, and . . . to enact and frame such just and equal laws, ordinances, acts, . . . and offices from time to time, as shall be thought most . . . convenient for the general good of the colony; unto which we promise all due submission and obedience. In witness whereof we have undersigned our names, Cape Cod, 11th of November, in the reign of our sovereign King James, the year of Our Lord 1620.

Incorporation of a modern city has much the same purpose of "better ordering," and this concept of a civic association for self-government is in distinct contrast to Spanish colonies directly ruled by the mother country (despite the slogan of St. Augustine, founded in 1565: "America's oldest city").

Five natural harbors determined the location of the principal colonial cities: New York (1609); Boston (1630); Newport (1639); Charleston (1670); Philadelphia (1682). The New England towns grew outward from the common to encompass the surrounding farmland. In contrast, Charleston was a planned community with a regular grid pattern and grew inward from the fifty-odd plantations surrounding it. These two growth patterns—outward expansion and growing together by surrounding settlements—can be seen in today's increasing urbanization.

The corporate, or governmental, existence of the colonial city was based upon a charter granted by the royal governor or by the proprietor of the colony. Municipal authority was concentrated in a council made up of the mayor, aldermen, and councilmen. Possessing both executive and judicial powers, the city's legislative body was bicameral, only the councilmen being directly elected, with the aldermen chosen by the councilmen or perpetuating themselves by deciding their own successors.[1] The mayor, usually appointed for a year, from among the aldermen by the aldermen or by the colonial governor, presided over the council but had little executive power. To vote, citizens had to be men who owned property and met racial and even religious qualifications, which reduced the municipal electorate to a relatively small percentage of the inhabitants.

Because of the city's limited functions (social welfare was a responsibility of the church), revenues were sufficient. The property tax furnished income, as did fees from municipal docks, ferries, and other enterprises. New York used the special assessment (whereby property owners pay for adjacent improvements) for the first time in the late seventeenth century. Citizens were expected to volunteer their services and equipment, which included a fire bucket in each house. Colonial balls and other benefit drives were held to raise money for public purposes, such as buying a fire engine. In short, many of the main municipal revenue sources of today were established in colonial times.

The Revolution and Jacksonian Democracy

If colonial government does not sound democratic and equalitarian, remember that the American Revolution started in the cities. During the Revolution, obviously a charter granted in the name of the Crown had no standing; it was replaced by the legislative bodies of the states or by revolutionary councils. Where the city had formerly been the creature of the executive will in the central government, it now became a creature of the legislative will. Some important municipal offices were filled by the new state legislatures. We will explore the relationship of cities to states in the next chapter.

The structure of municipal government was not drastically affected by the Revolution; the mayor was still often indirectly elected. City hall tended to be dominated by a rather select circle of merchants and professional people. In a predominantly agrarian society, many shared Thomas Jefferson's view that "the mobs of great cities add just so much to the support of pure government, as do sores do to the strength of the human body."[2] It was not until the late 1820s, in Jacksonian Democracy, that the rights of every man were extended to local government. Property restrictions for officeholding and the exercise of the franchise were removed, and most mayors became popularly elected. Virtually all municipal offices were made elective, usually with the only qualifications being the number of votes, since according to the Jacksonian creed any average citizen was competent to perform any public office. This belief has had an important influence upon modern municipal management; the will of the people was expressed at frequent elections, with many elective administrators each independent of one another and a diffusion of executive authority in separately elected boards and commissions. Structurally, this weak-mayor system, examined further in chapter 5, dominated municipal government for a century and is still frequently found in cities today.

Machines and Bosses

Following the Civil War, cities rapidly expanded, swelled by migrants from rural areas and immigrants and by the new network of railroads. Into this atomized power vacuum stepped the political boss, with power centrally wielded in his hands: Boss Tweed in New York City, King McManes in Philadelphia, and Col. Ed Butler in St. Louis are well-known examples. Distinguishing characteristics of boss rule, which flourished until World War II were several.

First, the boss, often building upon ethnic affiliations, organized tight party control, including nominations, to win offices at each election (see box). Second, the classic boss usually did not hold public office, being accountable only to his followers in "the machine" and hence invulnerable to external political attack. In exchange for votes, to fill all the offices of Jacksonian Democracy, the boss delivered the goods in the form of social welfare and public improvements. He used patronage (city jobs) to control votes, and he held out the promise of lucrative city contracts to build support among businessmen. The result, in its best form, was unprecedented building of needed public works and, at its most corrupt, city halls resembling palaces, with price tags to match. After all, the boss had to get his payoff from construction costs.

In this excerpt Boss George Washington Plunkitt describes organizing a party machine in

How to Become a Statesman

There's thousands of young men in this city who will go to the polls for the first time next November. Among them will be many who have watched the careers of successful men in politics, and who are longin' to make names and fortunes for themselves at the same game. It is to these youths that I want to give advice. First, let me say that I am in a position to give what the courts call expert testimony on the subject. I don't think you can easily find a better example than I am of success in politics. After forty years' experience at the game I am—well, I'm George Washington Plunkitt. Everybody knows what figure I cut in the greatest organization on earth, and if you hear people say that I've laid away a million or so since I was a butcher's boy in Washington Market, don't come to me for an indignant denial. I'm pretty comfortable, thank you.

Now, havin' qualified as an expert, as the lawyers say, I am goin' to give advice free to the young men who are goin' to cast their first votes, and who are lookin' forward to political glory and lots of cash. Some young men think they can learn how to be successful in politics from books, and they cram their heads with all sorts of college rot. They couldn't make a bigger mistake. Now, understand me, I ain't sayin' nothin' against colleges. I guess they'll have to exist as long as there's bookworms, and I suppose they do some good in a certain way, but they don't count in politics. In fact, a young man who has gone through the college course is handicapped at the outset. He may succeed in politics, but the chances are 100 to 1 against him.

Another mistake: some young men think that the best way to prepare for the political game is to practice speakin' and becomin' orators. That's all wrong. We've got some orators in Tammany Hall, but they're chiefly ornamental. . . . The men who rule have practiced keepin' their tongues still, not exercisin' them. So you want to drop the orator idea unless you mean to go into politics just to perform the skyrocket act.

Now, I've told you what not to do; I guess I can explain best what to do to succeed in politics by tellin' you what I did. After goin' through the apprenticeship of the business while I was a boy by workin' around the district headquarters and hustlin' about the polls on election day, I set out when I cast my first vote to win fame and money in New York City politics. Did I offer my services to the district leader as a stump-speaker? Not much. The woods are always full of speakers. Did I get up a book on municipal government and show it to the leader? I wasn't such a fool. What I did was to get some marketable goods before goin' to the leaders. What do I mean by marketable goods? Let me tell you: I had a cousin, a young man who didn't take any particular interest in politics. I went to him and said: "Tommy, I'm goin' to be a politician, and I want to get a followin'; can I count on you?" He said: "Sure, George." That's how I started in business. I got a marketable commodity—one vote. Then I went to the district leader and told him I could command two votes on election day, Tommy's and my own. He smiled on me and told me to go ahead. If I had offered him a speech or a bookful of learnin', he would have said, "Oh, forget it!"

That was beginnin' business in a small way, wasn't it? But that is the only way to become a real lastin' statesman. I soon branched out. Two young men in the flat next to mine were school friends, I went to them, just as I went to Tommy, and they agreed to stand by me. Then I had a followin' of three voters and I began to get chesty. Whenever I dropped into district headquarters, everybody shook hands with me, and the leader one day honored me by lightin' a match for my cigar. And so it went on like a snowball rollin' down a hill. I worked the flathouse that I lived in from the basement to the top floor, and I got about a dozen young men to follow me. Then I tackled the next house and so on down the block and around the corner. Before long I had sixty men back of me, and formed the George Washington Plunkitt Association.

What did the district leader say then when I called at headquarters? I didn't have to call at headquarters. He came after me and said: "George, what do you want? If you don't see what you want, ask for it. Wouldn't you like to have a job or two in the departments for your friends?" I said: "I'll think it over; I haven't yet decided what the George Washington Plunkitt Association will do in the next campaign." You ought to have seen how I was courted and petted then by the leaders of the rival organizations. I had marketable goods and there was bids for them from all sides, and I was a risin' man in politics. As time went on, and my association grew, I thought I would like to go to the Assembly. I just had to hint at what I wanted, and three different organizations offered me the nomination. Afterwards, I went to the Board of Aldermen, then to the State Senate, then became leader of the district, and so on up and up till I became a statesman.

That is the way and the only way to make a lastin' success in politics. If you are goin' to cast your first vote next November and want to go into politics, do as I did. Get a followin', if it's only one man, and then go to the district leader and say: "I want to join the organization. I've got one man who'll follow me through thick and thin." The leader won't laugh at your one-man followin'. He'll shake your hand warmly, offer to propose you for membership in his club, take you down to the corner for a drink and ask you to call again. But go to him and say: "I took first prize at college in Aristotle; I can recite all Shakespeare forwards and backwards; there ain't nothin' in science that ain't as familiar to me as blockades on the elevated roads and I'm the real thing in the way of silver-tongued orators." What will he answer? He'll probably say: "I guess you are not to blame for your misfortunes, but we have no use for you here."

From *Plunkitt of Tammany Hall: A Series of Very Plain Talks on Very Practical Politics, delivered by ex-senator George Washington Plunkitt, the Tammany Philosopher, from his rostrum—the New York County Court House boot-black stand*, recorded by William L. Riordan (New York: McClure, Phillips, 1905), pp. 13–18.

The Age of the Reformers

When British ambassador Lord Bryce wrote *The American Common-wealth* in 1888, he concluded that "municipal government is the one conspicuous failure of American democracy." Journalists such as Lincoln Steffens (*The Shame of the Cities*, 1904), were muckrakers who revealed the extent of municipal corruption: graft, bribery, waste, and electoral manipulation. Starting in the 1880s, some politicians were elected as reformers: Buffalo mayor Grover Cleveland went all the way to the White House.

What did the reformers want? Typical is the 1894 platform of the National Municipal League. Many of these planks remain reform issues today:

● Simplified municipal organization to reintegrate the administrative fragmentation resulting from Jacksonian Democracy. This "short ballot" movement wanted to reduce the number of elective offices to important posts readily identifiable to the voters and hence to break the electoral grip of the political machines.

● A strengthened office of the mayor, to be achieved by increasing his management powers as the city's chief executive. Under a strong-mayor plan, he would be held accountable for city administration.

● Municipal ownership of utilities would not only give citizens cheaper service in the "age of the robber barons" but would also reduce favoritism in granting exclusive and profitable franchises to private operators favored by the machine. The issues involved in present day municipal ownership are presented in chapter 10.

● Free public services, such as parks, streetlights, libraries, and fire protection, were goals for reform also designed to win electoral support from the urban masses.

● Professionalism of public employment and development of a career merit system were desired not only to improve municipal services but to attack the patronage base of the machines.

● Municipal home rule, or the right of a city to run its own affairs largely free of state legislative interference, was introduced in the Missouri constitution of 1875. Adopted by a number of states, as we shall see in the next chapter, it also weakened the ties by which the city machine delivered the party vote to the state administration in return for favors granted, including tolerance by the state of machine corruption.

● Nonpartisanship and at-large election of council members were designed to break the power base of the political machines. Without party identification by each candidate's name, the machine could not control the nominating process nor have its followers vote a straight party ticket. At-large elections from the city as a whole allowed the reformers to bring their strength to bear and to undercut the political machine's block-by-block geographical organization, described by George Washington Plunkitt.

• The devices of popular democracy allowed outraged citizens to participate directly in civic affairs. The initiative enables a certain number of citizens to petition that a proposed law or an amendment to the city charter be placed directly upon the ballot to be decided by the voters, thus bypassing the municipal governing body. The referendum allows voters to review legislation proposed by the city government to decide whether it should go into effect. The recall permits elective officials to be voted out of office prior to the expiration of their terms.

• City planning was not merely a "city beautiful" movement by reformers but a desire for orderly civil growth and elimination of health hazards and corrupt private land speculation.

• Efficiency, economy, and responsibility in government, or the "business approach," was the battle cry of the reformers, who were mainly concerned businessmen and taxpayers appalled by civic waste.

Most of the old-time bosses disappeared by the time of World War II. Despite the reformers' organizational remodeling, however, Frank ("I am the Law") Hague, on the Jersey City Commission, and Tom Pendergast in Kansas City, Missouri, which had a city manager form of government, were proof that a machine can flourish regardless of the organization structure. Chicago mayor Richard Daley, who died in office in 1976, was cited as the "last boss" because of his control of the Cook County Democratic organization. In addition to controlling the party, Mayor Daley held public office, and his reelection to a sixth four-year term in 1975 underscores the celebrated observation "Chicago ain't ready for reform yet." Pictures taken by a civic reform group demonstrated that the patronage payroll was huge. Five service department workers were needed to replace a single streetlight: an electrician on a ladder removed the globe; a second electrician unscrewed and replaced the bulb; a third worker held the ladder; a fourth stood by to provide any needed tools; and a foreman supervised the other four. Why was Mayor Daley one of the most durable figures on the American political scene? A newspaper poll revealed that while only half the voters believed what Daley said, 84 percent believed that he could get things done, and 77 percent thought he was doing a good job; the election results returned him to office.[3]

"Service to the people" was Boss Plunkitt's watchword, and if he made money for himself on the side, why, that was a privilege of office. Only the techniques have changed: computerized graft was recently uncovered showing that employees of a Long Island town paid 1 percent of their annual salaries to the Republican party and the computerized record was used to enforce contributions from those holding town jobs.[4]

Cities Today

The number of municipalities has grown slowly, compared with special districts which provide service functions such as water, sanitation, fire protection, transit, and public housing. The number of cities varies greatly by state, depending upon incorporation laws (see table 1.1): Illinois has more than 1,200 municipalities, but Hawaii and the District of Columbia have 1 city each. An important fact is that most municipalities are very small: half of all the cities in the United States have a population of 1,000 or less. This may mean a high degree of informality in American city government.

Table 1.1. A Statistical Profile of American Cities

	Municipalities						
	1977	1972	1962	1952	1942		
	18,862	18,517	18,000	16,807	16,220		
Population size	100,000 or more	50,000 –99,999	25,000 –49,000	10,000 –24,999	5,000 –9,999	1,000 –4,999	Under 1,000
Number of cities	163	230	514	1,212	1,461	5,668	9,614

Note: Data shown are for 1977.

Source: U.S. Bureau of the Census, Census of Governments, 1977, vol. 1, *Governmental Organization* (Washington, D.C.: U.S. Government Printing Office, 1978).

Such wide variations in the numbers and sizes of cities present twin problems of growth and government. The built-up urban area can be clearly seen from the air and a number of growth patterns on land use have been identified (see figure 1.1). Parkin and Burgess's concentric circles view, based on the growth of Chicago, has the central business district at the core, surrounded by rings of different land use. Hoyt's sector theory explains land use by dominant function. Maurice Davies sees urban growth occurring along transportation arteries from the core, resulting in star-shaped patterns. The Harris and Ullman multiple-nuclei thesis sees clusterings of specialized areas, or concentrated diverse use such as regional shopping centers. The patterns drawn are models; the configuration of a particular city will depend on its situation.

The government of urban areas may be fragmented among several governmental jurisdictions: counties, municipalities, and special purpose districts. Depending on its location, a municipality may be a core

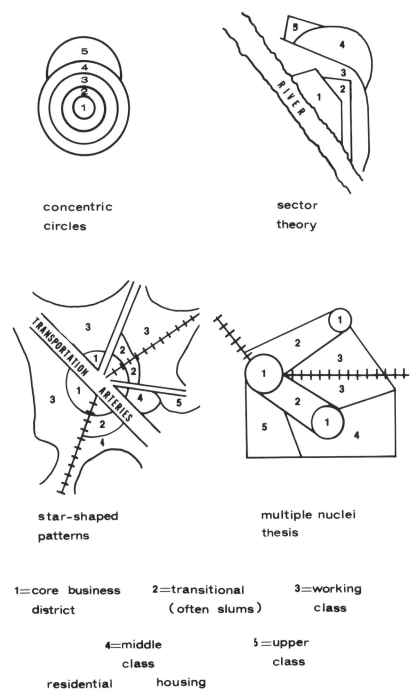

concentric
circles

sector
theory

star-shaped
patterns

multiple nuclei
thesis

1=core business   2=transitional   3=working
   district   (often slums)   class

4=middle   5=upper
   class   class

residential   housing

Figure 1.1 Patterns of Urban Development

city, a satellite suburb, or a rural town. The view from city hall will be different in each.

The remaining chapters will examine the political dynamics of municipal administration. Chapter 2 describes the legal foundations upon which municipalities operate, and chapter 3, on metropolitics, examines relationships within the larger community. Chapter 4 explores city politics, and chapter 5, municipal leadership. Work at city hall, public safety, and municipal social services are subjects treated in chapters 7, 8, and 9. Chapter 10 concludes by discussing how public works, transportation, and planning shape the city's future.

Notes

1. The terms "aldermen" or "councilmen" are still legally used to describe the members of a council, which is now a single body. (The only important exception is New York City's Board of Estimate, whose budgetary powers make it function like a second house.)

2. *Notes on Virginia* (1782), reprinted in *The Portable Thomas Jefferson*, ed. Merrill D. Peterson (New York: Viking Press, 1975), p. 217. The quotation is from "Query 19; Manufactures" of the unpaginated original.

3. William E. Farrell, "Daley Is Silent on Seeking Sixth Term as Mayor," *New York Times*, October 7, 1974, p. 22.

4. Mary Breansted, "L.I. Officials Accused of Using Computer to List Pay Kickbacks," *New York Times*, December 5, 1974, p. 1.

For Further Reading

Gist, Noel P., and Fava, Sylvia F. *Urban Society*. 5th ed. New York: Crowell, 1964. (Discusses patterns of urban growth)

Glaab, Charles N. *The American City—A Documentary History*. Homewood, Ill.: Dorsey Press, 1963. (Readings on colonial cities to the present)

International City Management Association. *The Municipal Year Book*. Washington, D.C., 19–. (Published annually, it contains articles written by experts in municipal government and is the main reference book of current information.)

Riordon, William L., ed. *Plunkitt of Tammany Hall*. New York: E. P. Dutton, 1963. (Reprints Plunkitt's observations on politics)

Robinson, Frank S. *Machine Politics: A Study of Albany's O'Connells*. New York: Transaction Books, 1977. (A modern city political organization)

Teaford, Jon C. *The Municipal Revolution in America, 1650–1828*. Chicago: University of Chicago Press, 1975.

U.S. Bureau of the Census. *Census of Governments, 1977*. vol. 1, *Governmental Organization*. Washington, D.C.: U.S. Government Printing Office, 1978. (A basic statistical reference that was published at five-year intervals [1972, 1977, etc.])

2: A Creation of the State:
Cities and Municipal Law

Whatever a city and its officials wish to accomplish depends upon its authority to act. Those coming into office quickly learn that their powers to act are circumscribed by the complex body of state statutes and court decisions which make up municipal law. The urban political arena is defined by legal interpretation.

Given the American heritage of popular sovereignty and natural rights expounded by Jefferson two centuries ago, one might assume that there is an inherent "right" to local self-government.[1] To be sure, a number of colonial settlements were founded—and were self-governing—before the establishment of states in which they were located. But the powers assumed by the state legislatures during the American revolution and the political benefits to be reaped from rapidly growing cities led to extensive state controls over local governments by the mid-nineteenth century. State intervention was prompted not only by patronage and partisan considerations but also by the appeal of civic reformers seeking to curb local corruption.

City-State Relationships

The prevailing legal view of the city as an instrumentality or subdivision of the state was neatly summarized in an 1868 opinion by Justice John F. Dillon of the Iowa Supreme Court. Dillon's Rule reads:

> It is a general and undisputed proposition of law that a municipal corporation possesses and can exercise the following powers, and no others: First, those granted in express words; second, those necessarily or fairly implied in or incident to the powers expressly granted; third, those essential to the accomplishment of the declared objects and purposes of the corporation—not simply convenient, but indispensable. Any fair, reasonable, substantial doubt concerning the existence of power is resolved by the courts against the corporation, and the power is denied.[2]

The practical importance of Dillon's Rule is that the city government must prove that the activity it wishes to pursue is within this definition; otherwise the power will be denied by the courts. Dillon's reasoning was this:

> Municipal corporations owe their origin to, and derive their powers from the state legislature. It breathes into them the breath of life, without which they cannot exist. As it created, so it may destroy. If it may destroy, it may abridge the control.[3]

This view of cities as "the mere tenants at will of the legislature" was refuted by other state judges, notably by Judge Thomas M. Cooley, who stated, "Local government is a matter of absolute right, and the State cannot take it away."[4] However, this position was never widely recognized by the state judiciary, and Dillon's Rule became the traditional doctrine. Thus, when the city of Trenton, New Jersey, sought federal protections against impairment of contracts to retain water rights which the state wanted, the U.S. Supreme Court ruled:

> The City is a political subdivision of the State, created as a convenient agency for the exercise of such of the governmental powers of the State as may be entrusted to it. . . . The State, therefore, at its pleasure may modify or withdraw all such powers, . . . expand or contract the territorial area, unite the whole or a part of it with another municipality, repeal the charter and destroy the corporation. All this may be done, conditionally or unconditionally, with or without the consent of the citizens, or even against their protest. In all these respects the State is supreme, and its legislative body, conforming its action to the state constitution, may do as it will, unrestrained by any provision of the Constitution of the United States. . . .[5]

The scope of legal authority enjoyed by the municipalities in each state depends upon whether they have been granted constitutional or statutory home rule (discussed below) and the interpretive rulings made by that state's courts.

The strict constitutional construction given by Dillon's Rule of municipalities as creations of state sovereignty has meant only a few limitations of the state's plenary power. First, there may be a state constitutional prohibition against "special" or "local" legislation applying only to a specific city. Such constitutional provisions were designed to prevent legislatures from passing "ripper bills" discriminating against one town or else giving special favors to another. This has been circumvented by the technique of "classification" whereby an ostensibly general statute applies to all cities falling into a category defined in the act. The favorite means of classification is by population category: "This act applies to all cities in the state between 500,000 and

1,000,000 persons." Sometimes classification may be as narrow as a few hundred people, and only one city falls into the narrowly defined class. The courts will generally uphold classification if:

• The classification is germane to the purpose of the law and based on substantial distinctions making one class different from another. (For instance, a city license requirement for plumbers might be invalidated if it were based on general population but upheld if it were based on the number of plumbers to be licensed and the fee charged on the amount of business that they do within the city.)

• The classification established must be based on existing circumstances rather than on future possibilities (or else the courts will void it as moot).

• The classification applies equally to each unit within the class. (A city reaching 100,000 population must comply with the requirements for cities in that category.)

• The classification is based on characteristics sufficiently different to draw the distinction between separate classes. (Such acts usually begin with a recital of unique circumstances that necessitate local legislation.)

A second and also narrow limitation on state power over municipalities comes from the protection granted by the United States Constitution. The Supreme Court has retreated from its 1933 ruling by Justice Cardozo that "a municipal corporation, created by a state for the better ordering of government, has no privileges or immunities under the federal constitution which it may invoke in opposition to the will of its creator."[6] The Supreme Court's intervention has been mainly in voting rights cases under the Fourteenth and Fifteenth Amendments, of which the *Gomillion* v. *Lightfoot* (1960) case is typical. During the civil rights struggle the Alabama legislature redrew the city boundaries of Tuskegee with twenty-seven different sides so as to exclude all but a handful of black registered voters. Both the federal district court and the circuit court of appeals, following Dillon's Rule, had thrown out the blacks' suit before the U.S. Supreme Court on appeal held the redrawing to be unconstitutional.[7]

Municipal Powers

The powers exercised by a municipality, whether under narrow judicial interpretation of Dillon's Rule or a more flexible grant of home rule (see below), fall into three major categories:

- Corporate powers include
  (a) perpetual succession: the officeholders may change, but legally there remains a mayor and common council or city commission of the town
  (b) the legal ability of the city to sue (and be sued, as discussed in the section on tort liability)
  (c) the legal ability of the city to make contracts and to acquire and hold property.
- Governmental powers include such compulsory activity as policing, taxation, regulating commerce, and other enforcement executed by the municipality as an agent for the state.
- Proprietary powers are undertaken on behalf of local inhabitants for which the city is providing services in a variety of money-making enterprises, charging fees to users rather than general taxes. Since the city may be in competition with private businesses in providing services (such as garbage collection), its authority may be more limited and its liability for damages greater.

The incorporated municipality as a general purpose government is thus usually distinguished from quasi-corporations of local government serving as administrative agents of the state, such as townships, school, and other special districts limited by purpose. While the municipality's powers are strictly construed, civic unanimity on an issue can muster considerable political muscle in support of legal authority to act.

Forms of State Control

The states monitor municipal activity in three major areas: legislative, administrative, and judicial.

Legislative prescription and supervision are exercised through:

- Enactment of statutes. General statutes relating to municipalities usually occupy a full volume in the state's legal code, while local legislation may consume a considerable portion of the legislative workload.
- State appropriations for subsidies and grants in aid. The proportion of state financial support for municipalities varies with the state and size of the recipient city. Cities which actively seek financial aid for their needs from the state must also accept state policy direction. Financial support is probably the strongest inducement for cities to meet state standards, although pressure from the legislature may prompt local protest against "outside interference" in civic affairs.
- Legislative investigations focus public attention on local corruption, city needs, and other urban problems.

• There are usually standing committees in each house or legislative commissions on municipal government. They may hire expert staff and make reports along with the bills they consider. Sometimes a special or "select" committee on specific city problems (such as a select committee on city welfare costs) will hold hearings around the state and will report its recommendations back to the legislature.

Finally, it should be noted that while reapportionment of state legislatures has given more representation to large cities, it has also meant many more voices (not always in agreement) speaking for urban areas. Some core cities have encountered more opposition from suburban representatives than from rural legislators before reapportionment. In order to promote legislation enabling the city to act (local bills, state financial assistance, authorization to participate in federal programs), a great amount of city officials' time must be spent to secure the support of the local delegation to the state legislature. The importance of politics in this task is easily seen, considering that local legislators are frequently of opposite parties, may want to run for mayor at the next election, or suspect city politicians of coveting their legislative seats.

Administrative Controls. While some states have created departments of local affairs,[8] most state oversight is on a functional basis: the state highway department deals with city planning, engineering, or street departments. Techniques used by the state bureaucracy range from persuasion to coercion. Frequently used devices in ascending order of state supervision are:

• Reports and inspections. The state may ask for periodic reports from local officials or may send around its own inspectors (to take samples of the community water supply, for example). State inspectors may be used if the city complains that too much of its manpower is required for state reports. Standardized reporting gives the state the data base necessary for policy formulation and to spot areas of potential trouble and allows city officials, the media, and interest groups to compile a body of comparable information for reference.

• Advice and technical assistance may be offered as a result of the findings. The advice may be sought informally by a phone call from a city worker needing help or by a formal request that the criminal investigators of the state police help solve a local crime. The state invests many manhours in combating local problems, and this serves as an important local input into operating policies. State technical aid takes several forms. In small communities employees may lack experience; in larger towns, the few highly paid professionals (engineers, planners) that the city can afford are overworked. The state can lend qualified technicians and also expensive equipment for a specialized job. A long-range solution for training (often undertaken in conjunction with state universities) is continuing education courses for municipal employees. State agencies frequently develop curriculum materials for the schools, provide computer checks for missing persons or stolen property, compile and validate civil service exams, do engineering tests for municipalities, and perform other technical tasks at minimal charge or below cost.

• Grants in aid. State financial subsidies act as a carrot rather than as a stick. With a local matching requirement, they are designed to stimulate community expenditures for that purpose. While grants in aid can be withheld if the standards prescribed by state or federal law (when the money comes from Washington) are not complied with, the purpose of financial assistance is to answer the city's critical needs and provide a minimum floor or standard of service. State controls on finance are discussed further in chapter 6.

• State review and approval. State law may provide for compulsory state agency review of local activity. The city may need the state's prior permission (to issue bonds, for instance), and state permits (for construction) may be withheld if the prescribed standards are not met.

• Administrative rules and orders. State agencies generate a wide array of regulations with which the community must comply, ranging from municipal accounting procedures to engineering specifications for public buildings. State agencies can even obtain court orders shutting off a town's water supply until the community spends enough to bring its purification up to safe standards.

• Appointment or removal of officials. Certain city appointments may have to be approved by the state or to meet certain qualifications (e.g., city health officer). In some cases, the state reserves the right to remove city officials without going through impeachment proceedings (for example, in the case of city judges who have run afoul of the law).

• Functional transfers. If the city proves financially unable or inept in the performance of a service, the state may simply transfer responsibility to another unit of local government (such as a special district or the county) or have a state agency take over. Thus education is often in the charge of an independent school board; tax assessment performed by the county; sewerage treatment by a regional sanitary district; and public assistance by a state welfare agency. Municipalities have eagerly sought to be relieved of some of these functions (usually because of the financial burden), but the question of who will assume other services, such as regional planning or rapid transit, remains a hot political issue.

• Substitute administration is an extreme measure when the state takes over because the city is incapacitated. Martial law may be declared by the governor in the wake of natural disasters or civil disorders when the city authorities are unable to cope with the situation. In rare instances of extreme civil corruption, indictment of virtually all city officials has prompted state administration until new (and honest) elections could be held.

The degree of state involvement in local government is determined by continuing political compromise as circumstances change. Americans take a pragmatic approach to service delivery, and the degree of state intervention depends upon the state and the size of the municipality and its needs.

Judicial Controls. Because of the subordinate legal position of municipal governments, controversies over their powers are always being litigated. Local ordinances are subordinate to both federal and state statutes. The preemption doctrine holds that if a state enacts a law covering a topic, the municipality, as a government of delegated powers, cannot pass a contradictory law. Most state constitutions contain a provision like the following: "The legislature shall not have the power to authorize any municipal corporation to pass any laws inconsistent with the general laws of this state."[9] In case of conflict, the judiciary will find that the state law prevails. This causes headaches in local regulation. The city may pass local ordinances which are stricter than the state statute but not unreasonably so.[10] If, for example, a state law says alcoholic beverages may be served from 8:00 A.M. to 2:00 A.M., a local ordinance might reasonably allow the city's bars to be open from ten in the morning to midnight. But narrower restrictions might invite legal challenge. Until the U.S. Supreme Court adopted "community standards" in the definition of obscenity in the early 1970s, many local ordinances were voided as being too restrictive of federal First Amendment freedoms. State preemption remains an issue in such regulatory areas as adult entertainment and prostitution.

Between the strict construction of Dillon's Rule and the necessity to show officials are not acting ultra vires (beyond the scope of their authority), the city has the burden of proving in court that it has the power to act. A favorite tactic of interest groups, corporations or disgruntled citizens to challenge proposed civic policies is to file a taxpayers' suit. This type of class action seeks, on behalf of the plaintiff and others similarly affected, to enjoin the city from committing acts which are illegal or ultra vires and to protect the municipality's interests where its officers have not acted. Successful taxpayer suits have voided franchises and contracts which were not awarded by due process, have blocked municipal expenditures not for public purposes (even compelling officials to make personal restitution of city funds that they illegally spent), have improved city sewage treatment, and have advanced other environmental concerns. While many taxpayers' suits are dismissed by the courts as lacking standing, the threat of such action forces city officials to proceed with caution. Since any nontraditional activity taken by a municipality will invite an ultra vires challenge, cities will frequently arrange a "friendly suit" to validate the action legally before it is undertaken. Such a precaution minimizes subsequent judicial intervention when a taxpayers' suit can tie up in litigation a project half completed. Smaller towns without full-time legal counsel frequently wait until larger cities have gained new powers in a test case and then enact an ordinance similar to the one which was upheld by the courts.

Incorporation: The Birth of a City

Through the nineteenth century, municipalities were incorporated and controlled by an individual special act of the legislature. Some states still use special acts because localities wishing to incorporate prefer tailor-made acts. The major disadvantage of such acts is that state legislatures are deluged by local legislation.

Municipal creation usually occurs with incorporation by general act. The citizens of a community initiate incorporation proceedings. There must be a "sense of community" with a grouping of population. In the words of the Florida Supreme Court: "two elements are essential to [municipal] existence; a community of people, and the territory they occupy. The Legislature can create neither."[11]

However, the state legislature specifies the conditions for incorporation in a general act on municipal formation, such as:

● There must be a minimum number of inhabitants, registered voters, or a minimum population density per square mile. Usually the requisite number of citizens of an unincorporated place petition a court, county board, or other local agency formation commission designated by the state for an order of incorporation. The number of petitioners required by many states is too small, leading to "defensive incorporation" by groups of individuals seeking to avoid annexation by neighboring municipalities or to the creation of low-tax industrial enclaves with names like "City of Industry." Lax statutory requirements for incorporation explain why most American metropolitan areas are fragmented into many separate jurisdictions.

● The proposed municipality must have some area, but usually not too much. Some states require that the property owners of a certain percentage of the affected land signify their consent by signing the petition for incorporation. Some municipal boundaries have acquired peculiar shapes, as a few large landowners did not wish to be included because of city taxes.

● The boundaries must be reasonably compact in form, with a contiguous area. Unlike some special districts which may have separate service areas, all portions of the proposed city must be joined together. Of course, many municipalities have acquired unusually shaped city limits through subsequent annexations of territory.

The incorporation petition goes to a court or board of proper jurisdiction for review (perhaps with public hearings), and if the state's conditions are met, an election must usually be held. If a majority of the votes cast by residents of the petitioning community favor incorporation, the judge or other responsible official issues an order declaring the municipality incorporated.

Besides procedures for incorporation, state general municipal acts may provide for:

• Classification of municipalities by various criteria such as size of population, area, and tax base (financial resources). These may be permissive options (a village under 300 people *may* have a police department) or mandatory obligations (a city over a certain size *must* have a fire department).

• Structural forms of government and policy parameters such as a maximum tax rate which can be levied. Depending on its size, the municipality may have to elect certain officers and appoint others.

• Optional charters that compromise between prescribed structure and home rule. This type of general act provides a smorgasbord of municipal charters with various organizational arrangements: mayor-council, city manager, or options within classification categories. By referendum, the citizens may choose among the forms of government for which their community qualifies.

• The strict interpretation of local powers by Dillon's Rule may be relieved by home rule, which is granted either by legislative enabling act or by statutory or state constitutional provision. Home rule, simply defined, is the power of a local government (city or county) to draft and control its charter, and to run its own local affairs. The arguments for and against home rule are numerous (and are given in the separate box). Briefly, its practical advantage is that it frees the state legislature and the courts from local chores. Disadvantages are popular fears of increased taxation, the possibility that the home rule charter (which serves as a miniconstitution for the city) may be more difficult to change after adoption, and the lack of uniformity among different municipalities. The experience of the more than forty states which grant home rule to at least some of their municipalities is that these powers are most frequently used in the three following areas: licensing and regulation of businesses and land use; financial self-management with respect to taxes levied and borrowing; and reorganization of governmental structure to meet administrative needs.

Home Rule for Municipalities?

Some of the most heated battles fought at state capitals occur between supporters who see home rule powers as a panacea for governmental problems and opponents who view such independence as reckless license. Given the following arguments on each side, which home rule powers would you grant as a state legislator?

Pro

1. Home rule power is necessary to achieve reorganization of government. Local units can alter their structure to meet their individual needs, giving flexibility for management. Offices can be combined or consolidated as necessary to reduce personnel costs. Duplication and unclear overlapping of functions mandated by state law at different times can be streamlined. Local citizens and their elected officials can decide the form of government best suited to their needs.

2. Home rule units may create urban service areas, thus containing the proliferation of special districts. By establishing high service areas at the request of inhabitants and increasing taxes or imposing user charges to pay for these services, creation of single-function governments (independent special districts) can be avoided. Home rule allows increased intergovernmental cooperation between local units: they may freely enter into interjurisdictional agreements, joint contracting, and financing of joint projects.

3. If the state constitution provides that home rule should be "construed liberally," court interference can be avoided. Such a clause avoids a shopping list of home rule powers, leaving munici-

Con

1. Home rule may be defeated on the issue of structural reform. The electorate may lack information or be opposed to a new form of government rather than decide on the merits of home rule itself. Officials who might lose their jobs under reorganization often oppose home rule politically or successfully demand that a new local charter protect their position. Self-determination in matters of governmental structure may not include a substantive grant of regulatory power, meaning reorganization in form but not in operation, where it counts.

2. Home rule necessarily results in lack of uniformity among units of government. If at local option some jurisdictions have home rule powers and others do not, conflicts of applicability will inevitably arise. Eminent domain powers of special districts still take precedence over local home rule zoning ordinances, and state enabling legislation may be necessary to establish special service areas (especially outside city limits).

3. While the courts have followed constitutional provisions to "construe liberally," fights do occur over the precedence of home rule actions. If the state legislature enacts preemptive limitations,

palities free to act as necessary unless there is state legislative preemption. Home rule units have the powers needed to carry out daily governmental functions without being second-guessed by the judiciary after expensive litigation.

4. Home rule provisions can define method(s) for state preemption, concurrent exercise of powers, and identifying a local as opposed to a statewide concern. An alternative is to leave this definition to the legislature or the courts to be decided on case by case, taking individual circumstances into account. Preemption can occur as the need arises, concurrently exercised powers can be shared, and changing circumstances will dictate whether it is a matter for local or statewide concern.

5. Home rule without revenue-raising power is a hollow shell. Home rule units should be allowed flexibility in spending, incurring debt, and the ability to tax themselves to the limit their citizens desire. Financial referendum requirements are ineffective controls for fiscal management because so few voters turn out—unless there is a taxpayers' revolt. Any fiscal irresponsibility is the fault of elected officials, not a consequence of home rule itself.

6. Reorganization allowable under home rule will lead to greater efficiency. Administrative authority can be concentrated in the mayor or city manager, rather than a host of officials separately elected for each function. Home rule flexibility in operational procedures will allow experimentation for greater economy. If the people

home rule units may challenge such restrictions in court. Previous state laws may conflict with actions taken under home rule and could be declared invalid. State legislators may resent judicial interpretation declaring statutes inoperative.

4. The distinction between statewide and local concerns is a source of endless litigation. Home rule becomes what the judges say it is. Political compromises determine the assumption of specific functions by local governments. The legislature can intervene by declaring an area to be of state concern, constantly shifting the balance of power. Efforts to allocate functions according to primacy of state or local interests result in an arbitrary and incomplete division of responsibilities.

5. Home rule with taxing authority erodes the state's revenue base and can lead to irresponsible local spending without state financial oversight. Home rule appears as a blank check to taxpayers who are reluctant to let local government's hands dig deeper into their pockets and are skeptical about how the money will be spent at local discretion. Public opinion surveys taken after home rule referenda appear to indicate that a major reason for rejection is voters' fear that home rule would mean new or increased taxes.

6. Incumbent officeholders and groups who feel they have a favorable position under the existing system are likely to oppose home rule. To gain political support necessary for adoption, the charter may specifically protect their positions. It may be more difficult and expensive to amend a home rule charter subsequently if a popular referen-

Pro	Con
desire more checks and balances in government, under home rule they can decide the limitations necessary and write them into the city charter.	dum is required than it would be to obtain new local legislation from the state legislature: To make a change under home rule requires convincing the voting electorate, not just the local delegation to the state legislature.
7. Home rule allows greater discretion in making routine decisions. City officials do not need the state legislature's authorization of everything. Without home rule, large cities have to submit a large volume of complex local legislation each session, while small towns will find it expensive to lobby at the state capital for the acts they need. Locally elected officials should have freedom to act in behalf of local government.	7. Home rule charters may be complex and highly technical. Voters are likely to be apathetic or else confused by charter amendments—plus some local interest group can lobby successfully for a change favoring it. State controls ensure that locally organized groups (such as public employee unions) do not use home rule to win special favors in charter amendments. Finally, those unsatisfied with local decisions under home rule will try to persuade the state legislature to intervene.
8. Municipalities (and counties) vary widely in their governmental needs. Home rule gives flexibility to deal with different population sizes, growth problems, urban rural makeup, and socioeconomic composition. Without it, most state legislation passed has a classification basis, making a "general" statute of narrow local applicability.	8. Of the many units legally eligible for home rule, only some have exercised the option. The calls for home rule often come from a relatively few large jurisdictions which need additional powers to meet citizen demand for urban services (which could be authorized by individual local legislation). Many local governments do not want and cannot afford additional responsibilities. Home rule may result in withdrawal of state financial support for certain functions.

Annexation and Extraterritorial Powers: Extending the City's Limits

Annexation means enlarging the city limits into unincorporated territory not part of another municipality (although the area of a quasi-municipal corporation such as a county, township, school, or other special district can be annexed). In a few states, annexation still

Pro	Con
9. Home rule relieves local governments from partisan discrimination by a state legislature controlled by the opposite political party. Without home rule, jurisdictions may not obtain necessary statutory authority because local legislation is tangled by party quarrels, legislative apportionment disputes, and carving up the city between legislative districts which give one party or another electoral advantage. In such partisan fights, it is tempting to block legislation crucial to local government's operation in order to obtain political compromise on other issues.	9. Local governments with partisan elections may (or may not) obtain home rule because of their political complexion rather than upon the merits of their situation. Home rule may be granted or refused on the basis of political loyalty, not need. Even with nonpartisan local elections, certain special interests may seek or oppose home rule, depending on whether it favors or might regulate them.
10. Home rule is a device allowing local initiative. It requires a psychological attitude as much as the legal formality for success. Home rule units have exercised their powers responsibly: only a tiny number have lost this power subsequently because of incapacity. Most state legislators hate to be charged with interfering in local affairs; moreover they can become entangled in local political squabbles. Denying home rule is really saying that local citizens are not capable of self-government.	10. Local pride biases consideration of alternatives. A system of strict state control does have its uses: legislators reap political rewards from sponsoring local bills. But even if one is disenchanted with local legislation, home rule is not a complete cure. Home rule may give some relief from inappropriate legislation, but it cannot undo adverse judicial decisions against the city. Since home rule powers are interpreted by the courts in light of national and state constitutional provisions, it is politically more difficult to reverse a judicial decision than to replace a legislator whose local bills do not please his constituents.

requires a special act of the legislature, while in others, a court or boundary commission reviews the proposed annexation and makes a determination. Most states require that annexation occur only after an election called for that purpose in which a majority of the voters (sometimes limited to property owners) both in the city and in the area to be annexed must consent (concurrent majority). Unless the area is "technically uninhabited" (with minimal population), unilateral annexation is unusual. However, a few states allow unilateral annexation of land by a simple vote of the city council without an election by the inhabitants.

Annexation is a highly charged political issue often stoutly resisted by the area to be annexed, especially if it suspects that the city is seeking additional tax base. The quest for this assessed valuation has sometimes resulted in contorted boundaries as the city limits probe outward. Expansionists believe that the urban fringe needs to be politically (as it is economically) integrated with the municipality, and city services are offered as an inducement for annexation. Those to be annexed are often those who originally moved out of the core city to escape its problems, and they do not want to be gobbled up again and pay higher city taxes. Annexation is a competition with important stakes: political representation is affected by changing the socioeconomic composition, and it determines the amount of land which may be subdivided subject to city zoning requirements. Occasionally, an area petitions to be separated, but it is rarely successful, especially if the city has made expensive public improvements, so that bondholders must consent. The state may impose certain standards for municipal annexation, such as compactness, and in certain states under the federal Voting Rights Act, all boundary changes must be submitted to the U.S. attorney general for review of representation impact before they become final.

"Extraterritorial powers"[12] refers to municipal authority which may extend beyond the city limits. Cities can own property outside their boundaries (including facilities such as airports) and can tax people who live outside the city on the income they earn and the purchases they make in town. In some states, municipalities can regulate and license businesses in a limited peripheral zone called the "police jurisdiction." The most controversial extraterritorial power is the right in a few states to regulate land use beyond city limits. This can include subdivision control, approval of street plans, and zoning of land use. Development along its fringes obviously affects the city, and such coordinating powers may eventually result in annexation. Thus such regulation is not merely a question of economic cost to developers but also affects the city's relations with its neighbors.

Death of the Municipality

The municipal corporation enjoys perpetual succession, unless positive action is taken: the city may vote to dissolve itself if taxpayers feel that services are too expensive and can be performed by another level of government or if it is in civic self-interest not to be incorporated any longer. (For instance, when state laws have restricted gambling at local option, a number of towns have given up their reason for being.) Second, a municipality may be abolished by the state legislature by special act but is usually abolished by the state attorney general for nonuse of powers. State law usually provides that if a depopulated ghost town has ceased collecting taxes, electing officers, and performing other vital functions (such as keeping its streets in repair), it becomes legally extinct after a specified time. Finally, the corporation may be consolidated when two or more cities join together, perhaps with a county, in an entirely new local government. Such metropolitan governments assume the assets and liabilities (such as bond obligation) of the original entities.

Suing the City: Municipal Tort Liability

A tort is a wrongful act, not involving breach of contract, which can result in civil suit. (Cities are subject to the provisions of contracts they enter into, since noncompliance is even more damaging to public confidence in terms of broken faith by a public entity. In extraordinary circumstances, a contract may be broken by the city under the police power or by use of eminent domain.) The torts that might lead to suits against the city include operations creating a nuisance, personal injury, property damage resulting from gross negligence or an illegal act (see box).

Tort Liability

POTHOLE VICTIM GETS
$150,000 FOR INJURIES

A pothole cost the city $150,000 Thursday in the settlement of a damage suit in state court.

James Williams, who sustained neck fractures and internal injuries when his rented car struck the depression on Covert Street, had sued the city for $500,000.

His lawyer contended that the pothole between Central and Evergreen Avenues had been a hazard to motorists for several months prior to the accident and that the city had taken no steps to repair it.

Does the citizen have a right to safe streets? Would the city be liable if it repaired the fault in a reasonable time or posted a warning? The city has traditionally been held responsible for torts dealing with the maintenance (but not the construction) of public ways, even though this is recognized as a governmental function.

Traditionally, neither the city nor its officers may be sued for tort unless:

1. there has been a statute authorizing such an action[13]
2. the function where the alleged tort occurred is
   a. proprietary rather than governmental
   b. ministerial rather than discretionary. (The city can be sued for damages from its performance, but not for its discretionary choice of policy.)

These restrictions in common law on suing the municipality stem from the medieval king, who as the fountainhead of justice could do no wrong. This doctrine of sovereign immunity was transferred by the courts to national governments, and ultimately to states and municipalities, on the theory that these governments were acting on behalf of their people: by suing his government (without its consent) in tort, the citizen was in effect suing himself, a legal impossibility.

Thus the division of governmental and proprietary powers examined earlier is important in setting the limits of city liability. If the city is exercising its police powers to protect public health, safety, or welfare, it can avoid suit by pleading sovereign immunity. On the other hand, if the city is engaged in a proprietary enterprise at its own volition (or corporate acts for its own convenience) it may be held legally liable for its actions. In states following this common law, a considerable body of case law was built up but was not always consistent from state to state. Can a citizen hit by a city dump truck sue because the municipality has entered the garbage collection business, or is the city performing a governmental function in protecting the public health by better sanitation?

Many states have sought to end this confusion literally resulting from "precedents by accident" by declaring the city responsible for *all* its actions, like a private corporation or individual. This course has been taken by state statute or by a decision of the state supreme court (which often leads to frantic municipal lobbying for a state constitutional amendment reasserting sovereign immunity for local governments). The erosion of municipal tort immunity will undoubtedly raise the costs of the government. The city must buy insurance policies from commercial companies or else self-insure by putting aside a sum each year and hope that there are no large claim judgments until the insurance reserve fund is built up. (The second alternative avoids political brawls over which local agent(s) win the city's insurance business, and it may be more economical than paying premiums to a commercial carrier. The key to self-insurance is whether the city can afford to keep large amounts in reserve to settle claims). Tort liability also means that the municipality will bear the legal burden of defending itself, even if it wins. The city has always been vulnerable to lawsuits, a tempting target for those with real or fancied injuries.

A tort is a wrong against an individual, and immunity obviously does not extend to a public servant who commits a crime against society. A municipal employee may act so as to render himself criminally liable, for example, by embezzling public funds or driving an official vehicle in a patently negligent way.

Civil Liability of City Officials

City officers, and on occasion city workers, may be individually sued in contract or tort action arising from their duties. In contract disputes, the court must decide whether the official made further commitments in interpreting the contract, if his actions were justified by changing conditions, and if the original terms can be performed. Was the officer or employee guilty of a tort? Personal liability depends upon whether the officer was acting within the law or ultra vires. A policeman making a valid arrest upon probable cause is not liable should the suspect be found not guilty by the court, but if there is illegal detention from spite, the officer may face tort action for false arrest. In the case of subordinate employees who are reasonably carrying out orders, the common-law rule of *respondeat superior* applies: "the master is responsible for the actions of his servant." Rather than suing the worker, who is doing his job, the city may be liable to tort action *if* it is a suable function. To be on the safe side, many city employees buy liability coverage at group rates through municipal officers' associations, unions, or police-fire benefit societies, which may also provide legal assistance as an inducement to membership.

In 1980, the U.S. Supreme Court ruled 5 to 4 in *Owen* v. *City of Independence*[14] that cities are not immune from liability for actions by city officials which violate an individual's constitutional rights. In 1981, the justices ruled 6 to 3 that compensatory damages (but not punitive damages) could be assessed against a city.[15] Municipalities have thus become responsible for decisions made by public officials on behalf of the city.

Finally, municipal officers may be named as defendants in the taxpayers' suits discussed earlier. Pending settlement of the case, legal action may be taken against an individual municipal officer by so-called extraordinary writs issued by a court of proper jurisdiction.

1. Injunction—a writ of prohibition, seeking to restrain or prevent an action. It may be temporary, pending a hearing of the case, or

permanent, entered as a final judgment (e.g., the city will not pollute under pain of contempt of court).

2. Mandamus—a writ to compel an official to act or perform a certain duty (e.g., the court may order striking police or firemen to return to work in the interests of public safety).

3. Quo warranto—an action to test the right of a public official to exercise his office. (Is it within the scope of his authority or ultra vires?)

4. Habeas corpus—officials must produce evidence of someone held in detention in court (subpoenas may be issued to compel attendance in court of witnesses or municipal records).

5. Certiorari—petition a higher court for review of the case (file an appeal).

A Final Judgment

The legal terrain examined in this chapter shapes many of the political battles waged at city hall. Even the threat of legal action can alter the outcome of public policy decisions. Risk management has become a field with important financial consequences as municipal liability to suit has widened. In an increasingly litigation-conscious American society, the judge has become an important arbiter of civic actions.

Notes

1. For an examination of the development of these concepts, see Anwar Syed, *The Political Theory of American Local Government* (New York: Random House, 1966).

2. John F. Dillon, *Commentaries on the Law of Municipal Corporations*, 5th ed. (Boston: J. Cockroft, 1911), vol. 1, p. 448.

3. Ibid.

4. *People* v. *Hurlbut*, 24 Mich. 44 (1871).

5. *City of Trenton* v. *State of New Jersey*, 262 U.S. 182, 185–86 (1923).

6. *Williams* v. *Mayor* (of Baltimore), 289 U.S. 36 at 40.

7. 364 U.S. 339 (1960).

8. Such departments are often part of the governor's office and advise the chief executive and state legislature on local government problems, act as a research and information center, coordinate state efforts to help municipalities, encourage intergovernmental cooperation and, if they do not financially monitor units of local government, at least collect and publish fiscal data (comparative tax rates, revenues, and expenditures).

9. Alabama Constitution, Sec. 89.

10. See *U.S. Fidelity and Guaranty Co.* v. *Guenther*, 151 F.2d 189 (1945).

11. *State of Florida ex rel. Davis atty. gen.* v. *Town of Lake Placid*, 109 Fla. 419 (1933).

12. Not to be confused with diplomatic immunity extraterritoriality.

13. The United States Supreme Court in *Monell* v. *Dept. of Social Services of the City of New York*, 436 U.S. 658 (1978), held 7–2 that local government officials can be sued under 42 United States Code 1983 for violating a person's civil rights. Thus tort immunity does not protect municipal actions which involve unconstitutional discrimination.

14. *Owen* v. *City of Independence* (Mo.), 455 U.S. 622 (1980).

15. *City of Newport* (R.I.) v. *Fact Concerts*, No. 80-396, decided June 27, 1981.

For Further Reading

McCarthy, David J., Jr. *Local Government Law in a Nutshell.* St. Paul: West Publishing, 1975.

Rhyne, Charles S. *The Law of Local Government Operations.* Washington, D.C.: National Institute of Municipal Law Officers, 1980.

Syed, Anwar. *The Political Theory of American Local Government.* New York: Random House, 1966.

3: Metropolitics:
Cities in Search of Community

The city forms part of a larger political community, and this chapter focuses on its relationships with its governmental neighbors. While not attempting a survey of urban problems, it examines the administrative responses which have been offered as answers—or at least as politically feasible solutions.

Municipalities and the Federal Government

During the urban crises of recent years, the answers given at city hall usually include waiting for "word from Washington." American cities are relatively independent of control by the national government compared with similar jurisdictions in most other countries. Although American civic ideology has rejected parenthood by the central government, the terms of partnership undergo constant political tension and realignment. While the popular image of rugged individualists founding democratic communities across a continent remains, Daniel Elazar, a noted writer on the subject, has traced a long history of federal-local cooperation during the nineteenth century.[1] Settlements grew up beside the national roads; army forts and railroads were built along rights-of-way of public lands; rivers and canals were improved by federal efforts. Direct technical assistance was provided by the U.S. Army Corps of Engineers for any local project of national interest, provided that the community contributed a fifth of the money, material, or labor. Vast tracts of public land were given by the federal government to states and local governments to endow schools and provide money for internal improvements. In Alaska, America's "last frontier," federal land was still being surveyed during the 1970s for future settlements.

The scope of federal financial support greatly widened during the great depression of the 1930s, when one-fourth of America's workers were out of a job. The unemployed were put to work on a variety of Works Progress Administration projects, including the WPA murals which decorate some of our older city halls and post offices. Many cities have auditoriums, parks, curbs and gutters, and water and sewage systems which were federally financed by the Public Works Administration. Under the Housing Act of 1937, the federal government loaned municipalities as much as 80 percent of the construction costs of public housing projects.

Today there is hardly an area of municipal activity in which the federal government cannot be involved. No one can tabulate all the forms of federal assistance available: an estimate made in 1980 distinguished nearly 500 separate grant programs administered by more than fifty federal agencies. As congressional representation has grown steadily more urban, even cabinet-level departments, such as Agriculture and State, have found it expedient to develop programs with a municipal orientation (such as water systems for rural communities and foreign exchanges of local government officials). A satisfied mayor is a favorable witness at an appropriations hearing before a congressional committee. The myriad programs of the Department of Housing and Urban Development and the Department of Health and Human Services have led them to be described organizationally as "domestic conglomerates." Whether the federal funds should go directly to municipal applicants or "pass through" the states has been a source of political controversy; the golden rule in government has been described as "they who provide the gold, rule."

What have been the administrative controls on municipalities exercised through federal programs? The usual requirements include a plan describing what the applicant intends to accomplish, progress reports (usually quarterly), massive instructions on operational procedures, and inspection or audits of the funds expended. The volume of paperwork required by the federal bureaucracy is a cause of constant local complaint. How effective is the federal monitoring? Experience indicates that superior professional resources dominate in the policy-making process, resulting in what Deil Wright calls "picket fence" federalism, with direct technical contact in each functional area (health, highways) through the horizontal levels of federal and state government.[2] The cash route of intergovernmental assistance has been taken in America because the grants can be made with strings. While some local waste of funds has occurred, given the magnitude of expenditure, federal monitoring has often seemed to emphasize control at the expense of results. The concentration of urban population causes problems with service delivery. A major criticism of many federal programs is that they are well administered—with a large staff for control—and deliver less to the recipients.

Often overlooked is the indirect federal presence that extends beyond massive and direct assistance programs for criminal justice, highways, hospitals, housing, mass transit, pollution control, urban renewal, welfare, and other urban needs. The location of federal installations, procurement contracts, or the closing of a local military base can have a tremendous impact upon a city's economy. The spillover effects of federal programs can also have unforeseen and sometimes counterproductive consequences. Often cited are federal mortgage guarantees, which subsidized the middle-class flight to the suburbs, and urban renewal programs, which attempt to increase the attractiveness of core cities.

Table 3.1. American Federalism and Urban Fragmentation: Layers of Governance at Whitehall, Pennsylvania

17. United States of America
16. Commonwealth of Pennsylvania
15. Air Quality Control Region
14. Southwestern Pennsylvania Regional Planning Commission
13. Western Pennsylvania Water Company
12. Allegheny County
11. Allegheny County Port Authority
10. Allegheny County Criminal Justice Commission
9. Allegheny County Soil and Water Conservation District
8. Allegheny County Sanitary Authority
7. City of Pittsburgh
6. South Hills Area Council of Governments
5. South Hills Regional Planning Commission
4. Pleasant Hills Sanitary Authority
3. Baldwin-Whitehall Schools Authority
2. Baldwin-Whitehall School District
1. Borough of Whitehall: Population 16,607

Note: The resident of Whitehall, a small suburban community, pays taxes or user charges to support the services of seventeen governmental entities.

Source: Advisory Commission on Intergovernmental Relations, *Substate Regionalism and the Federal System,* vol. 1: *Regional Decision Making: New Strategies for Substate Districts* (Washington, D.C.: U.S. Government Printing Office, 1973), p. 3.

State involvement has paralleled the federal role as a fiscal transfer mechanism to apply general tax revenues to urban needs. Also, at federal instigation, many states have set up coordinating bodies at either the state or regional level to administer the distribution of both federal and state assistance (such as the Council of Governments shown in table 3.1). Since most federal programs require a matching contribution from either the state or the recipient local government, state creation of an agency for each functional area not only indicates program commitment but also provides a useful political lobby. The city hospital administrator seeking federal construction funds is in constant contact with the regional health service planning body, the state public health department, and likely members of Congress in making application.

Municipalities frequently engage in direct lobbying. Their efforts range from the city attorney's attendance at sessions of the state legislature in support of local legislation to fully staffed municipal "embassies" in Washington, D.C. These liaison offices serve as information channels on proposed bills affecting cities, arrange testimony before legislative committees or the courts, cultivate administrators to discover possible new categories of funding, shepherd city grant applications through the bureaucracy, and even arrange visiting junkets for government officials or private businessmen who might wish to locate in town.

There are two major municipal lobbying organizations. The National League of Cities is composed of affiliated state leagues of municipalities and also has more than 500 direct member cities. The U.S. Conference of Mayors consists largely of cities of 30,000 or more population. About two-thirds of those cities eligible to join are members. The political importance of these organizations' annual conventions is obvious. Candidates for state or national office frequently address these gatherings with major announcements of domestic policy. Delegations of big-city mayors sent to the governor or president put their message across through media exposure.

Metropolitan Reorganization

We have seen that federal and state financial assistance mainly addresses specific functional problems. Governmental responsibility has thus been fragmented, leading to calls for organizational reform. The federal definition of a "Standard Metropolitan Statistical Area" is based on cities, with the SMSA named after the largest. This is a jurisdictional approach; each SMSA must contain a city of at least 50,000 (or adjacent cities totaling that population), covering an entire county (or New England township), plus adjoining counties meeting the same criteria. At least 75 percent of the labor force in each county in the SMSA must be in nonagricultural occupations, and the U.S. Bureau of the Census also evaluates commuting patterns and other evidence of economic integration.

The salient feature of the American metropolis is that it has outgrown its political framework. Through the nineteenth century municipal annexation roughly kept pace with urban expansion, but modern transportation outstripped government's reach. The result is that often the county area is too small, with metropolitan areas growing across state lines. Although municipalities are used as SMSA building blocks and two-thirds of all Americans live in them, the typical metropolis has a satellite configuration of suburbs. Half of these cover less than three square miles and have fewer than 3,000 inhabitants.

This fragmentation into separate incorporations has been criticized for:

- Resulting in differing and uncoordinated levels of service
- Creating overlapping jurisdictions as municipalities, counties, special districts, and various authorities struggle to provide necessary services
- Fragmenting the tax base into competing jurisdictions with a race for assessed valuation
- Exacerbating governmental competition for finite resources such as physical space, economic wealth, and even trained personnel
- Duplicating similar municipal facilities; the economies of scale are lost.

Structural Alternatives

A house divided against itself cannot stand, and many of our metropolitan areas are crumbling. Several structural reforms have been tried:

Special districts and authorities have been commonly used to meet the need for urban services, with the result that SMSAs *average* thirty (nonschool) special districts each. The independent special district[3] or authority with its own elected board and taxing powers sometimes becomes a rival to municipalities as a service provider. The usefulness of special districts is that as quasi-corporations they can legally cover other governmental jurisdictions in the metropolis. Often responsible for only a single function (providing water, mass transit, and so forth), they sometimes have multipurpose and usually interrelated services (such as water and fire protection or hydroelectric power generation).

The advantages of special districts over municipalities for service delivery are the following.

- The special district can cover the service area needed (not always with contiguous boundaries). School districts and public housing authorities are most likely to have boundaries coterminous with the municipality; other types have territory based on their own needs.
- Most states legally view special districts as separate bonding vehicles which can borrow to build the necessary facilities without a charge against the city's debt limit.

• Independently elected district directors argue that they are held more strictly accountable for their performance. They note that a city council member whose action in utility service matters may be disapproved by the electorate may make decisions in other areas that are sufficient to overcome such objections. Municipal or county utility operations permit these governments to tax the people indirectly by charging high utility rates and skimming off the profits to pay for other functions. Special districts charge the consumers only enough to cover the costs of providing the service.

• The cost of providing service is directly assessed in the areas covered by the special district, and the existing political boundaries of counties and rival municipalities are undisturbed.[4]

This political feasibility of formation has made the special district the most frequently used of these structural alternatives.

Major criticisms of this organizational approach are:

• Special districts are invisible layers of government whose separately elected directors are unknown to the voters or form an appointed board insulated from the public.

• Special districts are spending mechanisms, creating overlapping tax burdens on the property owner. The issue of whether the district should be financed from user charges or property taxes can be very controversial, and the outcome may favor certain interests (e.g., large landowners at the expense of urban residents).

• Special districts can become "special dynasties" with uncontested offices if they are elective and a patronage sinecure if they are appointed.

• Separate special districts plan only according to their tasks, without metropolitan coordination. Lack of policy coordination becomes obvious to the public when recently paved city streets are torn up for a new district utility line.

Since certain problems associated with delivery of urban services (such as mass transit, water supply, and sewage disposal) can best be handled on a metropolitanwide basis, many municipalities have favored constituent-unit representation—a city official sits on the special district or authority board.

City-county Separation. Detachment of a city from a county, sometimes with territorial enlargement, was used in the late nineteenth century but has not occurred recently except in Virginia. Municipalities reaching a specified population are legally detached and perform all the functions of both city and county within their boundaries. Opposition by county officials and residents left to depend on their own resources has made such severance politically unfeasible.

City-county Consolidation. Used in the nineteenth century, this method of merging governments regained popularity after World War II. However, only about 25 percent of the consolidations proposed since then have been approved. Most have occurred in the southern United States, where the county has traditionally been the strongest unit of local government.[5]

As cities grow outward through annexation, the amount of unincorporated county area diminishes. Even if municipalities do not occupy the entire county, settlement along their fringe requires expensive urban services. In time, a local governmental reorganization movement forms and draws attention to duplication of effort, lack of intergovernmental cooperation, the need for areawide solutions to problems, and the cost efficiencies which would result from unified services. Expert studies are commissioned, often with outside foundation or federal planning money, which detail the advantages of consolidation with precise logic. A citizens' committee draws up an organizational charter, any necessary enabling legislation is obtained from the state, and the proposed consolidated government is presented to the people in a referendum. Why is it turned down about three-fourths of the time?

Most arguments for consolidation are presented in abstract terms of estimated savings (which inflation tends to consume if plans are implemented), while the voter is familiar with the existing municipality and identifies with it. Adoption usually requires a concurrent majority in both the city or cities and in unincorporated areas, and county residents are likely to oppose higher taxes for extension of consolidated services. Minorities may suspect that consolidation is a tactic for diluting their strength when they are on the verge of electoral control of the inner city.[6] Political representation and a basis for taxation which are perceived to be equitable are the two ingredients necessary for adoption at the polls. Successful consolidations are most likely to occur when the existing political system has failed with a major breakdown in service delivery, or where an energetic elected leader has adopted governmental reform as his political vehicle.

Urban counties are a compromise to provide the service delivery without consolidated political integration.[7] Incorporated municipalities remain intact, but they and urbanized fringe areas receive their services under contract. In many situations, municipalities defensively incorporated to avoid annexation, or to gain control of their own taxation and zoning, but were already receiving urban services from the county. Thus the county, special districts, and large municipalities may all be in competition to provide services to newly subdivided or industrially developed areas. The county, with existing water and sanitary lines, and fire and police protection facilities, may serve these new customers who do not wish to be annexed by special districts or municipalities. Service delivery under contract is covered in the following section on interjurisdictional agreements.

Metropolitan federation, or "two-tier government," has been advocated as the optimal solution because of Canada's success in Toronto. Federation (as yet untried in the United States) envisages a comprehensive metropolitan government covering the entire built-up area. The central metropolitan government handles areawide services and encompasses the entire revenue base. Constituent units (municipalities? boroughs?) direct activities local in scope in accordance with community desires and share concurrent responsibility for other functions. The metropolitan council is composed of officials of the constituent units who are directly elected. The attractions of federation are its scope, which harnesses the financial resources of the entire metropolis (rather than producing competing jurisdictions hemmed in by each other and by prevailing socioeconomic patterns) and that it, like the original United States, could be created from existing political units. However, the Canadian federations were imposed unilaterally by provincial governments, without a vote by the inhabitants, whereas the only American consolidation created directly by legislative action (Unigov in Indianapolis) retained the existing townships, school districts, and suburban municipalities. The major controversies likely to arise over federation appear to be the division of functions between the two tiers, the allocation of political representation among constituent units, and especially whether part of the metro council should be directly elected.

To sum up, why have municipalities retained the allegiance of the American people rather than the innovations for structural reform? A metropolitanwide government

- Fixes responsibility for governmental decisions by merging the county(ies), municipalities and special districts
- Eliminates jurisdictional financial inequities with a metropolitan tax base
- Realizes economy of service delivery, with elimination of duplicate facilities
- Offers employment for trained specialized personnel and planned development for the future.

However, these technical advantages do not appeal to the average citizen for the following reasons.

1. Political integration is an unknown quantity, whereas the voter knows the representation and access afforded by his present local

governmental structure and identifies with it. Suburban officeholders and newspapers almost always oppose consolidation on these grounds. The structural status quo is a balance of accommodation arrived at over many years of political compromises.

2. Many suburban residents moved there to escape the core city and its financial burdens. The present fractionated system provides public choice. Not all suburbs are wealthy, and many unincorporated urban areas are so poor that existing municipalities do not want to annex them. Even many city employees do not live in the jurisdiction in which they work, unless there is a residency requirement.

3. Middle- and upper-class inhabitants are not interested in the economies of service delivery: What they want is control of their own facilities at the level which their income permits them to afford. This is the political essence of suburban gracious living. Successful metropolitan governments such as Toronto, Baton Rouge, and Nashville have recognized this by establishing differential taxing areas which provide various types or levels of service in accordance with community desires.

4. Most residents want response from governmental administrators, not technical specialists. An anonymous, cold bureaucracy is not appealing to people who feel secure with "concrete" decision-making rather than "abstract" planning.

In short, many of the features which make a particular community an attractive place in which to live and work are decided by private enterprise. Initiators naturally prefer to exert influence in smaller political arenas, where challenge from opposing interests is less likely than in the metropolis. The political independence afforded by separate jurisdictions allows people a sense of personal effectiveness in community affairs and permits them to insulate themselves from others whose mores they do not share.

Techniques for Metropolitan Cooperation

While metropolitan advocates have lost most of their battles for major structural reorganization, their ideas have influenced these less complete methods for interjurisdictional coordination: extraterritorial power, annexation, interjurisdictional agreements, functional transfers, and councils of governments.

Extraterritorial power is a means of bringing the unincorporated urban fringe within reach of the city's police powers, as discussed in the previous chapter. For municipalities not surrounded by others, such power extends regulatory influence, but as soon as satellite towns and villages incorporate, the effectiveness of extraterritoriality diminishes. Besides the rights granted by law (such as abating nuisances, ownership of land outside the city, and control of land use, examined in chapter 10, "Planning and Land Use"), certain extraterritorial privileges may be allowed, although they may not be specified. This "extralegal" authority includes the extraterritorial effects of city taxation and the discretion to extend utility service beyond the city limits. By taxation and inspection of those doing business in the city and by its policy of providing services for a fee to its neighbors, a municipality extends its influence beyond its boundaries.

Annexation. As noted in the previous chapter, urban growth has outstripped annexation procedures. There are three main problems with annexation as a vehicle for metropolitan governmental integration. First, a city can annex only unincorporated territory, which means that those surrounded by existing municipalities cannot expand. Most state laws prohibit annexation across county lines, and annexations across state boundaries are impossible. Second, annexation usually requires approval by the inhabitants, and opponents may find it easy to incorporate defensively or even to annex along a corridor to a municipality further away which has fewer taxes or regulations. Third, the city may offer services as an inducement for adjacent areas to annex, adding their assessed valuation to the city's tax base. But such races for assessed valuation result in patchy growth, with sprawling boundaries, and may not take into account the ultimate costs of providing city services. Will the revenues from the annexed area meet the capital costs of utility feeder lines, fire stations, and street lighting which must be extended?

The usefulness of annexation to meet metropolitan needs often depends upon the amount of state intervention. There are five procedural approaches to annexation.

● Legislative determination. Municipal boundary changes are made by special acts of the state legislature. Annexation can be encouraged if the legislature forbids further incorporations within the metropolitan area. However, it seems unlikely that a metropolitan legislative delegation would be so unified politically that it could agree on an areawide annexation policy.

● Unilateral municipal annexation without the consent of the area to be included will certainly stimulate civic growth. However, the few states (like Texas) which have granted this power usually circumscribed it after there were complaints of "land-grabbing" rivalry and overextension without services. This freedom encouraged municipalities to annex revenue-yielding areas and to ignore populated high-cost ones.

● Judicial determination, that is, cases in which the courts decide on proposed boundary changes, is used in Virginia. While it allows for an impartial determination, popular criticism of judicial activism in other metropolitan crisis situations makes it unlikely that judges would seek continuing responsibility for annexation squabbles.

• Electoral determination (the inhabitants in the affected area vote) is the most popular and widely used method. However, if a concurrent majority is required, a small number of opponents in the area proposed for annexation can stymie the larger metropolitan interest.

• Administrative determination. An independent nonjudicial tribunal or quasi-legislative board, often composed of representatives from the local governments, is empowered to decide boundary changes. Several states have successfully established such permanent bodies, which often hold public hearings on the desirability and feasibility of proposed municipal incorporations, annexations, and the formation of new special districts.

Interjurisdictional Agreements. Now permitted by most states, these informal understandings or formal compacts permit local governments to receive or provide certain services to other jurisdictions. They may range from reciprocal mutual aid pacts for lending personnel or equipment to a neighboring jurisdiction in time of emergency, to a formal contract for providing specified services over a period of time. Formal contracting is also known as the "Lakewood Plan," after the Los Angeles suburb which pioneered in receiving virtually all its municipal services in a package from the county for a negotiated price.

The voluntary nature of interjurisdictional agreements, stressing consolidation of services rather than governmental units, has made them popular. A 1972 survey[8] found that nearly three-fourths of the local governments in metropolitan areas and more than half of other municipalities had entered into such cooperative arrangements. The most frequently cited reason was cost economies of scale. As a vehicle for metropolitan cooperation, such service agreements have the following advantages.

• Services can be provided at financial savings more efficiently than through separate efforts (e.g., why build small suburban jails within a mile of another municipality?).

• Mutual action (often through joint construction and financing or leasing agreements) can be taken by the participating governments on common problems or projects (such as suburban crime rings or construction of a joint facility where there is limited area available for it). Voluntary agreements can be negotiated and adopted by local ordinance without being contingent upon voter approval, and in fact the public may be unaware of their existence.

• Most importantly, such schemes maintain the identity and autonomy of each of the units. Locally elected officials retain discretionary control over the functions which are provided cooperatively. If an agreement becomes too expensive, an unsatisfied jurisdiction can discontinue participation, letting the contract expire, and seek other arrangements or go on its own.

Besides counties and cities, cooperative arrangements have also developed between municipalities and independent school districts, such as recreational programs on school grounds after hours and internal administration such as purchasing or payroll services.

While service agreements allow a range of options which a city on its own resources could not provide, they can also have adverse metropolitan effects. The availability of basic services under a contract package may encourage the proliferation of minimunicipalities. Such tiny suburban entities are formed for defensive self-interest and otherwise would not be viable. Their only employees are contract negotiators, so that the idea of local self-government is vitiated.[9] Such governmental fragmentation also does not remedy fiscal inequities: poor jurisdictions may not be able to subscribe to available basic services, such as adequate sewage treatment facilities. Finally, the voluntary nature of interjurisdictional agreements confines them to routine housekeeping chores rather than permitting needed but controversial arrangements to solve metropolitan problems.

Functional Transfers. Governments in the metropolis may agree to—or the state can impose—a permanent reallocation of services. In many cities, responsibility for education is vested in an independent school district, public housing in a separate authority, and welfare administration in a state agency for public assistance. The degree of autonomy varies by function: the service and taxing authority for it may be taken out of the city's hands entirely; the municipal government may appoint to the agency members who then have complete discretion; the city may have to levy whatever tax or charge is necessary to support the activity or may have to approve a separate budget but not the items on which the budget is spent.

State assumption of responsibility usually occurs if local performance does not meet state minimum standards or if the cities ask to be relieved of the burden, usually for financial reasons. Most social welfare functions are now state administered, and other responsibilities such as pollution regulation and court management have been assumed by some states. There can also be horizontal shifts to other units of local government. Counties may handle voter registration and elections or property tax assessment. Other municipalities with available landfill may take over solid waste disposal. Sewage treatment, water supply, and mass transit services may be performed by other municipalities or special districts. In contrast to the voluntary nature of interjurisdictional agreements, functional transfers are usually permanent and state mandated by authorizing legislation covering the metropolis.

Councils of Government. COGs are composed of representatives of the governmental units in the metropolis (not directly elected members). Originally consultative vehicles for metropolitan planning, many of them in the 1960s became clearinghouses for federal (and often state) grant applications. Under regulation A-95, applications for federal funding must be reviewed by a regional body to ensure that requests by competing City X, City Y, and County Z are not duplicative or counteractive in effect. This review requirement stimulated formation of COGs and put teeth in their efforts at regional planning.

Most COGs are advisory in nature and require unanimity for any decisions. With rare exceptions, most have no taxing authority and rely on member governments' dues plus a few state or federal planning grants. Their twin weaknesses are representation and financing. Many metropolitan areas consist of a giant core city and many pygmy suburban jurisdictions. Contributions to finance the COG are usually assessed from member units according to population or tax base, which means that the central city or county foots most of the bill. However, the pygmy suburban municipalities (and perhaps special districts) will not join unless they have a majority of voting strength. The political compromise is usually that the mayor or a member from each unit's governing body sits on the COG, with voting strength weighted so that a broad coalition must be achieved to get anything accomplished. Decisions, such as a regional plan, may not necessarily be binding on all jurisdictions in the metropolis.[10] However, the typical COG, like the United Nations, provides a forum for debate on subjects of common concern and is useful for liaison between members. The metropolitan policy recommendations of the COGs depend upon member action for implementation.

Optimism in Diversity

Can the multiple jurisdictions which fragment American metropolitan areas produce solutions? One distinguished observer concluded: "Once an indivisible problem is divided, nothing effective can be done about it."[11] The metropolis may be ungovernable in a unified sense: functional activities are the responsibility of many entities. In this governmental framework hundreds of decisions are made, many with spillover effects into other jurisdictions. But each of these actions was taken to fulfill a pragmatic need. If the effects turn out to be counterproductive, political forces come into play. Rather than constituting a weakness, the elasticity provided by these multiple political agencies allows adaptation to the diverse segments of the metropolitan population.

Notes

1. Daniel J. Elazar, *The American Partnership: Intergovernmental Cooperation in the Nineteenth Century United States* (Chicago: University of Chicago Press, 1962).

2. Deil Wright, "Intergovernmental Relations: An Analytical Overview," *Annals of the American Academy of Political and Social Science,* vol. 416 (November 1974), pp. 1–16.

3. Dependent special districts are governed by county officials or by a board appointed by the local governments covered.

4. Under interstate compacts (agreements made between two or more states), a few special districts even cover adjoining states.

5. For a list, see Parris N. Glendening and Patricia S. Atkins, "City-County Consolidations: New Views for the Eighties," in *The Municipal Year Book, 1980* (Washington, D.C.: International City Management Association, 1980), pp. 68–72.

6. The 1974 Detroit integration ruling by the U.S. Supreme Court that school pupils cannot be bused across county boundaries has in effect drawn the lines of white resistance and has thus frozen the chances for multicounty metropolitan government.

7. Several successful city-county consolidations were preceded by merger of functional services.

8. Advisory Commission on Intergovernmental Relations and International City Management Association, *Survey on Intergovernmental Service Agreements* (Washington, D.C., 1972).

9. Although service agreements avoid problems with city personnel, a public employee strike in the serving unit could also have much wider effects.

10. Whether or not they are depends on the articles of organization and the amount of authority with which the state has endowed the COG.

11. Luther H. Gulick, *The Metropolitan Problem and American Ideas* (New York: Knopf, 1961), p. 24.

For Further Reading

The volume of literature on metropolitan areas is tremendous. The following recommendations deal with the main topics covered in this chapter and suggest works that contain extensive bibliographies.

Advisory Commission on Intergovernmental Relations. This federal agency publishes many studies on urban affairs and intergovernmental responses, including several volumes of case studies of metropolitan government.

Bollens, John C., and Schmandt, Henry J. *The Metropolis.* 3rd ed. New York: Harper and Row, 1975.

Elazar, Daniel J. *The American Partnership*. Chicago: University of Chicago Press, 1962.

Farkas, Suzanne. *Urban Lobbying: Mayors in the Federal Arena*. New York: New York University Press, 1971.

Gulick, Luther. *The Metropolitan Problem and American Ideas*. New York: Knopf, 1962.

Haider, Donald H. *When Governments Come to Washington: Governors, Mayors, and Intergovernmental Lobbying*. New York: Free Press, 1974.

Martin, Roscoe C. *The Cities and the Federal System*. New York: Atherton, 1965.

National League of Cities/U.S. Conference of Mayors. *Urban Affairs Abstracts*. (Published weekly; summarizes articles and urban topics from hundreds of periodicals.)

Shank, Alan. *Political Power and the Urban Crisis*. 3rd ed. Boston: Holbrook Press, 1976.

U.S. Bureau of the Census. *Census of Governments*. Washington, D.C.: U.S. Government Printing Office. (A basic statistical reference that was published at five-year intervals [1972, 1977, etc.])

4: City Politics

Politics, identified as activity resulting from differences in policy preferences, is found everywhere in the city. Ask what the city should be doing about something, and there will be conflicting opinions expressed along Main Street, in factories, churches, bars, civic clubs, and various neighborhoods. Edward C. Banfield and James Q. Wilson in *City Politics* identify a dual function of government: supplying services and managing conflict.[1] These roles are intertwined and can be positive or negative: Should a service be performed or not? Where should a facility be located? How will the costs of government be apportioned? Should an existing policy be changed or not?

Civic Ideologies: Views of the City's Purpose

Ideology, a set of political beliefs held in common, is more often studied at the national than at the municipal level. Yet public perceptions of what the functions of city government *ought* to be define the nature of the problems brought to city hall for public resolution. A pioneering study by political scientists Oliver P. Williams and Charles R. Adrian,[2] identified the following views of city government.

- An instrument for community growth. Civic boosterism ("growth is progress") is championed by the chamber of commerce, retail merchants, financiers, and developers who stand to benefit from expansion. Personnel and budget increases for city departments can be justified by growth.
- The provider of life's amenities. Rather than seeking growth as the highest goal, some communities are intensely concerned with their quality of life or atmosphere as a place to live. Civic expenditures are made for extra facilities and services in residential neighborhoods (e.g., sanitation scooters may come into the yards to collect trash from camouflaged bins so that garbage cans need not be lined along the curbs for street pickup).

- A minimal caretaker. "Businesslike" government without frills is desired by people on fixed incomes, those advocating small government and low taxes, and suburbanites whose mortgage and family expenses take all their income. If residents receive what they consider essential services, government is best which takes the least from personal or business profits.

- An arbiter of conflicting interests. Government performs a brokerage role in allocating resources among various segments of the community. Large cities with active interest groups, ethnic minorities, and diverse economic interests will seek political accommodation at city hall.

Williams and Adrian caution that these are pure types; these and other philosophies coexist in any community. Political scientist Everett Ladd, by measuring attitudes toward the public sector (what should be the political objectives of the community? how should resources be allocated for each project?), suggests the ideological poles of cosmopolitanism and parochialism: "The scope of public life is broadest in the central city, narrowest in the small town."[3] The locals' influence rests upon a network of personal relations and concern with booster issues such as civic beautification or clean city campaigns. The cosmopolitans' influence is derived from expertise rather than from personal contacts, interest in metropolitanwide or national social issues such as urban renewal or open housing, more detached from local sentiment. Which civic ideologies prevail in a town? Clues can be found in letters to the newspaper editor, local conversations, debate in the meetings at city hall, and seeing who benefits from the decisions made.

Community Power: Who Runs This Town?

The role expected of city government—its intervention to resolve a problem and the values by which people expect a decision to be made— is conditioned by prior local history and social composition. Hundreds of studies of community power have been made by sociologists and political scientists without consistent findings. Case studies, of course, are only a picture of a community at a certain point. The distribution of community power forms a continuum ranging from a monolithic structure in which decisions are made by a few economic or social notables to a pluralistic framework of contending factions.

Three basic methods of measurement have been used. The positional (or structural) approach identifies those who occupy key decision-making positions in the community; the local newspaper editor is invariably listed as influential. The reputational (or sociometric) method asks community respondents to identify powerful figures. The mayor is thus perceived to wield influence by virtue of his official position. The decisional-event (or issue-relevant) analysis observes how the issues deemed most important to the community were decided and who gained or lost. All three of these methodologies have strengths and weaknesses. Structural analysis defines key decision-makers but tends to ignore middle management or local bureaucracy. The little decisions made daily by specialists can have a snowballing effect upon public policy. The reputational method is useful in discerning perceived power, especially that exerted by private groups outside the public arena, but suffers from hindsight: past influence can evaporate in the face of present events. The decisional approach measures outcomes, but the selection of issues examined can give either monolithic or pluralistic results, depending on whether or not the issues chosen overlap (see figure 4.1). One of the major difficulties is how to measure nondecisions. These can be either "settled" questions which everyone in the community seems to accept (and which usually favor the group(s) in power, who benefit from the status quo) or issues so controversial that they cannot be brought into the political arena lest they tear the town apart. In neither case is there public discussion, yet influence is being wielded in this mobilization of bias.

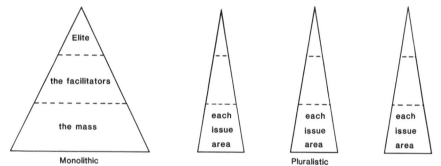

Figure 4.1. Theoretical Constructs of Community Power. MONOLITHIC: a socioeconomic elite at the top makes most community decisions. Its members' preferences are implemented by facilitators who hold public office, and the mass of people accept. *Studies:* Floyd Hunter in *Community Power Structure* found that in "regional city" (Atlanta) a group of forty top businessmen determined policy. The town in Robert and Helen Lynd's *Middletown* (Muncie, Indiana) was controlled in the 1920s and 1930s by the X (Ball) family, who owned the major industry (a canning jar factory). PLURALISTIC: There are still relatively few influential individuals, but one group does not make all decisions. Instead, there are shifting coalitions, depending upon the issue arena: schools, transportation, housing, and so forth. *Studies:* Robert Dahl in *Who Governs?* (New Haven, Conn.) and Arnold Rose in *The Power Structure: Political Process in American Society* found power more widely distributed through various voluntary associations—which also divide loyalties.

The titles of the case studies often indicate the pluralistic or mono-lithic conclusions of the researchers. Since sociologists as a discipline study institutions in society, they have tended to see power more concentrated than do political scientists, who focus on shifts and com-petition. However, one should not conclude that every sociologist takes a monolithic view, while every political scientist is a pluralist.

Can any pattern be pieced together from the many analyses of community power? Claire Gilbert examined 166 case studies,[4] and Terry Clark analyzed decision-making structures in 51 cities.[5] They agree that small towns tend to be more homogeneous politically, with elite dominance, while the larger the community, the more pluralistic the power structure. Economically, a one-mill textile town will be more monolithic than a city with a diversified industrial base. Labor unions and plants of nationwide corporations (rather than locally owned firms) when present will provide alternative leaderships. Competition among different elements of the power structure will encourage citizen participation rather than a single elite deciding what's best for the community. Socially, the more heterogeneous the inhabitants (in terms of religion, race, age, and family income), the more diversified their policy demands. A well-developed system of voluntary associations (churches, civic organizations, social clubs, and so forth) will articulate these interests and will contribute to a pluralistic structure.

These are enormously simplified conclusions; each community will handle consensus or conflict along channels of previous interaction. A community tradition of tolerance may facilitate compromise; past polarizing controversies may split new issues along old lines of cleav-age. Two vehicles are especially important in shaping citizens' views of city issues: political interest groups and the communication media.

Interest Groups and the Media: Shaping the Civic View

Voluntary private (or secondary) associations may have different bases: concern over a function or problem (good schools); ethnic heritage (a sense of identity); occupation (unions or the chamber of commerce); territory or neighborhood (downtown businessmen's asso-ciations); religious (an agency for social change); or general civic (good government) concern. No matter how much such groups may profess to be "above politics," sooner or later the regulative (licensing, zoning) or extractive (taxing) policies under consideration at city hall will excite their attention. How effective group intervention will be depends on a number of factors. First, only a minority of members will actively exert themselves down at city hall (usually they will be prompted by personal interest or their duty as officers of the organization). Second, an individual may belong to a number of voluntary associations and have other commitments which divide his loyalty. A parent wanting good schools may also be a homeowner worried about increasing property taxes. Third, not sheer numbers but the degree of motivation of organizational members to engage in political activity is the measure of strength. Fourth, the legitimacy of the organization in the eyes of others is important. The group promotes their cause as being parallel to the public interest, even though it may not be. Their reception at city hall will depend upon the perceived social values of their demands: while in some cities operators of adult entertainment have formed groups to protest "harassment" by the city, the political response has been cool because of an absence of "shared values." Churches may be influential on certain types of civic issues involving "morality," but less so on decisions concerning public works. Fifth, the pooled resources of groups seeking to affect mass public opinion (by media publicity, packing the audience at public hearings, or lawsuits) will have more clout than a few "crackpots" will. Sixth, successful lobbying depends upon the personalities of group spokesmen: are they articulate, truthful, and willing to compromise to advance their cause? Seventh, interest groups may assist by sharing needed information which government cannot gather (e.g., details on private investment in the city may be provided by financial institutions). Finally, government officials need lobbying support from private groups in the community (a fact which the schools recognized long ago in encouraging the PTAs). Interested groups who feel that they are ignored in city policy formulation can stir up political opposition which cripples its implementation.

What tactical factors mobilize the influence of the group for political action? Drawing skillfully upon the potential organizational support listed in the preceding paragraph means several things. Long-standing or "recognized" groups in the community have privileged access, and official attention is paid to their views. New or minority groups (of whatever kind) may have to demonstrate at city hall to show their strength. In contrast, notables enjoy access and deference to their views deriving from their economic or social standing in the community. Since elites may have divided interests, they may openly (by check) or covertly (by cash) contribute to both sides in political campaigns to insure access: their views must be taken into account, because without their participation a policy may fail.

Group activists must spend their time and energy, the negotiating resources necessary for political bargaining. The prestige and legitimacy necessary for participation give the group the image of having popular support and acceptable views. If public response to a proposal is uncertain, a "trial balloon" exposure of an alternative is aired to test reactions. The group cultivates strategically placed allies and friends at key (public or private) decision-making points. Favors can be traded off for reciprocal political support.

Group leaders in bargaining must husband their potential resources and must calculate the costs involved in committing them, the relative influence of opponents, and the magnitude of any negative public reaction. The congruency of the group's position and the costs of compliance by the bureaucracy must be acceptable before it will be adopted as a city policy. The group must show expertise or at least accurate information if its ideas are to be taken seriously. Also crucial to a political success is the right timing, knowing when the issue is coming up for a decision.

Interest groups serve to focus public demands; the communications media by disseminating information on the issues creates the climate of opinion in which these are considered. Often ignored in the praise of freedom of the press is the fact that the number of media outlets at the local level is extremely limited. Between 1970 and 1981, the number of cities with two or more separately owned and competing newspapers dropped from 70 to 55.[6] The limited number of frequencies (and opposition by current licensees) has prevented establishment of new radio or television stations. Virtually all citizens depend on the media for coverage of city events, and if they are not reported, most of us never know what happened. The type of coverage given shapes the city's policy agenda by focusing public attention on perceived needs and creates a long-term popular impression about the operation of city government.

No matter how conscientious their reporting, the media have two inherent biases. They operate under time constraints (press deadlines and news show schedules) which permit limited space, necessitating simplification of complex issues. Second, newsworthy items are likely to be coverage of sensational and controversial events rather than more routine, predictable items. To remain in business, reporting must sell newspapers or build the TV and radio audience ratings upon which advertising revenues are based.

Around city hall, human interest requires the media to report more on a politician's style and personality than on policy substance. Since most newpapers or stations can only afford a single reporter on the city hall beat, they are dependent upon prepared press releases or sources who want the story told in a manner favorable to them. If a reporter does an independent critique, these leaks may dry up. While editorial thunder has on occasion driven corrupt rascals from city hall, on issues which truly polarize the community a weak, underfinanced newspaper may hesitate to take an editorial position for fear of losing advertising. In the case of TV and radio, under the licensing "fairness doctrine," reply can be made to a station editorial on the air, where glib opponents can confuse the issue, even if the listener heard the station's original opinion. Even if the broad public reads (and remembers) an editorial, the endorsement may be counterproductive if the paper has been identified with one side in the past. Editorials may be more influential in the absence of other cues or public information on the issue or candidate.

Political Participation

Political activity at city hall appears to be proportional to the effect of official action on a person's activity. For the majority of citizens, their personal stake in city decision-making is small.[7] Expressing a political opinion makes a surprising number of people socially uncomfortable. It risks antagonizing friends, neighbors, and co-workers or eliciting criticism for lack of logic or understanding of the issue. The average citizen is likely to doubt the efficacy of his individual intervention. The outcomes at city hall appear more determined by the imperatives of the situation, financial constraints, and pressure generated from those more powerful than people like the rest of us. This attitude is summed up in the cliche "You can't beat city hall." Yet many elected officials stress that most of their public meetings take place before an empty chamber. Nothing is more politically embarrassing than to make a routine decision and then to find that it has stirred up a political hornet's nest. Even if the meeting room is packed, the policy-maker must question whether this is the "true voice of the people" or simply a vociferous minority.

Limited political participation by the general public is most noticeable in voting. Usually only a third of the electorate turns out for separate municipal elections, an even lower proportion than that at the state or national level.[8] Since many adults in our mobile American society do not meet residency requirements or fail to take the initiative of registering to vote for local elections, relatively few inhabitants of the municipality decide at the ballot box. There are several structural reasons for this. Sixty percent of city elections are timed by law to be held separately from others. Reformers have claimed that such a timetable focuses attention on local issues and prevents interference from other contests. Even if municipal elections are consolidated by being held concurrently with others, the ballot may become too long for the voter to make all the choices: bond issues, school board or other special district members, judges, or county, state, or even federal offices.

A major variable affecting municipal voter turnout is whether or not city elections are nonpartisan (candidates on the ballot are not identified by party label).[9] Turn-of-the-century reformers advocated non-partisanship to break the grip of the big-city party machines. With separate elections, there would be no possibility that national or state

---

Should municipal elections be nonpartisan?

Yes	No
1. Local government is less concerned with social policy than with efficient administration: "There is not a Republican or a Democratic way of treating city sewerage."	1. The expansion of municipal activity beyond public improvements and basic services has sharpened policy issues between the parties.
2. Local issues should be decided on their merits. The injection of national party loyalties into the local scene merely confuses the voter: consolidated elections on the same day mean that party landslide victories carry over into a local avalanche.	2. Nonpartisanship nurtures the myth that public decisions can be made outside politics. It results in a special kind of group politics with low visibility. Voter turnout may be lower (Lee found 40–60 percent less in California) without party interest.
3. Nonpartisanship enables members of the minority party to participate in public decision-making. On a nonpartisan council or city commission, those representing a minority viewpoint may secure passage of useful measures which, in a partisan body, the majority might feel compelled to defeat for strictly party reasons.	3. Nonpartisan elections may be so in name only, with parties actively engaging in behind-the-scene endorsements and maneuvering. For example, Chicago's fifty city aldermen are elected on a legally nonpartisan basis, but no one who knows Chicago politics would suggest that it is nonpartisan!
4. Nonpartisan elections may enable well-qualified members of the minority party in the community to be elected, when they would be unlikely to stand a chance in a party contest. "Blue ribbon" citizens can be induced to run for city office "above the politics" of a partisan campaign: businessmen may not wish to run under a party label which might lose them clients.	4. Knowledge of a candidate's party orientation is a far more significant guide to the voter than such information as their occupation, which may appear on the nonpartisan ballot. Nonpartisan elections may tend to segregate political recruitment and finance into partisan or nonpartisan channels, making it harder for the individual candidate to raise campaign resources.
5. Nonpartisanship encourages voting for the person, not the party.	5. Without party labels, voters search for other cues and may vote

voting shifts would create a party tidal wave, sweeping all the offices at city hall. These expectations were amply fulfilled: the incentives for local party organization were lost, so that few cities today have block,

Yes	No
Americans are increasingly identifying themselves as independent voters, without party affiliation.	their prejudices: a nonpartisan at-large ballot may make it more difficult for candidates with an identifiably ethnic name rather than an Anglo-Saxon one to be elected. Voters' familiarity with names alone favors the incumbents in nonpartisan races.
6. The so-called interest of the community as a whole is obscured by party labels. Nonpartisan candidates will uphold "what's right" without fear of party retaliation.	6. Nonpartisanship encourages the avoidance of policy issues in local campaigns: Candidates prefer to take an ambiguous stand or no stand on issues to avoid possible loss of potential electoral support. Nonpartisanship tends to frustrate protest voting, since there are no identifiable "in" and "out" groups.
7. Both major political party organizations have been guilty of ignoring local problems and issues to concentrate on holding city hall for use as an organizational and patronage base.	7. There is no collective responsibility in a nonpartisan body, since the members are elected as individuals rather than as members of a slate of nominees dedicated to a party platform.[10]
8. In predominantly one-party communities, nonpartisanship allows choice by all voters in a general election rather than by the majority party's primary, nominating convention, or caucus of party bosses.	8. Without parties as a recruiting mechanism, nonpartisan candidates may be chosen by special interests such as the remaining incumbents, the local press media, and so forth.
9. Sections of the city do not receive special favors for "voting right" or else are penalized in civic improvements for failing to support the party in power.	9. The combination of nonpartisanship with elections at large (citywide) weakens the power of minority groups which obtain their strength from bloc voting. A party seeks to balance the ticket with candidates from all segments of the community to attract the widest support at the polls.

precinct, or ward party workers. With the party-column type of ballot being replaced by the office-block type, voters have to hunt to find the candidate's name, and many never reach the bottom of the sheet.[11] The relative merits of nonpartisan elections, which are used by two-thirds of the nation's municipalities, have been hotly debated, and the arguments are listed in the separate box.

Parties and Civic Administration

What is the role of political parties in many of the nation's largest cities where partisan elections are used? With fewer Americans professing allegiance to either of the major political parties, personality rather than platform captures the most campaign attention today. The test of a successful politician is knowing how to get things done—and getting others to do them. The political party is a means of mobilizing others to action. The decline in party attachments by the public seems to have an anemic effect upon the running of city hall as teamwork gives way to individual candidacies.

The party's two main functions are selecting candidates and delivering the votes to elect them. In communities of diverse composition, the party functions as a social integrator by reconciling different interests. This can include "ticket balancing," selecting candidates to represent various ethnic, religious, and geographical segments of the city. The ultimate test on election day is, of course, whether the party has attracted a majority at the polls.

People become party activists because they have a continuing passion for playing the political game in concert with others. Loyalty is what distinguishes theirs from transient interest in one candidate or campaign. The partisan politician is an organizational person who remains faithful to a party.

As a voluntary association, a party must offer rewards satisfying to its members. Social respectability in gaining seats of power was important for immigrant groups as they became assimilated into American life and is presently sought by the "newest" large-city ethnic groups: blacks, Chicanos, and Puerto Ricans. For economically underprivileged groups, patronage (city jobs but often state or federally funded) may be sought. Such patronage positions may be outside a merit system, being designated "temporary" but being regularly renewed at six-month intervals. While legally open to all, public jobs may in practice go to those with a party recommendation. In return, they are expected to vote "the right way" and in some cases kick back part of their salaries to an elected official or political party. The party may also be financed by "contributions" from businessmen who want special favors (such as city business) or do not want the city to enforce certain inspections or other regulations. In cities where such corrupt practices occur, a political party, because of its neighborhood organization, becomes the go-between. The party hack, or ward heeler, becomes the bagman, or collector of graft for redistribution to dishonest city employees, department supervisors, or elected officials. An entirely honest broker's role, which party leaders would defend as being true in 99 percent of the cases, is that of the partisan politician acting as a simple facilitator. Knowing whom to contact in the municipal bureaucracy on behalf of a constituent with a problem is an effective way to gain the support of many citizens baffled by the maze at city hall.

Devices for Direct Democracy

In many states municipal voters may directly make decisions. The three devices, initiative, referendum, and recall, allow municipal government by plebiscite. They were often adopted as a reform package, although some states do not allow all three (for instance, some bar recall of judges as impairing the independence of the judiciary).

Initiative. The initiative allows the citizens to propose legislation directly and takes two forms. In the first, the political action group must draft the proposed ordinance, which appears on a petition signed by the number or percentage of registered voters prescribed by state statute or city charter. If the group obtains the required number of valid signatures, the text of the law appears on the city ballot, and if a majority votes for it, the ordinance goes into effect after the election as a city law or as an amendment to the city charter. If the city's governing body refuses to enact a measure the citizens want, they can legislate directly around their elected officials. In the second form of the initiative, the group does not draft the actual text; they petition the governing body to take action in passing a law covering the topic. The city council or commission may be obligated to act, or the request may be left to their discretion.

The initiative can be used by a politically active group to start policy change at regular elections or to force an issue at a politically opportune time at a special election held on the proposal. This device has also been used to legislate special treatment for certain groups, such as specifying that minimums in city wage scales be tied to pay of similar employees in surrounding jurisdictions. The mere threat of an initiative petition may stimulate action by the city council. After the initiative measure has been passed by the electorate, it cannot be altered or repealed by the city governing body for a specified period of time.

Referendum. The referendum refers proposed municipal ordinances or charter amendments to the electorate for decision. There are three types of referenda. The "compulsory," or "mandatory," referendum must, according to the state constitution, statute, or city charter, be decided by the people. Financial referenda to authorize city borrowing or increase tax rates are usually subject to voter approval, often with extraordinary majorities required. Issues deemed of great civic importance (such as city charter amendments, annexations of territory, whether the town will be "dry" or "wet") may be legitimated through popular sovereignty by compulsory referenda. In contrast, an "advisory," or "optional," referendum is sought by the city's governing body, either as an advisory nonbinding expression of public opinion or as assurance that a measure will not go into effect unless the voters approve. While proclaiming that the people should decide, elected officials avoid the political hot seat by letting controversial issues be decided by referendum. An animal leash law may be submitted to the electorate, since the community is evenly divided on the question. "Petition" referenda provide that specified measures enacted by the city governing body can be challenged during a period of time (thirty, sixty, or ninety days) after passage if a protest petition is filed. If the petition contains the required number of signatures, the measure must be ratified by the voters in a special referendum or at the next regular election in order to take effect.

The referendum is the most widely used of the three methods for direct democracy. It provides a check upon city legislative actions in contrast to initiating changes, and it can considerably delay decisions. If a bond issue fails, city operations may be financially crippled until an acceptable measure is passed at a subsequent referendum. While providing safeguards against unwise machinations by the city fathers, it can also thwart their discretion (e.g., voter approval may be required to sell any city property; see figure 4.2). Amendments proposed to the city charter may be highly technical, may add to a complex ballot, or may even contain contradictory measures (in such a case, the one passing with the most votes takes effect). Referenda raise election costs and may prompt expensive campaigns. Firms can be hired to circulate petitions at an agreed price per signature. The number of signatures required for initiative, referendum, or recall efforts if it is set too high may discourage their use and if it is too low may permit abuse by small factions of the community. The signatures must be verified against the list of registered voters, so that an extra margin is usually sought by the gatherers. An absolute number of signatures (e.g., 250) may be required, or the minimum may be a specified percentage of the registered electorate or of those voting in the last city election. In both the initiative and referendum, the negative forces may enjoy the upper hand, for people tend to vote no if they are unsure about a ballot proposition. A two-thirds majority requirement means that two yes votes count the same as a single no vote; or if passage requires a majority of all those voting at the election, those issues at the bottom of

| PROPOSED PROPOSITION NO. 2: DISPOSAL OF CITY PROPERTY: Approval is hereby given to the Mayor and Common Council of the City of San Bernardino to dispose of certain properties of the City by sale for cash or by exchange for other valuable property, as described in City Resolution No. 10994, and generally located south of Fifth Street between Arrowhead Avenue and Mt. View Avenue in said City. | YES |
| | NO |

SYNOPSIS

Proposition No. 2 seeks approval of the voters of the City of San Bernardino for the disposal by sale or by exchange for other valuable property cf real property owned by the City. The real property is described in Resolution No. 10994 and is generally located between Fourth Street and Fifth Street and between Arrowhead Avenue and Mountain View Avenue in said City.

ARGUMENT IN FAVOR OF PROPOSED PROPOSITION NO. 2
(MEASURE "D" ON BALLOT)

Existing facilities at the Hall of Justice are outmoded and grossly inadequate for Police Department use and to accommodate the equipment and personnel required to serve the needs of San Bernardino's expanding area and population. The land involved is ideally located with respect to the downtown area and would be a very marketable piece of real estate.

The site on which the Central Fire Station is located, while a less valuable parcel of property, is immediately adjacent to the Hall of Justice. If considered for sale, together with the Hall of Justice, it would have a potential value greatly in excess of its value if considered separately.

While there are no immediate plans to undertake the relocation of police and fire headquarters, voter approval would be necessary before the present property could be sold. Funds realized from such a sale would help significantly in financing new and needed facilities elsewhere. Adequate vacant land and space to house Police or Fire headquarters is now owned by the City of San Bernardino.

Authorization to sell or otherwise dispose of the Hall of Justice and/or Central Fire Station would give City government the flexibility necessary to properly plan for the most economical and effective location or relocation of these two important facilities and would not make the move mandatory until suitable quarters are available.

We urge a Yes vote on Proposition No. 2.

/s/ Edward S. Wheeler, Jr.
Edward S. Wheeler, Jr.
Councilman, Second Ward

/s/ William Katona
William Katona
Councilman, Third Ward

/s/ Robert L. Hammock
Robert L. Hammock
Councilman, Fourth Ward

/s/ Lionel E. Hudson
Lionel E. Hudson
Councilman, Fifth Ward

/s/ Russell E. Lackner
Russell E. Lackner
Councilman, Seventh Ward

ARGUMENT AGAINST
PROPOSITION FOR SALE OF CENTRAL FIRE STATION
AND/OR HALL OF JUSTICE
PROPOSITION NO. 2
(MEASURE "D" ON BALLOT)

Voters should not approve this measure.

A thorough feasibility study should be undertaken and public hearings held to determine the need for relocation of our existing Central Fire Station and/or Police Station.

The present location of the Fire and Police Departments within the Central City complex and the property now owned by our citizens is of prime value. Future needs may require a further expansion of our City government facilities and what we now own may never be replaced at a cost which is consistent with the revenue of our city.

/s/ Norris Gregory, Jr.
Norris Gregory, Jr.
Councilman, Sixth Ward

This publication is pursuant to Article XI, Section 8, of the California Constitution, relating to city charters and amendments to city charters, and to State Laws relating to measures.
DATE: March 30, 1972

LUCILLE GOFORTH, City Clerk

Figure 4.2. A Referendum Ballot

the ballot receive fewer votes than the candidates who fill the top of the ballot. Politicians call this voter "drop-off."

Recall. The recall is designed to remove an elected official prior to the expiration of his term, in contrast to the policy orientation of the initiative and referendum. Since it is directed against elective (not appointive) officials, the recall petition requires signatures equal to a certain percentage of those voting for the office or in the last city election. The number can range from 15 percent to 50 percent. Higher requirements discourage use, since verification of signatures and holding a special election are expensive. The recall ballot often contains the petition statement of the grounds on which the recall is sought, together with a rebuttal submitted by the incumbent justifying his conduct in office (see figure 4.3). The ballot asks: "Shall (incumbent's name) be recalled from the office of . . . Vote yes or no." If a majority of people vote yes, the official is removed from office. Some state laws permit a consolidated recall ballot, where opposition candidates may be listed below the incumbent so that if the voter wants a change, he can pick the replacement. Otherwise, if a recall occurs, a later separate election is held in which candidates have filed to fill the vacant office. If an incumbent survives a recall election, another petition cannot be made against him for a certain period, commonly six months. (A newly elected official is not usually subject to recall for an initial period of his term, so that opponents cannot immediately seek a recall.)

In contrast to impeachment, for which grounds are specified in law, recall is simply a matter of popular desire. The reasons may be purely political, and recall is often threatened as a retaliation. Policy differences are the usual cause, but the individual nature of the recall stimulates personal recriminations. A determined interest group can instigate vague or unprovable charges which can have very divisive effects. Proponents of the recall (such as Theodore Roosevelt, who described it as the "club behind the door") argue that it fosters continuing accountability of elected officials. While recalls may be threatened, the actual removal of officials is relatively rare.[12]

Administering the Will of the People

The importance of political parties in American cities has declined in this century[13] because many jurisdictions are dominated by one party or another or because nonpartisanship has spread. The result has been that the traditional distinction between parties seeking to fill political office and interest groups organized to influence public policy has been blurred. Good government groups may recruit and endorse candidates, while loyal partisans may use a local issue as a mobilizing vehicle for recruiting party supporters. A number of cities have local political

STATEMENT IN RECALL PETITION OF THE GROUNDS ON WHICH THE RECALL IS SOUGHT:

We petition for the recall of Robert J. Simpson, member of the San Bernardino City Unified School Board for his actions in opposition to the best interests of the education of the children of the district. The above named board member has consistently supported action to bring about mandatory cross-busing which in our belief shows neglect of the education standards, resulting in continual lowering of achievement levels in the community and continually costing taxpayers more for less.

STATEMENT SUBMITTED BY SAID ROBERT J. SIMPSON JUSTIFYING HIS COURSE IN OFFICE:

Mandatory busing is no longer a current issue with the Board. On March 16, 1972, the Board instructed the School Administration to formulate a plan of integration without the use of mandatory busing. The ultimate decision as to forced busing will be decided by the state and federal laws and court decisions.

Figure 4.3. A Recall Ballot

parties which grew out of ad hoc political groups in past conflicts. Party control of the statehouse, majority control of Congress, or the presidency may have more policy impact on local communities than control of city hall, given the financial scope of state and federal programs.

Both parties and the devices for direct democracy serve simply as vehicles for mobilizing citizens' preferences. The link between voting and public policy has long been a subject of research by political scientists. The fact that the old-time party machines have withered away does not mean an absence of brokerage politics in the city. There will be conflicts over goals and the priorities according to which available resources should be allocated as well as over whether private or public means should be used to solve community problems. Election results constitute a collective decision which may give clear answers in a referendum but which usually provides mixed verdicts in the candidates' races. If all incumbents are defeated (or win reelection by large margins), then the voters' mandate is relatively clear.

But many administrative actions have no such electoral link. Frequently they are implementational decisions which are highly technical and of which the public is not aware. An administrative course will be pursued unless it is challenged by a noisy demonstration at city hall protesting the "bureaucratic mess." This policy drift has worried some observers, who contend, "The modern city is now well run but badly governed because it is now comprised of islands of functional power."[14] Our social emphasis on professionalism has produced policy fiefdoms ruled by educators, social workers, policemen, firemen, and even sanitation workers. Can city politics provide adequate policy guidance?

One solution which has been suggested for large and diverse cities is administrative decentralization. Popularly called "neighborhood government" or the "little city hall" concept, it seeks resident input into the administration of programs needing local implementation. Advantages claimed are responsiveness to neighborhood needs, improved delivery of city services, and healing of political alienation by bringing government closer to the people. Decentralization involves two dimensions, political decision-making and administrative implementation. Various cities around the country have tried limited experiments.[15] New York City, with "community control" of certain schools and coterminous community districts for police, sanitation, parks and recreation, and a number of social services, tried a delegation of authority amid great political bitterness. Other cities have tried "mini city halls" where forms can be obtained, citizen complaints registered through a mayor's aide, and neighborhood desires for city services voiced (an increase in police patrols at certain hours, the need for trimming of a tree, and so forth). Such decentralization appears most effective in obtaining service or communicating problems directly to the police, sanitation department, or other department responsible for the area. But political progress is slow. City councilmen may resist a parallel structure for handling the constituent requests which build political support. Elections to community councils, urban renewal advisory committees, and federally funded community action boards have in most cases produced negligible neighborhood turnouts. Decentralization needs executive support to succeed but may be regarded by opponents as establishing a campaign or patronage organization to benefit the incumbent mayor. City civil servants stoutly resist any shift of authority (especially over appointments, promotions, or transfers) to neighborhood control. Administratively, the task of city politics remains to mediate between the extremes of centralized authority and the tyranny of arbitrary local majorities.[16]

Notes

1. Edward C. Banfield and James Q. Wilson, *City Politics* (Cambridge, Mass.: Harvard University Press and M.I.T. Press, 1963), p. 18.

2. Oliver P. Williams and Charles R. Adrian, *Four Cities* (Philadelphia: University of Pennsylvania Press, 1963).

3. Everett Ladd, Jr., *Ideology in America: Change and Response in a City, a Suburb, and a Small Town* (Ithaca, N.Y.: Cornell University Press, 1969), p. 139.

4. Claire Gilbert, "The Study of Community Power: A Summary and a Test," in *The New Urbanization*, ed. Scott Greer, Dennis L. McElrath, David W. Minar, and Peter Orleans (New York: St. Martin's Press, 1968), pp. 222–45.

5. Terry N. Clark, "Power and Community Structure: Who Governs, Where and When?" *Sociological Quarterly*, vol. 8 (summer 1967), pp. 291–316.

6. Jonathan Friendly, "Requiem for a View: News Executives Call Star's Demise Washington's and the Nation's Loss," *New York Times*, July 24, 1981, p. 9.

7. Local businessmen, realtors, developers, contractors, and municipal employees do have direct interests in city policy outcomes and thus are major participants in the political arena. Businessmen are crucial in determining local investment and, by heavy representation on city boards and commissions, exert a continuing influence in civic affairs.

8. Robert R. Alford and Eugene Lee found in 282 cities with population over 25,000 that turnout averaged 47 percent because of mayor-council and partisan elections. "Voting Turnout in American Cities," *American Political Science Review*, vol. 62 (1968), pp. 796–813. Howard D. Hamilton, "The Municipal Voter: Voting and Nonvoting in City Elections," *American Political Science Review*, vol. 65 (1971), pp. 1135–40, found that people in the top socioeconomic brackets are more likely to vote, the usual trend in political participation.

9. The two major studies (both done in California) are by Eugene Lee, *The*

Politics of Nonpartisanship (Berkeley and Los Angeles: University of California Press, 1960), and his student Willis D. Hawley, *Nonpartisan Politics and the Case for Party Politics* (New York: Wiley, 1973).

10. Charles R. Adrian, "Some General Characteristics of Non-Partisan Elections," *American Political Science Review*, vol. 46 (September 1952), pp. 766–76.

11. As a result, larger cities are under pressure to rotate the candidates' names in first place on different series of ballots.

12. In the mid-1970s a recall petition against Philadelphia's mayor was invalidated, and a recall election sparked by Seattle's fire fighters' union was won by the incumbent mayor. An attempt in 1978 to recall Cleveland mayor Dennis Kucinich failed by a narrow margin.

13. Chapter 1 related reasons for the decline of city machines.

14. Theodore J. Lowi, *The End of Liberalism* (New York: Norton, 1969), p. 201.

15. George Frederickson, ed., *Neighborhood Control in the 1970s* (New York: Chandler, 1973) contains conference reports.

16. See James Madison, *The Federalist Papers*, No. 10.

For Further Reading

Agger, Robert, Goldrich, Daniel, and Swanson, Bert. *The Rulers and the Ruled.* Rev. ed. Belmont, Calif.: Duxbury Press, 1972.

Banfield, Edward C., and Wilson, James Q. *City Politics.* Cambridge, Mass.: Harvard University Press and M.I.T. Press, 1963.

Bonjean, Charles M., Clark, Terry N., and Lineberry, Robert L., eds. *Community Politics: A Behavioral Approach.* New York: Free Press, 1971.

Callow, Alexander B., Jr., ed. *The City Boss in America.* New York: Oxford University Press, 1976.

Clark, Terry N., ed. *Community Structure and Decision-Making: Comparative Analyses.* San Francisco: Chandler, 1968.

Frederickson, George, ed. *Neighborhood Control in the 1970s.* New York: Chandler, 1973.

Gilbert, Claire. *Community Power Structure.* Gainesville: University of Florida Press, 1972.

Hawley, Willis D., and Wirt, Frederick M., eds. *The Search for Community Power.* Englewood Cliffs, N.J.: Prentice-Hall, 1968.

Ladd, Everett C. *Ideology in America: Change and Response in a City, a Suburb, and a Small Town.* Ithaca, N.Y.: Cornell University Press, 1969.

LaNoue, George R., and Smith, Bruce L. R. *The Politics of School Decentralization.* Lexington, Mass.: D. C. Heath, 1973.

Nordlinger, Eric A. *Decentralizing the City: A Study of Boston's Little City Halls.* Cambridge, Mass.: M.I.T. Press, 1972.

Rose, Arnold M. *The Power Structure* New York: Oxford University Press, 1967.

Sigal, Leon V. *Reporters and Officials.* Lexington, Mass.: D. C. Heath, 1973.

"Urban Black Politics," *Annals of the American Academy of Political and Social Science*, vol. 439 (September 1978).

Williams, Oliver P., and Adrian, Charles R. *Four Cities.* Philadelphia: University of Pennsylvania Press, 1963.

5: Who's Who at City Hall

Decision-making for the city takes place within a decentralized framework, described in this chapter with its implications for administration.

Forms for Municipal Government

The town meeting is still used by some smaller jurisdictions with population under 10,000, particularly in New England (see figure 5.1). In this form of pure democracy, all the adult residents meet once or twice a year to decide basic policies such as the tax rate, adoption of the budget, and so forth. The meeting is presided over by an elected moderator, and decisions are taken by voice vote or show of hands. In some communities where an open meeting has proved too unwieldy, delegates are chosen by neighbors on each block to vote at the representative town meeting held in the village hall, church, or lodge hall.

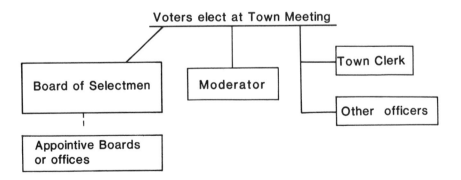

Figure 5.1. New England Town Meeting Form

Daily operations through the year are supervised by a few "selectmen" chosen at the annual town meeting. An elected town clerk usually serves as the only full-time paid administrator.

The city commission originated in 1900; a Galveston hurricane swept away the city and its government, and an emergency citizens' relief committee proved so efficient that it was continued by the governor and legalized by the Texas Legislature. The major characteristic of the commission form is that it fuses legislative and executive powers. Three, five, or seven commissioners are elected at large (citywide), serving collectively as the legislative body and individually as heads of the principal city departments including public works, public safety, finance, and others. They may be elected all at one time or may serve staggered terms (e.g., one commissioner may be elected each year for a three-year term). While not elected by geographical ward, in some cities they run "by place" for a specific office (e.g., commissioner of parks and recreation). In other cities, the commissioners after the election simply divide the functional responsibilities among themselves. Presiding over their meetings is the president of the commission, or "mayor," who may be elected by place or chosen by his colleagues or may be the commissioner who received the most votes or the senior member in length of service; or the commissioners may rotate the ceremonial duties in turn every year. The president does not have a veto, and commission decisions are made by majority vote.

The concentration of municipal authority in the city commission, combined with nonpartisan at-large elections, appealed to reformers, especially those advocating the short ballot of few elective offices. Other benefits claimed are four:

1. If commissioners are elected by place for a certain function, they can be chosen on their individual qualifications by the voters, or else the commissioners can give responsibility for finance and accounting to a commissioner who may be a banker or accountant in private life.

2. Administration is expeditious, since a commissioner can make a proposal, have it approved by his colleagues, and then carry it out with direct responsibility.

3. With election at large, there is no gerrymandering (politically skewed drawing) of council ward boundaries.

4. There is no rivalry or deadlock between a dictatorial mayor and the council. The voters can judge commissioners on the performance of their departments.

While it enjoyed initial popularity, the commission form peaked about 1920 and was gradually abandoned as the following disadvantages became apparent in its operation.

1. The absence of executive-legislative checks and balances may mean logrolling between the commissioners—each votes for the others' projects, so each commissioner acts independently without coordination.

2. Citizens lack redress for grievances: if the streets commissioner turns down a request to trim a tree, it is usually futile to appeal to the commission, since the other members will back their colleague, lest he similarly interfere in the operation of their departments.

3. Competition over the budget occurs, since each commissioner seeks funding for his domain. The result may be overspending without a chief executive to set priorities or a schism between the commissioners, with buck passing as criticized commissioners claim that the majority did not give their departments adequate funding.

4. The technical expertise demanded by city operations may mean hiring separate department heads, such as police and fire chiefs, making a public safety commissioner less economical. Or if the commissioner does act as the operational head, he may lack time to make joint policy decisions with his colleagues.

This lack of clear and coherent leadership led the reformers to switch allegiance to the council-manager form. Today the commission form is found only in smaller communities, predominantly in the South, where its simple structure and at-large elections (which make it more difficult to elect minority members) apparently have appeal.[1]

The mayor-council form is used by more than half of all American municipalities, from the smallest villages to the largest cities. While it separates legislative powers between a city council and a directly elected mayor as chief executive, there can be separately elected officers such as city clerk and treasurer. A frequent classification is between weak- or strong-mayor types (see figure 5.2), and the separate box lists relative measures of the mayor's authority. The council can be elected at large citywide or by geographical districts called wards,[2] on a partisan ticket or a nonpartisan ballot. The number of council members usually increases with the city's size, and larger city councils may be presided over by a council president either chosen by the members or directly elected by the people. Some city activities may be administered by separate entities such as water commissioners, library trustees, cemetery boards, or airport authorities, which enjoy various degrees of fiscal independence and autonomy in setting their operating policies.

The council-manager plan (figure 5.3) is used by 40 percent of American cities, and is especially popular in middle-sized (10,000–250,000) middle-class communities. Developed during the early years of this century, it reflects the business orientation of the reformers who pushed its ideology of professional management. The city is conceived

WEAK MAYOR TYPE

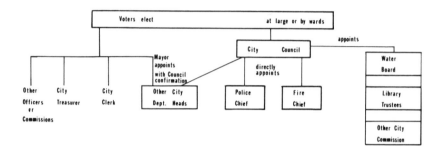

STRONG MAYOR TYPE

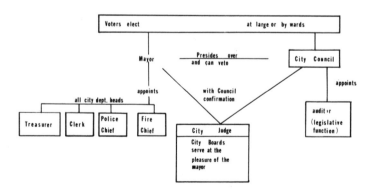

Figure 5.2. The Mayor-Council Form. Some organizational arrangements compromise between (a) the weak-mayor type and (b) the strong-mayor type.

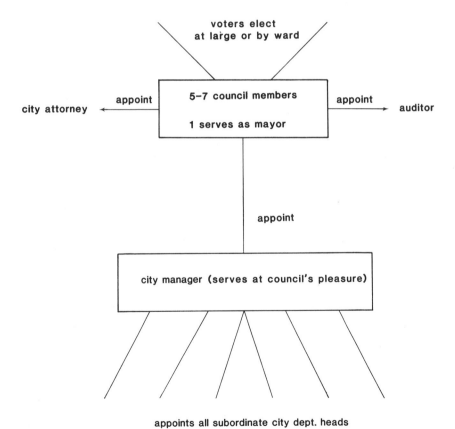

Figure 5.3. A Council-Manager Form, with All Authority Delegated to the City Manager

as a common concern in which the citizens are shareholders. They elect a board of directors (city council), which sets major policies and hires a professional city manager to carry them out. In pure form, the city council is small (usually a short ballot of five members), elected at large on a nonpartisan basis. Council positions are usually considered to be part time, paying a minimal salary or small allowance per meeting. The city manager, a trained professional, has complete administrative authority, hiring and firing all city department heads and responsible solely to the council. The council chooses one of its members to preside as mayor (the honor may go to the senior member or the one receiving the most popular votes), although nearly half the council-manager cities have a mayor directly elected by the people. The mayor usually does not have a vote, but his executive authority varies. The administrative hierarchy of the city is simplified, with the manager at the top: city boards or commissions lose their budgetary independence and become advisory only. The manager is responsible for preparing the city budget and making any recommendations to the council which he deems advisable, but he does not have a veto power (as a directly elected mayor may).

The council-manager form has been the favored adoption as city commission or weak-mayor arrangements have been abandoned. The International City Management Association (ICMA) has acquired its name as the system has been used in Canada, West Germany, Scandinavia, and even Yugoslavia. While there are fervent proponents of the plan, it has also drawn criticism (see box).

The City Manager Plan

Pro	Con
1. As city government has become more complex, it stresses professionalism, with administrators chosen on the basis of competence.	1. An appointive city manager is less responsive. All large American cities with population over one million have a politically elective chief executive.
2. Municipal administration is segregated from city politics.	2. It is naive to think that policy can be separated from its implementation and management.
3. The city manager gives expert advice to council, resulting in maximum efficiency and economy.	3. The council still has ties to the municipal bureaucracy, and potential political liabilities may outweigh the savings in cost recommended by the manager.
4. The city manager, as an appointed expert, can provide more impartial judgment.	4. The manager may lack political sensitivity, and if there is an elected mayor, their respective roles may be ambiguous.

The Mayor-Council Form

A Weaker Mayoral Office

1. Mayor is chosen by council; a council president may also be directly elected citywide. Council members elected at large.

2. Has a two-year term or one shorter than the council and is barred by law from succeeding himself.

3. Does not preside over the council, or if mayor does, has no vote or power to appoint council committees.

4. Can only vote in case of a tie and/or does not have a veto over any council action.

5. There are separately elected executive officials (clerk, attorney, treasurer), or the council chooses the major city department heads (police chief, fire chief, and so forth). The mayor may have limited appointive power (with council confirmation) but cannot remove any officials.

6. Important city activities (e.g., ports, water system, library, even police) are under control of various city boards or commissions which the mayor does not sit on or appoint.

7. City budget requests are formulated by city boards, commission, or council committees and are passed as a legislative budget.

8. Mayor's job perceived as mainly ceremonial, part time, with minimal compensation.

9. Mayor elected on nonpartisan ballot; must gather own campaign support and build political alliances wherever he can.

A Stronger Mayoral Office

1. Mayor is directly elected so has mandate from the people. Mayor is the only official elected by the entire city.

2. Four-year term or longer term than council, with no limitations on reelection.

3. Presides over council, sets its agenda, may vote on measures, and can appoint or serve ex officio on all committees of the council.

4. Can veto municipal ordinances passed by the council, can item veto financial appropriations, and can only be overridden by an extramajority vote of the council (three-quarters of membership or two-thirds present and voting).

5. The mayor appoints and dismisses all city officials not covered by civil service, without council concurrence.

6. City administration is integrated under control of the mayor as chief executive. City boards are advisory only, appointed at the pleasure of the mayor.

7. Mayor is responsible for presenting an executive budget and all financial requests must be submitted to his office.

8. Mayor's job considered full time with appropriate salary and staff proportional to the size of the city.

9. Mayor is recognized as leader of his party, which provides support, political influence in the council, and control through patronage over the city bureaucracy.

The préviously described structures are pure forms subject to considerable alteration according to state law and local desire. The governmental arrangement found in each municipality is a product of local tradition, borrowed features which worked for neighboring jurisdictions, past political history, and even officials' personality clashes at city hall. Thus town meetings can hire a "town (city) manager" who serves several nearby New England towns. City commissions or mayor-council governments can hire "city administrative officers" who are vested with varying degrees of management authority. The couplet "For forms of government let fools contest; Whatever is best administered is best"[3] ignores the fact that structure is formed by political compromise and determines the framework within which administration takes place. Moreover, form does not ensure admirable city government: the Hague machine operated in the Jersey City commission and Kansas City had a city manager during Boss Pendergast's reign. As important as official structure are the electoral rules by which the political struggle is waged.

Electoral Systems

Electoral systems affect voter influence at city hall and the scope and intensity of political conflict in the community. The essence of campaign strategy is to build electoral strength sufficient for victory. City elections have several aspects: voter qualifications, registration, and polling; methods of nomination; margins required to win; and trends in electing municipal officials.

Voter qualifications center on age and residence, unless an American citizen[4] has lost this civil right through criminal conviction or mental incompetence. The Twenty-sixth Amendment to the U.S. Constitution lowered the voting age to eighteen in all elections, federal, state, and local, and now that the U.S. Supreme Court has characterized voting as a fundamental right, the state must show a compelling state interest before it may impose any limitations. Traditionally many jurisdictions required lengthy residence to familiarize the voter with candidates and civic issues, but this also sharply reduced the local electorate. Today a jurisdiction requiring more than about one month's residency to vote is inviting court challenge, although candidates for public office may have to live in the city longer than the registered voter. Formerly, in some states the municipal electorate was further divided: all registered voters could vote for candidates, but only those who were property tax payers could vote on financial referenda. The U.S. Supreme Court, in two opinions delivered on the same day in 1969, said states could not restrict voting in a school district election to parents and property owners[5] and that limiting the franchise to property tax payers in revenue bond elections of a municipal utility in Louisiana violated the Equal Protection Clause.[6]

Since the financial burdens and benefits of taxes or bond issues are likely to fall indiscriminately on residents, statutes which selectively distribute the franchise are likely to violate the Equal Protection Clause of the Fourteenth Amendment. Any classification of voters requires a compelling state interest (there must be a rational basis for limiting the franchise to certain voters) before it will be upheld by the courts.

Citizens who qualify must register (usually in person) to vote. Registration is normally conducted by county- or state-appointed registrars, although some municipalities maintain separate registration lists or, occasionally (in small communities where everyone knows everyone else), none at all. Registration is possible until a few days before an election, when poll lists are being prepared, although in some jurisdictions where registrars are paid on a per diem basis the board may accept applications only a few days per month. Registration by postcard or even at the polls is currently being tried in a few states which have not had a reputation for vote fraud.

Registration may be either permanent or subject to cancellation if the voter does not appear at the polls for a specified number of elections. Permanent registration is more convenient for the voter but rapidly becomes inaccurate as people move and is also conducive to election fraud ("voting the city cemetery"). Periodic reidentification through checking obituary columns, property tax rolls, or utility billing rosters or by asking voters to send in a newspaper coupon in order to stay on the poll list is a time-consuming and expensive process.

In some states, party workers can be sworn in as deputy registrars to enroll anyone regardless of party, although such door-to-door voting drives are usually made in areas which appear favorable to the conducting party. The decline of parties at the city level has meant that in states using deputy registrars, retired persons supplement their income by enrolling voters at so much per name in local shopping centers and other public places. In cities electing officials by geographical ward, voting lists must be prepared for each polling place, which may be different from the voting precincts used in other elections.

State law usually specifies the hours the polls will remain open, although political machinations in big cities have occasionally resulted in too few voting booths or machines to accommodate waiting voters. Polling officials (clerks and inspectors) are often appointed from lists supplied by the parties (a vestige of minor patronage) and are frequently senior citizens or housewives who receive a small stipend. State law usually allows any political party which has candidates running to appoint a poll watcher to observe and challenge any irregularities in the voting or the counting. To reduce fraud and human error, some jurisdictions have replaced paper ballots with voting machines. These are expensive and may mechanically malfunction, so the newest innovation is to have voters punch a computer card (see figure 5.4), which then can be counted swiftly at a central location. If a voter knows he is going to be absent on election day, most states permit, for specified reasons, filing of an absentee ballot during a certain period before the election.

There are several methods for placing candidates' names on the ballot. The decline of party activity at the municipal level has ended the caucus (a meeting of political leaders to pick a slate) and city party conventions (although local party clubs may endorse individual candidates). Recruitment for city office has therefore become largely a matter of personal ambition. An individual may be urged to run for office by his friends and neighbors or may develop the political itch spontaneously. The first step is self-announcement by a release to the media or a form letter to constituents seeking their support. While this is the method used by write-in candidates, before the name can be printed on the ballot, nomination by petition is usually required. The aspiring candidate must collect the signatures of a stipulated number or percentage of registered voters as a testimonial that the person meets the qualifications for office (age, residency, and so forth). Such certification may be inaccurate, and courts are sometimes asked to disqualify candidates on various technical grounds. The candidate may also be required to deposit a filing fee along with his petition, which can be a flat sum ($100) or a percentage of the salary that the office pays. The purpose of the filing fee (and signatures) is to eliminate frivolous candidates, since the money will be forfeited unless they receive a minimal percentage (such as 5 percent) of the vote. Candidates who swore that they could not afford the fee have been placed on the ballot by the courts, although the chance that such candidates would be elected is slim, since voters are unlikely to place indigents in charge of public money. A number of perennial officeseekers often forfeit their petition deposits, but in contrast, if only a single candidate files for an office by the deadline, state election law may declare him the winner without an election.

While nominating petitions and payment of a filing fee can place an independent candidate on the ballot, these may also be used to qualify in the direct primary method. Primary elections are the most common means of selecting municipal candidates and may be partisan or nonpartisan. Partisan primaries may be "open," for all voters to participate in, or "closed," for only that party's members, so the opposition cannot

VOTING INSTRUCTIONS

STEP 1 Remove the Ballot card from the gray envelope.

STEP 2 Using both hands, slide the ballot card all the way into the Vote Recorder.

STEP 3 Be sure the two slots in the end of your card fit down **over the two red pins.**

STEP 4 To vote, hold the punch **straight up and push straight down** through the ballot card for each of your choices.

STEP 5 Turn the pages to continue voting.

STEP 6 After voting, slide the card out of the Vote Recorder and place it **under the flap** of the gray envelope.

If you make a mistake, return the ballot card and gray envelope to obtain another.

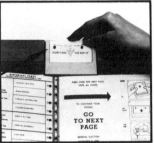

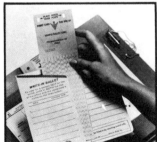

Instrucciones Para Votar

PASO UNO: Saque la papeleta de votar del sobre gris.

PASO SEGUNDO: **Usando las dos manos,** meta la papeleta de votar hasta el fondo en la voto-matica.

PASO TRES: Asegure que los dos hoyos en la parte superior de su tarjeta caigan **sobre los dos alfileres rojos.**

PASO CUATRO: Para votar, detenga el picador **derecho para arriba y pique directa-mente para abajo** por la papeleta de votar por cada una de sus selecciones.

PASO CINCO: Voltie las paginas para continuar votando.

PASO SEIS: Despues de votar, saque la tarjeta de la votomatica y pongala **debajo de la tapa** del sobre gris.

Si hace un error, devuelva la papeleta de votar y el sobre gris para obtener otra.

Figure 5.4. Ballot by Computer. The voter inserts the ballot in a plastic frame of overlapping pages which enables him neatly to punch out his choices. This method is cheap and error proof; its major disadvantage is that any write-in votes must be submitted on another sheet and tabulated separately. *Source:* Voting instructions prepared by the California secretary of state to accompany official ballots counted by computer.

infiltrate into the nominating process to pick the weaker candidate for the general election. In states which do not require voters to register by party affiliation, closed primaries are actually open, because voters can simply enter the polling place and pick the primary ballot of the party they wish to vote in (for areas dominated by one party, this is the only way voters of other persuasions can influence election to local office, since the minority party or parties will frequently fail to recruit a slate of candidates). Under some (especially Southern) state election laws, if no candidate receives a majority in the party primary, the top two will face a runoff. In areas dominated by one party, such nomination is tantamount to election, since opposition at the general election may be insignificant.

Nonpartisan primaries place all declared candidates, or those filing by petition, on the ballot without party labels. Usually the two highest vote-getters in the primary are nominated for the office and their names placed on the general election ballot, also without party designation. However, if a particular candidate gains a majority in the primary, he is usually declared the winner without the need for a general election to fill that office.

Single-member electoral districts provide geographic representation within a city and contribute to a short ballot. While promoting grassroots political organization as a means to win, in cities using partisan elections wards may tend to be one-party enclaves. Single-member district representatives may take a parochial view of civic issues and may trade votes with other council members to benefit their ward. Proponents of ward elections respond that small constituencies make possible an official voice for neighborhood or minority interests.

Citywide or at-large elections were promoted by Progressive era reformers believing in an indivisible civic interest. Often adopted along with nonpartisanship, at-large elections were used by reformers to defeat ward-based political machines. Running at large tends to favor candidates who possess greater "name recognition" (either by reputation or through the media) and those having money to campaign throughout the jurisdiction. Thus successful candidates may be drawn from a rather narrow geographic area or social elite.

At-large electoral systems can show several variations. Candidates may be required to live in and be nominated by district, although they are elected by voters of the entire jurisdiction. Or candidates may run by place for a specific council seat. The place system originated in the South and prevents the so-called bullet vote by a minority community. Thus rather than running against all other candidates at large, one of whom might receive the concentrated vote of a disciplined minority voting bloc, the candidate elected by place runs only against those who filed for that seat. A deeply divided U.S. Supreme Court, in *City of*

Mobile (Ala.) v. *Bolden,* 446 U.S. 55 (1980), overruled lower federal courts and held 6 to 3 that an at-large electoral system (by place) did not violate the Fifteenth Amendment rights of the city's Negro residents. The majority held that while the Equal Protection Clause of the Fourteenth Amendment confers the right to participate in an election on an equal basis with other qualified voters, it does not protect any "political group," however defined, from electoral defeat, nor does it require proportional representation in political organizations.

To provide continuity, many municipalities stagger (overlap) the terms of office of council members, although a change of public opinion at the polls will usually shift control to the new majority following an at-large election. A few cities combine both types of representation by electing some council members by ward and others at large.

Finally, an electoral system used in only a very few American cities is proportional representation (PR), in which voters indicate their choices of candidates in numerical order. Preferential voting ensures minority representation, which is both its strength and its weakness; when it was tried in New York City during the 1940s, it was dropped when communists—a tiny but solid voting minority—were elected to the city council. No nominating or runoff elections are needed; PR mirrors voter preferences, but counting the ballots is a lengthy process, depending on which system is used.[7]

Thus the margin for victory in a city election can vary, depending upon state election laws. A candidate may file for an office which is uncontested and win immediately. Or he may have to fight in a primary and runoff to gain his party's nomination and then face stiff opposition in the general election. In nonpartisan contests, the candidate may win outright with a majority in the primary or gain office with a plurality (more votes than any other candidate received, but not a majority of those cast). A survey[8] indicated that in more than half the American cities, candidates can win with a plurality at the general election, although other cities go to the expense of a runoff election to ensure a majority mandate. However, given the low turnout typical of municipal elections, most city officials are elected by a fraction of the populace.

The reapportionment revolution started by "one person, one vote" has been applied by the U.S. Supreme Court to counties and cities.[9] If a municipality decides to elect its governing body by wards or geographical divisions, then these must contain substantially equal population. Thus each citizen's ballot is theoretically equal, although demographic variables, numbers of registered voters, and propensity to turn out to vote can produce striking differences among the districts on election day. Even if all election districts are equal in population, their boundaries can be gerrymandered—arranged to produce certain political advantages or to divide the electoral strength of opposing interests (see figure 5.5).

A Profile of Civic Leaders

While electoral rules structure voting influence at city hall, the American trend is toward fewer elective municipal officials. The executive officers most likely to be separately elected are those concerned with finance: city treasurer (27 percent), assessor (17 percent), auditor (11 percent), or controller (10 percent). If there is no full-time mayor or city manager, the city clerk (18 percent) and occasionally the city attorney may be directly elected.[10] All these percentages have decreased over the past twenty years as the weak-mayor form has declined and the council-manager system has been adopted. The city clerk can vary from being a routine office manager to functioning as the only full-time administrator in small communities. The clerk ordinarily attends each council meeting taking its minutes, maintains municipal records required by law, and conducts city elections. In contrast to such ministerial duties, the city attorney (or corporation counsel) is often drawn into policy formulation as the council asks for legal advice. An independently elected city attorney can freely question the course of action proposed by a mayor or council. In smaller municipalities, the attorney is frequently hired part time on retainer from private practice. His major duties are to review all city enactments (including contracts) for legality, represent the city in any legal action (such as eminent domain or condemnation proceedings), and act as prosecutor of municipal violators in criminal court.

Table 5.1. Number of City Council Members

Population category	Average (mean) size
Over 500,000	15
250,000–500,000	9
100,000–249,999	8
25,000–99,999	7
5,000–24,999	6
Under 2,500–4,999	5
Total	6

Note: $N = 3,834$.

Source: International City Management Association, *The Municipal Year Book, 1976* (Washington, D.C., 1976) p. 70.

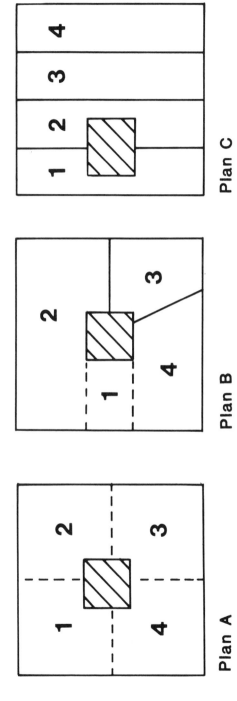

Plan A

Plan B

Plan C

Figure 5.5. Gerrymandering. The practice is named after Elbridge Gerry, a signer of the Declaration of Independence and fifth vice president of the United States. A legislative district in Massachusetts drawn when Gerry was governor was said to resemble a salamander, prompting Gerry's political opponents to dub it a gerrymander. In Plans A-C, all four districts comply with the "one person, one vote" requirement, but drawing of the districts determines party advantage or disadvantage. In the case of any minority party, or group X (shaded area), Plan A offers no electoral chance of winning; Plan B concedes one seat but prevents other seats from being won; and Plan C gives X candidates the maximum chance of winning seats 1 and 2.

The 1972 *Municipal Year Book* contained a profile of municipal governing bodies. (See table 5.1.) They consist predominantly of "councilmen"; only 20 percent of the cities reported having women on the council. Minority representation is exactly that: only about 1 percent of the members nationwide are nonwhite. The smaller the municipality, the less likely it is to have nonwhite council members. However, cities in the South report more nonwhite members—one in every four councils. In terms of age, the councilman is most likely to be in his forties, fifties, or thirties (in that order). In common with most political leaders, councillors are likely to have more formal education than their constituents' mean years of schooling. In contrast to state or national legislators, average incumbency is much lower: 60 percent of the council members have served four years or less, and only 2 percent have been in office more than eight years. More than half the council members in this 1972 survey were serving their first term in office.[11] Smaller municipalities (population under 25,000) had more turnover, probably because elective office is considered a part-time civic duty and personal business and family life suffer from extended periods in office. Any vacancies are filled by appointment by the rest of the council or in special elections. Since two-thirds of the cities have overlapping (or "staggered") council terms, it is difficult to "throw the rascals out" of city hall all at once.

A city council determines its own rules of procedure subject to state law or city charter requirements such as frequency of meetings. Larger bodies will necessitate more formal proceedings, but every council will have its own personality, depending upon the members elected. The larger the city, the more likely that the council will have specialized committees and that council members will have office space or even staff assistance.

How do councils spend their time? The most frequently reported activities in the ICMA survey were:

1. Considering proposals of the executive branch
2. Review of city operations
3. Zoning and planning decisions
4. Preparing and adopting the annual budget
5. Handling individual constituent requests
6. Appointments and personnel decisions.[12]

What does it mean for public scrutiny that councils are deliberating rather than initiating bodies? Virtually all councils are required by law to keep minutes of their meetings; three-fourths maintain official voting records; and two-thirds publish the council agenda in advance of the meeting.[13] A number of states have "sunshine laws" that call for all public business to be conducted in open session and announced in advance. Common exceptions are personnel matters involving discussion of employees' work records or discussions concerning acquisition of land or property (to prevent speculation). Although the practice borders on illegality, some councils may engage in an informal conference, or caucus, to resolve their differences in private before the official meeting, which then becomes a speedy ritual.

The most extensive study of council behavior was conducted at Stanford University during the late 1960s, and various books by the researchers are listed at the end of the chapter. The study covered eighty-seven cities in the San Francisco Bay area, almost all of which had the council-manager form of government. One of the researchers, Betty Zisk, has characterized local interest politics as a one-way street because three-fourths of the 435 council members were either merely tolerant of or downright antagonistic toward interest group activity. The local chamber of commerce and Jaycees were the most frequently mentioned groups in civic activities. Her findings closely parallel studies of state legislators as to how elected officials perceive their role:[14] 60 percent of the council members identified themselves as trustees using their own judgment in deciding issues. Only 18 percent characterized themselves as delegates carrying out the wishes of their constituents or responding to "public demand" (generated by interest groups). Twenty-two percent took the intermediate politico response of following public opinion if it was clear-cut but otherwise relied on intuition, advice of friends, party stance, or other cues to decide less visible issues. Since most members regard council service as a part-time civic duty, they appear disposed to make up their minds independently, having no ambition for a political career.

Discussion at council meetings is likely to impress observers as concern with trivia rather than vigorous debate over policy. The simple explanation is that most people, including council members, feel more comfortable discussing things that they understand from personal experience. Hence frequency of garbage collection will occupy more time than an application for a million-dollar federal grant which may change the face of the city. If the mayor or administrative bureaucracy appears to know what to do, and there is no public opposition, the council will ratify the proposed course of action. If there is a conflict between city department heads over available resources or their allocation appears unequally distributed over certain sections of town, the council is more likely to inquire into the matter (especially if the members are elected by ward, with district interests).

Social science research has indicated that small groups exert additional pressures for conformity.[15] Most council votes will be unanimous; disagreement frequently will not be made public until a majority consensus can force a change (e.g., "the police chief has to go"). An exception is the case in which the council is broken into open factions, and splits generally erupt in personality clashes rather than along policy cleavages per se. Such dissension manifests itself in voting against others' pet projects, refusing support unless there are reciprocal favors, or voting which follows the factional leaders. In the traditional sharing of power with the executive, city councils can exercise a blocking check or a facilitating balance, depending on the circumstances. If all the council members were elected together, they may react against discredited policies of the previous incumbents. With staggered terms, more newly elected members may feel that they have a more recent mandate from the people and disagree with the council members, mayor, or city manager who have held office longer. To secure enactment of executive proposals, the mayor or manager may have to spend considerable time cultivating a personal following on the council. Party allegiance and mutual economic or social interests such as neighborhood, ward, or ethnic ties may provide cohesion, if they are present. As a small group, a council may develop its own personality, with its own informal leaders, based on shared political struggles over time.

Council oversight of administration varies with the legal structure and the personalities involved. A city commission in which each commissioner runs his own bailiwick, or an active city manager, will probably mean a perfunctory legislative review. On the other hand, if the city council appoints department heads or boards or must confirm certain administrative actions of the mayor, supervision extending into daily operations may occur. For partisan reasons, or if one of the council members is intending to run for mayor at the next election, he may be more inquisitive—either to embarrass the incumbent or to build a reputation for knowing the details. If council members are elected by ward, or even have budgetary control over a "ward improvements fund" to allocate at their pleasure, they may dictate city activities in their district. Because governmental operations have become more complex, the city councilman may feel torn between the advice of technical experts and the "commonsense" opinions of his constituents. Both can be erroneous at times, producing political embarrassment on occasion. Except in a few large cities whose council seats are full-time paid positions, most members lack the time, energy, or resources to gather the information necessary to develop policy alternatives. Even if council members initiate a new approach, they must convince a majority of their colleagues to run any political risks in adopting it. In short, it is easier to let a single executive official such as the mayor assume the risks associated with change; an appointive city manager can also be sacrificed if opposition becomes too strong.

Professional Leadership: The City Manager

The role expected of city managers has changed over the past half century, as reflected in the code of Ethics of the International City Management Association, which in 1924 first stated, "No manager should take an active part in politics." The 1972 statement no longer denies a political role to a city manager but merely asks that he "refrain from participation in the election of the members of his employing legislative body and from all partisan political activities which would impair his performance as a professional administrator." Indeed, the city manager is exhorted to "submit policy proposals to elected officials [and] provide them with facts and advice for making decisions and setting community goals."[16] Studies have verified that most policies adopted by the council do originate with the manager. The shift is also shown by the academic background of managers: originally most of them were trained as technicians in engineering fields; today a majority hold advanced degrees in political science or public administration.[17]

Where do city managers come from? Typically, after graduation from college, a young person (now including an increasing number of women) enters the public management field by becoming an administrative assistant and then an assistant city manager. After a few years' experience, he or she is recruited as city manager in a small town and then usually moves on to the larger cities which pay more highly. Theoretically, the job market for qualified managers is nationwide, filled through advertisement in publications of the ICMA and the American Society for Public Administration (ASPA). The detailed nature of the manager's job requires intimate familiarity with applicable state statutes, however, so that recruitment usually occurs through reputation within the state or region. While the concept provides that a manager serves at the pleasure of the council, most managers prefer to be hired on a contract (like appointed school superintendents). If a council wants to dismiss a manager, the city may have to pay for the remaining time on a contract, an expensive process. If most council incumbents are defeated in an election, a prudent city manager will probably start looking for a new position, since prior city policies have been repudiated at the polls and their administrative implementation (by the manager) is likely to have come under attack during the campaign. In terms of retirement security, the city manager may join a retirement fund established by the ICMA or take out a private annuity which is transferable. (Managers can also be covered by federal social security or may be eligible to participate in the retirement systems of some states.)

Political scientist Deil S. Wright has characterized the city manager's position as having three facets:

1. Managerial: supervision and control of the municipal bureaucracy
2. Policy: preparation of recommendations for the city council
3. Political: articulation of community needs to the council, other units of governments, and the public at large.[18]

To succeed in the job, the astute city manager must reflect the expectations in each of these areas. Depending upon the manager's own personality and those of the employing council, he or she may limit attention to administrative routine (the first role) and avoid taking a stand on controversial issues. Other managers view themselves as policy innovators and believe that they have a duty to their council and the public to persuade them, even in the face of opposition.[19] Since no council likes to be upstaged and too vigorous advocacy may imperil the image of the manager as an adviser, most managerial lobbying will take place behind the scenes: by setting the council agenda, the manager influences the issues which will be raised. Unless their attention is called to them, many problems will not be visible to the council.

Most policy originates with the manager, since he presents the range of options to the council, usually with an indication of the preferred course of action. Since the manager's professional reputation is at stake, all possible alternatives may not be described, lest they "confuse" the council, and the disadvantages of the recommended plan may not be fully listed. Under this form, all council contacts with the municipal bureaucracy are supposed to take place through the manager. An adroit manager enjoys a near-monopoly of technical information, although most council members will heed unauthorized leaks from the potential voting bloc of city employees. Unless there is a directly elected mayor, or a council member with a vigorous personality to seize the policy initiative, the manager will guide the options considered and will deal with the questions raised. However, a council's regular acceptance of the manager's recommendations does not necessarily mean that it acts as a rubber stamp; the council may have hired a competent manager whose recommendations agree with community values and objectives.[20]

The Honorable Mayor

By virtue of the elected position, the mayor is expected to be a political spokesman. The extent of leadership will depend on both formal institutional powers and individual inclinations. While a diffident personality may not exercise the full potential of the office, a mayor weak in legal authority will have to utilize talents of persuasion to achieve the leadership that people expect in the formal position. Political resources depend upon a unified party organization (if any), accurate information which will allow intervention at the right time, experience in dealing with people, willingness to keep an open mind so as not to foreclose consideration of alternatives as a result of prejudices, and the ability to bargain to obtain desired results without compromising goals. All of these must be effectively mustered if the modern mayor is to achieve what the electorate expects, given the fragmented authority frequently found in municipal government. Mayoral response to the leadership challenge has ranged in the following policy styles, characterized by Duane Lockard:[21]

- The stooge, a front man for a political machine or power structure (even organized crime)
- The reformer, riding into office on a platform to end corruption and bring "businesslike" government
- The program politician, an activist innovator advocating his policies with a variety of promotional techniques
- The evader, seeking avoidance of conflict: such passivity may result from frustration of his plans by the council or municipal bureaucracy.

As Robert Dahl observed, the mayor's position "was not the peak of a pyramid but rather at the center of intersecting circles . . . He negotiated, cajoled, exhorted, beguiled, charmed, pressed, appealed, reasoned, promised, insisted, demanded, even threatened, but he most needed support from other leaders who simply could not be commanded. Because the mayor could not command, he had to bargain."[22]

As a power broker, the mayor does enjoy several advantages as a result of the position. People expect the office to handle civic crises, and even ceremonial occasions can give media attention to the mayor's remarks. Mayors commonly have the right to submit messages to the council and may testify before state and congressional legislative committees to air policy views, even if they did not originate the proposals. Major civic disputes will eventually gravitate to the mayor's desk: mayoral policy preferences will be taken into account in resolving them even if the office lacks binding enforcement authority. The mayor can appeal for energetic action and accuse obstructionists of having special interests to protect. Threats are rarely effective because the typical mayor does not have the sanctions to back them up. But most people come to city hall wanting something, giving the mayor an opportunity to collect political IOUs. Even without granting favors, the audience gives them an impression of access. The longer a mayor listens, the more inclusive a script for compromise may appear.

All of this, especially when there is no staff to handle routine matters, takes enormous amounts of the mayor's time. The mayor of a big city, or even a small one, coping with crises,[23] is subject to grinding personal strain. A high proportion never seek reelection, and rather than being a stepping-stone to higher office, the mayoralty has gained a reputation as a political graveyard. Lyndon Johnson is reported to have remarked during one of the more trying moments of his presidency, "Things could be worse; I could be a mayor."[24]

The Municipal Judiciary

The courts serving municipalities are part of the state judicial system which defines their jurisdiction and increasingly their internal operation, prescribing, for example, minimum qualifications and salaries for judges. The municipalities may be mandated to contribute toward court support but exercise little discretion over their operations. Such courts are at the bottom rung of the trial ladder, and are called by various names—police court, traffic court, magistrates (or justice-of-the-peace) court, or small claims court, depending upon their functions. If it is designated "municipal," the court usually has both minor criminal jurisdiction (state misdemeanors or violation of city ordinances where the punishment cannot exceed six months in jail or several hundred dollars' fine) and civil jurisdiction (where the amount in litigation between the suing private parties does not exceed $500 or another limited amount). Except in courts in large cities, which serve as courts of general jurisdiction, trial by jury is not available; cases are heard before the judge, who makes all decisions.

Municipalities are usually authorized to establish an "inferior court" which has jurisdiction to try offenders who have broken city ordinances: the city magistrate has authority to issue warrants, set bail, and levy fines within limits prescribed in state law. In addition, many states allow municipalities to try under state statutes misdemeanor offenses which occur within its jurisdiction. In such cases, the fines or court costs levied may be retained by the municipality to defray its expenses and may even prove an important revenue source: the traffic speed trap of some small towns is occasionally notorious.

Formerly, the duties of the mayor as chief magistrate might include presiding over the municipally established court. However, in 1972 the U.S. Supreme Court ruled in *Ward* v. *Village of Monroeville, Ohio* that a mayor cannot act as a judge where municipal fines constitute a substantial portion of city revenues, since his impartiality might be questioned.[25] The ruling has forced cities to select a separate judge (see box), often a local attorney who hears cases part time, and has intensi-

Judicial Selection

Judges of courts serving municipalities may be directly elected or may be appointed by the governing body of the municipality or by the governor with legislative consent. Terms of office vary from one year to service "during good behavior" until age seventy. A "merit plan" utilized by some states means that the governor selects a judge from a list submitted by a nominating committee on qualification. To retain the office, a judge runs on his record without opponents:

> FOR JUDGE, MUNICIPAL COURT
> Shall [incumbent's name] be   Yes
> elected to the office for the
> term prescribed by law?   No

If a majority of people vote no, the incumbent loses and the governor makes another merit appointment.

> JUDGE REMOVED
> July 11, 1975—The controversial "miniskirted" Judge of Los Angeles Municipal Court, Noel Cannon, yesterday became the third judge in California history to be removed from the bench by the state Supreme Court.
> Judge Cannon, who was criticized for wearing seemingly exotic costumes in court and bringing her pet poodle to sit on her lap while she rendered judgments, was cited earlier this year for 24 allegations of willful misconduct by the state Commission on Judicial Qualification and she was suspended.

From Albin Krebs, "Notes on People," *New York Times*, July 11, 1975, p. 8. Judges may be removed, depending on the state, by impeachment on specified grounds, by recall of elective judges, or as a result of state investigation, which may recommend censure or even removal from office.

fied the debate as to whether all judges should have legal training. Advocates of the elective justice-of-the-peace system (dating from medieval England) prevalent in many small towns maintain that it provides speedy and inexpensive resolution of personal disputes which require only common sense and not legal technicalities. There may not be lawyers practicing in rural areas, and the low volume of court cases could not support an attorney. Critics contend that the seriousness of judicial actions and the need for due process of law require more qualifications than mere success at the polls. Horror stories of questionable hearing practices or sentencing abuses by nonlawyer judges frequently make legal training seem indispensable. However, requiring all judges to be licensed attorneys does not necessarily guarantee quality on the bench: several large cities have been notorious for making judgeships a reward for party services rendered. Some judges can confer the offices of clerks, bailiffs, process servers, and court-appointed guardians as forms of patronage. Many attorneys have discovered that a law practice and activity in city politics can be mutually beneficial.

Courts in urban areas may be large enough to attract qualified judges but face problems of delay and jurisdictions that overlap with state-established inferior (e.g., county) courts. The municipal court may not have time to handle the caseload,[26] since the city magistrate frequently begins the process of criminal justice by holding the preliminary hearing, at which arrested suspects are either discharged for lack of evidence or are routed to other courts (e.g., family court), the grand jury for felony indictment,[27] or the prosecutor's office for further disposition. In addition to the fact that "justice delayed is justice denied," many municipal tribunals are not "courts of record" (the proceedings are not transcribed), so that any appeals have to be tried all over again, with evidence and witnesses produced in the higher court.

Many residents expect their local courts to be self-supporting from fine revenue and dispense justice reflecting community standards. These expectations can make the bench a political hot seat. The courts are frequently called upon to resolve conflicts on appeal from executive or legislative action: relief from zoning or land use regulation, business license or other permits, municipal powers, and procedures in nominations or elections.[28] Appeal to the courts has delaying effects and has also served as a lever for those at a disadvantage in city legislative or administrative conflicts.

Courts whose jurisdiction covers the geographical area of the city can affect its policies in several ways. The extraordinary writs described in chapter 2 can be sought, enjoining administrative action until the case is heard. In ruling on the admissibility of evidence and by his power to dismiss criminal cases, the judge can regulate police procedure and officers' behavior. Since only a small fraction of cases are appealed beyond the initial trial court, judicial sentencing can affect the whole tone of city law enforcement: what are the penalties for disorderly conduct, public drunkenness, or the relative values placed on protection of persons or property? Easy release on bail, insignificant fines, or suspended sentences may discourage law enforcement officers and other city inspectors from pursuing repeated violators.

While judges cannot initiate policy change and must wait to have cases brought in litigation, once the question is before the court, their decisions can have far-reaching impacts. A taxpayers' suit may challenge municipal legal authority to do something or to spend public money; indeed the city administration may seek a friendly validation suit, allowing the courts to legitimize a new policy. A city ordinance or departmental regulation as applied may be challenged as being incorrectly interpreted; the courts must decide. Further, the administrative practice in question may not comply with procedural requirements. A finding of improper procedure by the courts will greatly change the day-to-day operation of whatever program is involved: from internal personnel management to property condemnation proceedings for city urban renewal. Courts may even find cities violating federal and/or different state constitutional rights ranging from taxation policy to freedom of speech in demonstrations. While judicial intervention which has produced major changes in local life frequently arouses great criticism, court orders have been complied with and the independence of the judiciary maintained.

Notes

1. In 1976, a federal court ordered Mobile, Alabama (population 190,000), to replace the commission form, which "precludes a black voter from an effective participation in the election system" with a city council elected by districts.

2. In a few cities two council members are elected from each ward, but most are single-member districts. Sometimes part of the council is elected at large and the rest by ward.

3. Alexander Pope, "An Essay on Man," epistle 3, ll. 303–04. Such a view is often repeated by those stressing a "practical" approach in debates at city hall.

4. Before World War I, a few states permitted aliens to vote.

5. *Kramer v. Union Free School District*, 395 U.S. 62 (1969).

6. *Cipriano v. City of Houma*, 395 U.S. 701 (1969).

7. For details, see Jewell Cass Phillips, *Municipal Government and Administration in America* (New York: Macmillan, 1960), pp. 189–90. In the 1970s a Negro college professor was elected mayor of Ann Arbor, Michigan, which uses PR.

8. Eugene C. Lee, "City Elections," in *The Municipal Year Book, 1963* (Chicago: International City Management Association, 1963), p. 79.

9. *Avery v. Midland County, Texas*, 390 U.S. 474 (1968).

10. International City Management Association, *The Municipal Year Book, 1972* (Washington, D.C., 1972), pp. 274–78.

11. Ibid.

12. Ibid. The items in last place indicate the decline of party machines.

13. Robert Boynton, "City Councils: Their Role in the Legislative System," *The Municipal Year Book, 1976* (Washington, D.C.: International City Management Association, 1976), p. 76.

14. Betty Zisk, *Local Interest Politics: A One Way Street* (New York: Bobbs-Merrill, 1973), p. 99.

15. For political aspects, see A. J. Vidich and Joseph Bensman, *Small Town in Mass Society* (Princeton, N.J.: Princeton University Press, 1958).

16. International City Management Association, *City Management Code of Ethics* (Washington, D.C., 1972), p. 9.

17. Ronald O. Loveridge, *City Managers in Legislative Politics* (New York: Bobbs-Merrill, 1971), p. 46.

18. Deil S. Wright, "The City Manager as a Development Administrator," in *Comparative Urban Research*, ed. Robert T. Daland (Beverly Hills, Calif.: Sage, 1969), pp. 218–19.

19. See Ronald O. Loveridge, "The City Manager in Legislative Politics: A Collision of Role Conception," *Polity* (May 1968), pp. 213–36, and Robert J. Huntley and Robert J. Macdonald, "Urban Managers: Organizational Preferences, Managerial Styles, and Social Policy Roles," in *The Municipal Year Book, 1975* (Washington, D.C.: International City Management Association, 1975), pp. 151–53.

20. Perceptively noted by Charles R. Adrian and Charles Press, *Governing Urban America*, 4th ed. (New York: McGraw-Hill, 1972), p. 230.

21. Duane Lockard, *The Politics of State and Local Government* (New York: Macmillan, 1963), pp. 413–27.

22. Robert Dahl, *Who Governs?* (New Haven: Yale University Press, 1961), p. 204.

23. Good examples might include a water shortage, high local unemployment, or a strike by municipal employees.

24. Edward Kosner, "Troubled Cities and Their Mayors," *Newsweek*, March 13, 1967, p. 38.

25. 409 U.S. 57 (1972). In some states, mayors also have executive clemency powers to commute the sentences of violators of municipal ordinances.

26. The municipal governing body or the state legislature may be unwilling to expand municipal court operations for expense or other reasons (such as partisan squabbles over new judgeships).

27. That is, for serious crimes.

28. For a breakdown of cases considered in an urban New York county, see Kenneth M. Dolbeare, *Trial Courts in Urban Politics* (New York: Wiley, 1967).

For Further Reading

Banfield, Edward C. *Big City Politics*. New York: Random House, 1966.

Bollens, John C., and Ries, John C. *The City Manager Profession: Myths and Realities*. Chicago: Public Administration Service, 1969.

Boyd, William J. D. "Local Electoral Systems: Is There a Best Way?" *National Civic Review* (March 1976), pp. 136–40ff.

Caraley, Demetrios. *City Governments and Urban Problems*. Englewood Cliffs, N.J.: Prentice-Hall, 1977.

Eyestone, Robert. *Threads of Public Policy: A Study of Policy Leadership*. Indianapolis: Bobbs-Merrill, 1971. (Stanford city study)

Gilbert, Bill. *This City, This Man: The Cookingham Era in Kansas City*. Washington, D.C.: International City Management Association, 1978. (Portrait of a city manager)

Huntley, Robert J., and Macdonald, Robert J. "Urban Managers: Organizational Preferences, Managerial Styles, and Social Policy Roles." In *The Municipal Year Book, 1975*. Washington, D.C.: International City Management Association, 1975.

International City Management Association, *The Municipal Year Book*, published annually, contains a wealth of statistical information about each form of city government.

Jacob, Herbert. *Justice in America*. 2nd ed. Boston: Little, Brown, 1972.

Karnig, Albert K., and Walter, B. Oliver. "Municipal Elections: Registration, Incumbent Success, and Voter Participation." In *The Municipal Year Book, 1977*. Washington, D.C.: International City Management Association, 1977.

Kotter, John P., and Lawrence, Paul. *Mayors in Action: Five Approaches to Urban Governance*. New York: Wiley, 1974.

Loveridge, Ronald O. *City Managers in Legislative Politics*. Indianapolis: Bobbs-Merrill, 1971. (Stanford city study)

Maier, Henry W. *Challenge to the Cities: An Approach to a Theory of Urban Leadership*. New York: Random House, 1966.

Mulrooney, Keith F., ed. "Symposium on the American City Manager." *Public Administration Review*. vol. 31 (January–February 1971), pp. 6–46.

National Municipal League. *Model City Charter*. (Periodically revised, it reflects reformist beliefs as to the optimum structure for city government.)

Prewitt, Kenneth. *The Recruitment of Political Leaders: A Study of Citizen-Politicians*. Indianapolis: Bobbs-Merrill, 1970. (Stanford city study)

Rice, Bradley R. *Progressive Cities: The Commission Government Movement*. Austin: University of Texas Press, 1977.

Ruchelman, Leonard, ed. *Big City Mayors: The Crisis in Urban Politics*. Bloomington: Indiana University Press, 1970.

Stillman, Richard J. II. *The Rise of the City Manager: A Public Professional in Local Government*. Albuquerque: University of New Mexico Press, 1974.

Zisk, Betty. *Local Interest Politics: A One Way Street*. New York: Bobbs-Merrill, 1973. (Stanford city study)

6: Financing Municipal Government

Most of the issues discussed at city hall are eventually expressed in terms of money. The cost of a program is most easily computed in dollars and cents, and the expenditures for each item show the allocation of the community's resources. Because of the differences in wealth and needs in urban areas, because of the relatively narrow economic base within the city limits, and because of legal limits on the kinds and amounts of taxes that local jurisdictions can collect, financing municipal government is a continuing problem. In this chapter, we will examine where the money comes from, how it is raised, where it goes, when it is borrowed, and how the city purse strings are controlled.

Where the Money Comes from: Revenue Base

American cities, on the average, must raise two-thirds of their revenues from their own resources, with the remainder coming from the state or federal government. Thus the major sources of revenue of a particular city can greatly vary, depending on its location, its socioeconomic composition (as a residential suburb, a one-industry town, and so forth), the revenue sources that the state allows it to tax, and the desires of its citizens (a few towns receive most of the city treasury from traffic fines—from the infamous "speed trap" on those passing through). Table 6.1 gives the national breakdown for 1976–77.

Many municipal revenue sources have remained unchanged through the years. The reason for this is that candidates usually run for office promising more services at lower cost than their opponents offer. Thus no relationship is made in the public mind between service levels and taxation: "the government" pays for it. When a tax increase is necessary, however, politicians usually pledge the money for a certain purpose (such as a water system) in order to gain political support for the hike. Many local revenues are thus earmarked, or dedicated for

Table 6.1. Municipal Revenues

Source	Amount (%)	Total (%)
From own sources		67.3
Taxes	35.5	
Property (21.3%)		
Sales and gross receipts (7.9%)		
Income and Licenses (6.3%)		
Utility revenue	14.6	
Charges and miscellaneous	17.2	
(liquor stores, insurance trust)		
Intergovernmental revenue	32.7	32.7
State (19.1%)		
Federal (13.6%)		
Total	100.0	100.0

Source: U.S. Bureau of the Census, *Census of Governments, 1977,* vol. 4, no. 4, *Finances of Municipalities and Township Governments* (Washington, D.C.: U.S. Government Printing Office, 1979), pp. 9, 11.

certain purposes, and are levied in traditional ways. This produces a rather inflexible revenue system with the major sources described below.

The general property tax has been the major municipal financial support since colonial times. It is a levy upon real property (land, buildings, or other improvements) and personal property, either tangible (home furnishings, motor vehicles, business inventories) or intangible (bank accounts, stocks, bonds). Since portable possessions cannot easily be traced for tax purposes, the property tax is effectively levied on land, the buildings on it, and vehicles. It is the major tax allowed by all state governments in the belief that it most fairly taxes land values within the city. The landowner benefits directly from the city services available and indirectly through property values increased by growth and development of the community. Other reasons for its popularity are inertia ("an old tax is a good tax: a new tax is a bad one") and enforcement of collection. Real property cannot move, and if the owner fails to pay his taxes, the governments can auction off the land to a new owner. Although this tax is not levied according to ability to pay (many homes are owned by pensioners on fixed incomes), it is a stable revenue producer. Its adequacy is such that no substitutes are satisfactory enough to replace its high yield.

While it is dependable, the general property tax does not rapidly respond to economic prosperity. Since there is a finite supply of land, its values remain relatively stable. Moreover much of the wealth produced in the city may not be invested in real estate. We cannot have a comprehensive property tax because we have changed from an agrarian society where wealth was in the land into an industrial economy.

Universality is further eroded because substantial portions of the city's land may be tax exempt: owned by churches, charitable foundations, or educational institutions. In depressed urban areas where government-guaranteed mortgages have been foreclosed, or tenements abandoned by their owners and taken over by the city for nonpayment of taxes, government itself has become the largest landowner, and these parcels are also off the property tax rolls.

There are several policy considerations involved in levying the property tax. Property owners may oppose such taxes and may even raise rents to a greater extent than necessary to meet the increased property tax burden. Since improvements on the property will frequently mean higher taxes because they increase the market value, owners whose profits are marginal may ill afford any more investments and so may allow further deterioration. Critics charge that our system of property taxes encourages landlords to let buildings run down, since most improvements lead to higher taxes; in contrast, Britain levies upon the fair net income value of the property. In many American cities, the occupants have grown old along with the houses. And by the time they have paid off a twenty- or thirty-year mortgage, their home may represent the major asset of the retirees. With fixed incomes, they may not be able to pay property taxes, let alone maintenance or repairs—a further cause of urban blight. Government is faced with the choice of driving them out of their homes and likely onto welfare rolls, since rent will take a large portion of the pension, or, alternatively, reducing property taxes. A number of states have adopted a "circuit breaker" whereby the elderly poor pay only up to a certain percentage of their income, with the state paying the remainder of the property tax due.

A final controversy over property taxes is their uniformity. While the levy (so many cents per $100 value) must be uniform, cities or counties are often permitted to classify property (vacant lot, residential, commercial, industrial, and so forth) and provide for a different levy uniform within each class. This can lead to political battles between homeowners, apartment owners, and businessmen, and to property tax rivalry between cities to attract commerce and industry. Depending upon the state, property tax policy fluctuates between strict uniformity and presumed ability to pay. In 1978, California voters adopted Proposition 13, a constitutional initiative which limits property taxes to 1 percent of market value, and this tax revolt seemed likely to spread to other states.

Often ignored in the ruckus is that the property taxes paid, in whatever amount, often bear no relationship to the city services needed: one parcel of land worth the same amount as another, and even paying equal taxes, would require far more costly city services in the form of sidewalks, sewage, and police and fire protection if it were the site of an apartment house than if it served as a cattle feedyard. Such cost-benefit differences mean that for a well-balanced tax base, a municipality should have a blend of land uses.

The second major source of municipal revenue consists of subventions from the state and federal governments. The proportion of intergovernmental financial support is increasing. There are several reasons for this. Although state legislatures may require cities to perform more functions or meet certain standards of service, local tax resources may not match these responsibilities. Cities may already have reached tax or debt ceilings imposed by the state or local charter. Urban officials point out that certain social problems may be concentrated in their jurisdictions and that they are the "government on the spot" where people are moving in. Critics respond that outside money encourages careless expenditure and dilutes the political accountability involved when each jurisdiction decides how much to tax itself and how much to spend. Expenditure decisions are separated from political responsibility for raising the money.

State aid takes the form of shared taxes and grants in aid. Shared taxes can be a returned portion of the revenue produced within the local jurisdiction or distributed according to some legislative formula. Sometimes the shared tax must be used for a certain purpose (the city's share of the state motor fuel tax going for street repair), while in other cases towns can decide how to spend their slice of the state tax. There may be locally imposed taxes which the state collects for convenience (sales tax or auto license fees are common examples); we are talking here of a state-legislated tax in which cities might or might not share. Depending upon the political bargains which are often made when a shared tax is imposed in the first place, there is likely to be considerable haggling over the distribution formula. Frequent questions are: Should all cities share equally? Are some more deserving? How can they be defined?

Grants in aid can be either categorical grants for specified categories of programs or simply grants to support general city government, the use of which can be determined by local officials. In some cases, these may be matching grants: the city must put up a certain proportion in order to receive outside support. The idea is to assist the most acute areas of need or to encourage civic expenditure in areas where because of the local political climate it would not otherwise be made. Local officials, however, are likely to resent having such strings attached to the payment and fear that the state or national capitals will decide policy. Critics contend that matching requirements (for example, 10 percent) may distort expenditure priorities; if the local jurisdiction can put up one dollar and receive nine more from outside, the limited local funds will naturally go for the grant programs while other needs remain unmet. Finally, the degree of state assistance, in either shared taxes or grants, varies greatly from state to state and among sizes of municipalities within each state.

Federal assistance also takes the form of grants in aid and, since 1972, general revenue sharing. Subjects deemed of national significance have risen, so that cities are now eligible for hundreds of categorical grant programs administered by scores of federal agencies. Such proliferation has led to some consolidation into block grants; federal money is allocated for the field of criminal justice but local officials decide the particular purpose on which it will be spent.

Beginning in 1972, Congress appropriated $30.2 billion over a five-year period for general revenue sharing to states and general units of local government such as counties and cities. Renewed with an additional $25.6 billion to extend from 1977 to 1980, general revenue sharing is politically popular because local officials are free to spend the federal money with few restrictions. It was renewed again in 1980, with $4.6 billion allotted over a period of three years. Two-thirds of each state's allocation goes to local governments, including cities, based on formulas which take into account population, degree of poverty measured by per capita income, and amount of local tax effort.

The law also sets a floor and a ceiling on the amounts that local governments may receive, calculated at minimum and maximum percentages of the average per capita local share. Yet cities having the same population, or similar low per capita incomes, can receive different amounts under federal revenue sharing. Why is this so? Cities of the same size can be either poor or affluent, and this will affect the poverty factor of the allocation formula. Moreover, cities with a greater need may receive less per person than neighboring communities because their tax effort is less. This is not necessarily the poor municipality's fault. A jurisdiction may have exploited its meager tax base to the fullest, levied every local tax that it is authorized by the state constitution to the limit allowed by law, and still produce total revenue less than that received by a neighboring wealthy suburb from its share of a sales tax at one of its shopping centers. It cannot be said that the poor city is making less of a tax effort; it is deprived of revenue-sharing money by natural or economic factors over which it has no control. If a city relies heavily on nontax revenue (such as profits from municipally owned utility systems or even traffic fines), it will suffer in revenue sharing. Each time that revenue sharing is renewed in Congress, it seems likely that the distribution formulas will be discussed. Critics charge that revenue sharing is helping perpetuate fragmented local government because most of the receiving jurisdictions are very small: it is an incentive to incorporate a separate municipality in an urbanizing area rather than to consolidate. Supporters of revenue sharing laud its redistributive effects and the principle of sharing the national tax base as an intergovernmental source of revenue.

What uses have municipalities made of their revenue sharing funds? Fiscally hard-pressed jurisdictions have paid current expenses or have realized other substitutive effects such as keeping taxes down. New spending has been mainly for capital projects (construction and equipment) rather than new programs. This is politically safer than starting new services and then cutting people off should revenue sharing be reduced in the future.

A third major source of municipal revenue is user charges or fees for services. As cities reach their taxing or debt limits, it becomes very tempting to make as many activities as possible self-supporting through service charges. Those favoring taxation on the benefits-received principle see no difference between a customer of public services and those in private enterprise. Sometimes citizens have a choice as to whether or not they will use the city service (such as garbage pickup), while in other cases all must pay (those with a water connection must pay a sewer fee), making the fee more a general tax.

Whether an individual pays a charge or fee often depends on whether an individual benefit can be distinguished (e.g., weed cutting) rather than a general good shared by all (e.g., snow removal), plus a host of other political considerations. Will the imposition of a service charge fill a revenue gap and make the tax level appear lower than it is? Who will use the facility? Can people outside the city's taxing jurisdiction pay a fee for a municipal service which they enjoyed? Will a fee or charge unduly discriminate against those with less ability to pay: does the city fail to meet a moral obligation to furnish services to all citizens? Will imposition of charges promote equity in taxation where some user institutions are tax exempt or use the service provided (e.g., industrial sewerage) disproportionately? Will charging for a service prevent waste, ration user demand and, by the pricing mechanism, finance service levels to meet the need? Should the city's general bonding capacity be reserved to raise funds to build facilities which could not be self-supporting, so that user fees could be imposed to pay off the cost? Finally, can the municipality use its package of prices for service activities for fiscal control in line with community objectives? An example might be parking meters, vehicle license fees, and bus fares to shape forms of downtown transportation use.

City service charges may be levied according to use and may be a flat rate or a scaled fee. The most lucrative type is utility revenues from city-operated water and electric systems. Depending upon civic attitudes, pricing policies may be set only high enough to cover operating expenses, depreciation, and possible expansion, or utilities may be a significant money maker, with profits turned over to the city treasury.

Other service fees, such as city transportation fares, hospital charges, and rents from public housing, usually only partially defray costs, and the service may have to be subsidized. Tolls levied for construction of bridges and tunnels go for repayment and then may either cease or continue as a revenue producer (especially if outsiders use the service), depending upon the attitude of the townsfolk. License fees are often imposed upon business or commercial establishments, ostensibly to pay the costs of inspection, although the fee may bear no particular relationship to the costs of regulation. Many cities have begun levying an occupancy tax on hotels and motels, especially if the city has a significant outside tourist or convention trade, although this practice may be opposed by the operators, who become unpaid tax collectors for the city. The city may charge admission to municipally owned recreation facilities such as swimming pools and zoos. Some municipalities impose admission taxes on entertainment such as movies and the theater and sporting events. Rentals and concessions at city parks, stadiums, civic auditoriums, or municipal airports frequently are big money makers which help defray their own cost. Finally, fines charged to lawbreakers may be of significant help to the city treasury.

Under increasing financial pressure, more and more cities are levying municipal sales and income taxes, which many states used to forbid. Municipal sales taxes began during the Great Depression of the 1930s and can be levied either on general retail sales or on gross receipts of merchants. Selective sales levies or excises are increasingly levied by municipalities on such sumptuary items as liquor and tobacco. If the state allows such municipal sales taxes, the larger, more financially pressed cities are likely to collect first, followed by other municipalities as the practice becomes accepted. The rate varies from about ½ percent to 3 percent, often "piggybacked" on top of a state sales tax and so collected with low cost of administration. Some municipalities, however, do not trust the state's accounting and maintain their own collection department. Local sales taxes are very productive and offer a method of tapping nonresidents who make major purchases in the city. The consumer is less likely to notice paying the sales tax than making other lump sum payments. Political opposition to the municipal sales tax is likely to come from merchants, upon whom as unpaid collectors the accounting costs fall, and workers or those on fixed income (the sales tax is quite regressive unless food or other necessities are excluded).[1] A municipal sales tax may drive some shoppers to business establishments outside the city limits and may also increase resistance to annexation.

As property and sales taxes have failed to meet city financial needs, more states are allowing municipalities to levy an income tax to tap the wealth in our wage-earning economy. Municipal income tax rates are very low, often 1 percent, and (unlike the federal or state) are not graduated: the same rate applies to all. The tax is usually on gross salary: usually no exemptions or deductions are allowed. It has thus been opposed by organized labor, which sees it as regressive upon the wage earner, especially because it does not reach nonsalary income such as interest, rents, dividends, and capital gains. "Payroll taxes" do have the advantage of tapping suburbanites who earn their living in the core city and use its services daily. If the city has substantial numbers of commuters, the tax is likely to be popular with residents, since it is levied where the income is earned, not according to place of residence (which may be out of state, or even in Canada, in the case of Detroit). In the states which forbid municipal income taxes, some cities have adopted the legal subterfuge of levying occupational license fees on businesses, trades, and professions. Its effect on an individual is the same as an income tax, and it can be withheld by major employers in town and is often collected on a quarterly basis.

Finally, borrowed money may constitute a significant portion of civic revenue, although not indefinitely, as we shall see in the section on debt management. Many cities are forced to fill a revenue gap by borrowing because they have reached the limit or levied all the taxes or charges allowed by state law, city charter, or taxpayer opinion.

How Money Is Raised: Taxation Systems

A major political issue is likely to be tax equity, or the fairness and appropriateness of the tax burden as it is distributed. Depending on community attitudes, the burden may be distributed more or less upon the principles of the benefit received and/or ability to pay. The incidence of a tax or service charge can be either progressive or regressive in terms of the proportion paid by the individual in relation to his means. While local taxes may be regressive, local expenditures may be progressive, thereby offsetting the effect of the tax. The "proper" balance of support, the question of who should really pay, is a topic likely to excite public argument at city hall. The municipal governing body sets the levies in an ordinance which is passed in the same manner as other local laws. However, several "readings" of the ordinance, or public hearings on the rate increases, may be required. Interested groups affected by the charges may lobby for changes, especially because all the fiscal impacts may not be readily apparent in the bare wording of the law—precedents for the future may be set as the city seeks financial support.

Taxation involves two steps: putting a fair value on the property for tax purposes and setting the tax rate. The first step is the assessment process. Usually the law requires that property be assessed at full, or market, value. However, the assessed valuation (AV) for tax purposes may be less than 100 percent, such as 25 percent, which diminishes the effect of variation. It is quite possible that two objective observers might look at the taxable item, one appraising it at $60,000 and the second at $50,000. If the assessment is made at full valuation, there will be a wide variation in the amount of tax due, but if a fraction (say 25 percent) is used for AV, then the smaller difference is more likely to be acceptable. Also, some states have a policy of using different ratios for assessment, depending on what is being taxed, in the belief that utilities and corporations could be assessed at 30 percent, while people's homes and farmland should only be assessed at 15 percent.

After the assessment has been made, it can be altered in two general ways. If a citizen disputes the valuation, he may appeal it to a board of tax appeals, to the general governing body of the jurisdiction making the assessment,[2] and ultimately to the courts (if illegal procedures can be shown). If the city governing body acts as the appeal board, its members will find themselves sitting on a political hot seat, because any reduction in one person's valuation means assessments must be raised on the rest unless the tax base is to be eroded. It should be pointed out that in most jurisdictions, the taxpayer may object to an increase in assessed value only during an appeal period after the reappraisal is made, not later, when the tax rate has been computed and the bill is due.

A second way in which the assessment may be altered is through equalization, since the law requires uniformity. If assessment is below fair market value or the standard ratio throughout a jurisdiction, the equalizing agency raises it to the legally prescribed level. In many states, there may be a wide variation in assessment on similar property due to inadequate revaluation or political pressures on the local offi-cials. A state equalizing agency (or occasionally the courts) thus orders adjustments for uniformity and often handles assessments of large utilities and companies (e.g., railroads) operating throughout the state.[3] Sometimes citizens who have voted against additional taxes feel doublecrossed because their bills go up. The candidate elected may not have raised the tax rate, but assessments or equalization may rise, reflecting general inflation of values. Some jurisdictions for adminis-trative convenience raise assessments one year and the tax rate the next.

There are several problems in assessment. First, the assessment juris-diction (often the township or county) may not be coterminous with the municipality which depends on its evaluation of the tax base. The normal city is of relatively small area, whereas assessment should theoretically be broad so that it includes comparable taxable items for uniformity.[4] Second, making sure all taxable property is on the rolls at its current value is a never-ending task. Much personal property is never taxed because it is never recorded. To distinguish full market value, the assessor may resort to aerial photos to find changes in land use, check building permits for improvements, and record the prices of property transfers—fought in every detail by most owners who want to list items at their lowest worth for speculative purposes and avoid paying taxes on their profits. Third, exemptions in full for publicly owned property, churches, and charitable or educational institutions, and in part for certain individuals such as owner-occupied residential "homesteads," veterans, and senior citizens, seriously erode a tax base. A high concentration like this means that more than half the property in some cities is tax exempt. But achievement of a taxation goal that involves assessing property at its highest and best use may result in undesirable policy effects: urban sprawl, disincentive to make improvements upon deteriorating buildings, and regressive impact upon those who can barely afford to live where they are now. Fourth, the assessor's role requires a great deal of political tact in dealing with taxpayers, professional skill in appraisal, and knowledge of real estate. But most of our assessors are elected with no technical qualifications, and there have been periodic scandals where favoritism was shown. The International Association of Assessing Officials recommends that the office be made appointive under a merit system. Yet more than technical competence is necessary in such a politically sensitive post.   *2/59/1*

The second major step in tax administration is setting the tax rate. After the total tax base has been evaluated, a percentage must be applied in order to derive the amount to be paid. This rate is set by the city governing body; an example might be two cents per $100 of assessed value.[5] Theoretically the tax rate would be derived by dividing the assessed value of all property by the amount of money that the taxing jurisdiction needed to raise. In practice, determination of the rate may be limited by factors other than revenue need and political considerations of what the public will bear. First, there may be an overall limitation on the total rate imposed by the state, constitutionally or legislatively, or by municipal charter. Second, there may be specified limits for various purposes such as not more than one mill for a sewage tax, two cents per $100 for operating expenses, or 1 percent of assessed value to repay city debts. In many cases, the voters may have to approve any tax increases, so that there may be taxpayer revolts at the polls.

Thus there are several problems in setting the tax rate. First, the limits may be too low or too high for the city's specific needs. Second, many reformers, including some taxpayers' associations, seek removal of arbitrary tax limits or inequities. They contend that most local governing bodies are responsible and politically sensitive, but public suspicions linger, and some elective officials like to duck the responsibility and "let the people decide." Third, earmarked levies could be eliminated: designated tax rates for everything from firemen's pensions to support of libraries complicate city fiscal administration. If all tax revenues could go into a general fund, the setting of spending priorities would be clearer. Finally, the city can lower its tax levels by expanding its revenue base. Besides imposing other charges examined in the previous section, some cities seek voluntary contributions from tax-exempt institutions and attempt to attract new commerce and industry to town. But in granting these businesses tax advantages to relocate, the city must consider the long-range servicing costs and the political liabilities of such favored treatment.

Where the Money Goes: Expenditures

The city budget can be viewed as public policy spelled out in dollars and cents, and expenditure decisions represent the allocation of certain kinds of values (priorities) as well as resources. Major civic expenses for all American cities in 1976–77 are shown in table 6.2. These are combined expenditures: the states vary widely in the extent to which municipalities pay for education, public welfare, health, and hospitals because of the diversity of arrangements among the various types of governmental units providing services in these fields. In addition, cities may have to pay for debts and utility services.

Table 6.2. Municipal Expenditures

General expenditure functions	Percent
Education	14.1
Police protection	11.7
Public welfare	8.3
Highways and transportation	7.8
Sewerage	7.0
Other sanitation	3.4
Fire protection	6.3
Hospitals and health	6.1
Interest on general debt	4.7
Parks and recreation	4.5
Housing and urban renewal	3.2
General control	3.2
Financial administration	1.8
General public buildings	1.6
All other functions	16.2
Total	100.0

Source: U.S. Bureau of the Census, *Census of Governments, 1977*, vol. 4, no. 4, *Finances of Municipalities and Township Governments* (Washington, D.C.: U.S. Government Printing Office, 1979), pp. 9, 11.

The table shows that a major portion of municipal expenditures is the wages of employees: the payroll typically consists of one-half to three-quarters of the city budget. Since wage scales are different in each city, perhaps the most useful comparisons are per capita expenditure for each function and the ratio of city employees to population served. Figure 6.1, reproduced from the 1977 *Census of Governments*, shows that the amount spent per resident served varies by city size for each function. Small towns may spend more per citizen to provide initial equipment or minimum service. Additional highways, sanitation services, and more fire stations remain relatively constant in cost per individual, but police protection, education, and public welfare require more in larger cities, which are also more likely to go into debt and spend more on interest repayment. Because of state variations in whether municipalities assume public welfare costs, seven standard city functions are often distinguished for purposes of comparison: education, highways, police, fire, sanitation, parks, general and financial administration. The figures in table 6.3 were compiled by the Congressional Budget Office.

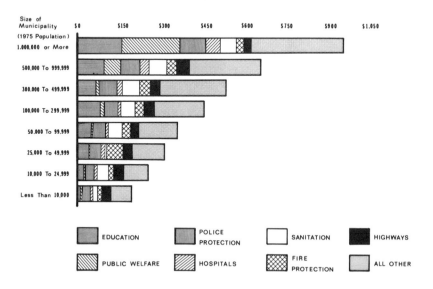

Figure 6.1. Per Capita General Expenditure by Function for Size Groups of Municipalities, 1976–77. *Source:* U.S. Bureau of the Census, *Census of Governments, 1977*, vol. 4, no. 4, *Finances of Municipalities and Township Governments* (Washington, D.C.: U.S. Government Printing Office, 1979), p. 10.

Table 6.3. Providing City Services

	Per capita expenditures ($)	City employees per 10,000 pop.
Baltimore	470	260
Boston	441	219
Chicago	383	208
Denver	375	219
Detroit	396	202
Los Angeles	408	206
New Orleans	260	217
New York	435	243
Philadelphia	395	255
St. Louis	360	214
San Francisco	488	225

Source: "Outlays Here and by Other Cities," *New York Times,* October 10, 1975, p. 44.

The second measure for comparison of expenditures is the number of city employees needed to service the population, although this will also be affected by the number of hours in the work week. While the levels of service or employee efficiency may vary, the number of people on the city's payroll will be the greatest item of expenditure. Calculation of full-time equivalents yields the largest operational cost, and also noteworthy is the number of retired employees to whom the city has pension obligations. The increasing unionization of municipal employees has meant negotiated contracts for higher salaries, reduced working hours, and more generous retirement plans. A study on municipal finances by the federal Advisory Commission on Intergovernmental Relations concluded that many municipal pension plans were underfunded, that is, employee contributions invested were only a small portion of the eventual benefits promised, with the city making up the difference. As cities face a fiscal crunch, it is inevitable that they are trying to reduce the number of city jobs and to renegotiate employee contracts.

A large number of analyses have been made in an effort to explain the factors which affect spending levels in local communities. It is very difficult to generalize determinants of fiscal behavior, since each community is different. However, demographic and socioeconomic composition of the community appears to be more influential than political variables. Robert Lineberry and Ira Sharkansky have identified seven socioeconomic factors which appear to affect spending levels.[6] Whether the resources are measured in terms of individual income or assessed valuation, if the city can tax this wealth, it will spend more than a poor jurisdiction. The economic base is a second variable, with manufacturing in town tending to be associated with higher levels of municipal expenditure. Industry not only increases service demands but adds to the tax base. Third, density, or population per square mile, has a varying relationship with expenditure. More people in a smaller area may mean less expense on streets to serve them but more in per capita costs to meet police and fire protection needs. Fourth, the effect of growth rates upon economies of scale is uncertain. Whether an increase in size means more expenditure depends on the function, and other political and external factors intervene: cities may "spread themselves thin" in service. Fifth, usually the greater the amount of owner-occupied housing, the lower are municipal expenditures, because of the lower density of single-family residences and homeowner concern over property taxes. Sixth, ethnicity and religious composition indicate greater expenditures if a city faces the high service needs of racial minorities and Roman Catholics. Seventh, metropolitan location indicates that a central city is likely to have higher per capita municipal expenditures than will suburbs located outside the core.

Finally, these factors may be influenced by governmental structure and other political variables. Municipal expenditures tend to be higher when local responsibilities are greater (other governmental units perform fewer functions), state debt and expenditure limits are unrestrictive (if the city can tax, it may spend more), intergovernmental aid is low, and previous expenditure levels have been high. This incremental effect of a city's spending history defines what is politically acceptable. It seems likely that the costs of government operations will rise with service demands and the ability of municipalities to finance activities on their own will be limited, so that expenditures will be carefully scrutinized.

When Money Is Borrowed: Debt Management

If needs exceed revenues, cities, like families, often borrow to make up the difference. Public attitudes about going into debt are influenced by several factors. The local political culture may favor a pay-as-you-go, or cash, philosophy. The project involved will be subjectively evaluated on its intrinsic merit and as to whether its cost ought to be passed on to future generations: if a public facility will be used for forty years, perhaps it ought to be paid off during that period by those who use it. Current interest rates which will affect the ultimate cost of borrowing and the extent to which indebtedness reaches the limit set by the state or municipal charter will affect the decision as to whether to borrow now. Finally, current economic conditions will shape opinion about the use of credit, since several local government jurisdictions may want voters to approve bond issues. An important point to remember is that municipalities do not enjoy the unlimited credit of the national government. State and local governments are forced to seek credit in the money market like other borrowers.

Why does a city borrow? First, to pay for capital (large, permanent) improvements. Second, in anticipation of receipts (tax payments or charges) which are due to come in later in the fiscal year. And finally, cities sometimes borrow because of unanticipated emergencies. A general principle is that borrowing should never be for current operating expenses, lest a city live beyond its means. Operating a city on a strict cash basis is nearly impossible using property taxes alone, since receipts come in only once or twice a year. A few cities are wealthy enough to pay current expenses and capital investments out of annual revenues, especially if they have budgeted in advance for capital improvements or have built up a revolving fund to meet unanticipated expenses. But few taxpayers are willing, or politicians dedicated enough, to build up a city surplus.

There are several types of municipal debt instruments. Short-term warrants or notes extend from three months to five years. Such certificates are very much like a person's signature note, a promise to pay. A typical example is tax anticipation warrants, issued by many cities until taxes come due. Occasionally, municipalities in financial distress pay their vendors (suppliers) or city employees in short-term vouchers which are cashed in at the bank, usually at a discount, but such a practice cannot continue for long.

Special assessment bonds are sometimes issued to pay for public improvements. Special assessments are levied when it is felt that the improvement (such as sidewalks, curbs, and gutters) will benefit the adjacent property owners more than the public at large, so they should pay all or part of the cost. The use of this technique varies with community philosophy: some towns may feel that street paving is a general good shared by all citizens, while others believe that the value of adjacent property will be significantly enhanced by such access, so owners should bear the cost. The share paid for by the city and the proportion borne by the property owners are often negotiated by political compromise, although once a majority of property owners have agreed to the project, usually all must share the cost.

The use of the special assessment has declined since the depression of the 1930s, although smaller and poorer communities are likely to use this technique. The city council may demand advance payment from property owners, but this may amount to several thousand dollars, depending upon the property frontage or other prorated share. Or a town may pay for the improvement from a revolving fund, with the owners paying back the added special assessment on their property

Interest exempt, in the opinion of counsel, from all present Federal Income Taxation.

$10,285,000

City of Paterson
New Jersey

6.25% Various Purpose Bonds

Rated: Moody's—Baa

Dated April 1, 1974   Due April 1 as shown below

Principal and semiannual interest (April 1 and October 1, first coupon October 1, 1974) payable at the First National Bank of New Jersey, Paterson, New Jersey. Coupon bonds in the denomination of $5,000 each, registrable as to principal alone, or as to both principal and interest.

These Bonds, in the opinion of counsel, will constitute valid and legally binding general obligations of the City of Paterson, payable from ad valorem taxes to be levied against all the taxable property therein without limitation as to rate or amount.

Amount	Maturity	Yield	Amount	Maturity	Yield	Amount	Maturity	Yield or Price
$375,000	1975	5.25%	$450,000	1980	5.50%	$ 525,000	1986	6.05%
375,000	1976	5.30	450,000	1981	5.60	1,150,000	1987-88	6.10
375,000	1977	5.35	500,000	1982	5.70	1,200,000	1989-90	6.15
425,000	1978	5.40	500,000	1983	5.80	1,250,000	1991-92	6.20
425,000	1979	5.45	525,000	1984	5.90	1,235,000	1993-94	100
			525,000	1985	6.00			

(accrued interest to be added)

These Bonds are offered when, as and if issued and received by us and subject to approval of legality by Messrs. Hawkins, Delafield & Wood, New York, New York, whose opinion will be furnished upon delivery. An Offering Circular may be obtained in any State in which this announcement is circulated from only such of the undersigned and other dealers as may lawfully offer these securities in such State.

HALSEY, STUART & CO. INC.
AFFILIATE OF BACHE & CO. INCORPORATED

JOHN NUVEEN & CO.
INCORPORATED

CONTINENTAL BANK
CONTINENTAL ILLINOIS NATIONAL BANK
AND TRUST COMPANY OF CHICAGO

BOLAND, SAFFIN, GORDON & SAUTTER

L. F. ROTHSCHILD & CO.

CHEMICAL BANK   **THE PHILADELPHIA NATIONAL BANK**

FRANKLIN NATIONAL BANK   **FIRST OF MICHIGAN CORPORATION**

GIBRALTAR SECURITIES CO.   **ABRAHAM & CO. INC.**   **ERGOOD & CO.**

HALPERT, OBERST & COMPANY   **A. S. HART AND, COMPANY, INC.**

RAND, McKAY & LYON, INC. **STEPHENS INC.** **STERLING, GRACE MUNICIPALS**
DIVISION OF STERLING, GRACE & CO., INC.

AUSTIN TOBIN & CO.   **G. WEEKS & CO., INC.**   **RAND & CO., INC.**
INCORPORATED

March 29, 1974

Figure 6.2. A Newspaper Advertisement for General Obligation Bonds

In the opinion of Messrs. Johnson & Thorington, Bond Counsel, interest on the Series 1979 Bonds is, under existing statutes, court decisions, regulations and rulings, exempt from Federal income taxation, and the Series 1979 Bonds and the income therefrom are, under existing statutes, exempt from all taxation in the State of Alabama.

NEW ISSUE

$36,200,000

The Hospital Authority of the City of Huntsville

(Alabama)

Hospital Revenue Bonds
Series 1979
(Huntsville Hospital)

Dated: December 1, 1979   Due: June 1, as shown below

The Series 1979 Bonds will be issuable as coupon Bonds in the denomination of $5,000 each, registrable as to principal only, or as to both principal and interest, and as fully registered Bonds without coupons, in the denomination of $5,000 or any integral multiple thereof. Coupon Bonds and fully registered Bonds without coupons will be interchangeable, subject to certain conditions. Interest on the Series 1979 Bonds will be payable on June 1, 1980 and semiannually on each June 1 and December 1 thereafter. Principal (unless registered) and interest (unless registered as to both principal and interest) on coupon Bonds will be payable at the principal corporate trust office of The Henderson National Bank, Huntsville, Alabama, the Trustee. Fully registered Bonds without coupons and coupon Bonds registered as to principal only will be payable, upon presentation, at the principal corporate trust office of the Trustee. The interest on fully registered Bonds without coupons and on coupon Bonds registered as to both principal and interest (except for the final installment thereof) will be payable by the Trustee by mail.

The Series 1979 Bonds will be subject to mandatory, optional, extraordinary and special partial redemption prior to their respective maturities as described in the Official Statement.

The Series 1979 Bonds will be limited obligations of The Hospital Authority of the City of Huntsville and will not constitute an obligation, debt or pledge of the faith and credit of the State of Alabama, the City of Huntsville, Alabama or any other municipality in the State of Alabama, nor will the Authority be liable for the payment of the Series 1979 Bonds except from the sources described in the Official Statement. The Series 1979 Bonds will be equally and ratably secured by a pledge of, and will be payable solely from, revenues derived by the Authority from the operation of Huntsville Hospital, located in Huntsville, Alabama (except to the extent that the Series 1979 Bonds may be paid out of money attributable to Series 1979 Bond proceeds, investment income or, under certain circumstances, proceeds of insurance or condemnation awards, if any) and will be additionally secured by a non-foreclosable mortgage on the facilities comprising Huntsville Hospital, all as more fully described in the Official Statement.

Amount	Maturity	Interest Rate	Amount	Maturity	Interest Rate	Amount	Maturity	Interest Rate
$365,000	1984	7 %	$440,000	1987	7.10%	$545,000	1990	7.40%
385,000	1985	7	475,000	1988	7.20	580,000	1991	7½
415,000	1986	7.05	505,000	1989	7.30	625,000	1992	7.60
						675,000	1993	7.70

$ 4,230,000 8¼% Term Bonds due June 1, 1998
$26,960,000 9   % Term Bonds due June 1, 2012
Price of all Bonds: 100%
(plus accrued interest)

Figure 6.3. A Newspaper Advertisement for Revenue Bonds. The price "100%" means each costs $5,000 with accrued interest to be paid at maturity. Some bonds are sold "below par" at a discount, so the yield is even higher: a $5,000 bond can be bought for $4,900 and redeemed at face value plus interest.

tax bill. Usually municipalities issue special assessment bonds for periods ranging from five to fifteen years which are paid back in installments by the extra assessment on the property tax bill. In addition, many cities pledge their full faith and credit for repayment if an owner cannot, so there is much less risk and hence lower interest. Few cities still issue property liens to the contractor who did the work, since he usually must sell them at a discount to a bank, which then demands payment from the property owners within a year.

Longer-term municipal bonds (more than five years) come in three forms. General obligation bonds usually require a popular referendum to approve their sale, since the "full faith and credit" of the local government is pledged for repayment (see figure 6.2). This means that taxes can be raised to whatever level is necessary to repay the debt, although frequently state-imposed limits have the effect of restricting this type of borrowing. Since the taxing power and other financial resources secure them, they are often called guaranteed bonds and hence bear the lowest rate of interest. This cost saving can be significant over a long borrowing period.

Revenue bonds are paid off from the income of the project for which they were issued: tolls, utility charges, fees, or periodic repayments from operating appropriations (figure 6.3). Revenue bonds, although nonguaranteed, constitute a large proportion of city borrowing because they usually do not count against a statutory or constitutional debt limit. They can be issued by the city's governing body either with or without voter approval, and citizens should watch, if this type of borrowing is engaged in, to see that the revenue from the facility will indeed be sufficient to pay off the bonds.

Mortgage bonds are used in the purchase or construction of a government-operated utility. Also nonguaranteed, they offer a mortgage on the facility as security. They usually bear a higher rate of interest and do not count against a debt limit. The type of facility obviously determines whether a mortgage bond can be used: lenders might be willing to finance a municipal swimming pool or utility which could be privately operated if the mortgage had to be foreclosed, but there is obviously little market value in a repossessed jail.

There are several techniques for debt retirement. The bonds may have a call provision, which means that they can be paid off at any time prior to the date of maturity, at the desire of the debtor. A premium might have to be paid for exercising this option. A municipality may decide on early repayment of its debt if it encounters a surplus or if interest rates are dropping so that the debt can be "rolled over" or renegotiated at a lower rate of interest.

Traditionally, bonds matured at the same time and were repaid from a sinking fund, or reserve account, where money was put aside to repay the debt. But several problems were encountered with such lump sum repayment. The city fathers might fail to make regular appropriations to the fund to build it up systematically. ("It isn't due for fifteen years, so let's make it up next year.") When the reckoning came due, they were no longer in office. Or the fund might be tampered with for political reasons—money might be "temporarily" borrowed from this reserve account. Sinking fund investments sometimes failed during a recession or even sank into somebody's pockets without a trace through dishonest bookkeeping.

For all of these reasons, most cities now issue serial bonds, which mature gradually, with a certain number coming due each year. The city governing body is thus responsible for funding the money for repayment of part of the debt each year. This method is similar to an individual's installment loan; each payment includes both principal and interest. Thus a $5,000 serial bond is divided into coupons to be detached and mailed to the city treasurer or bank acting as fiscal agent for repayment, which will be made on the date printed on them.

A new type of city financing is a lease-purchase arrangement whereby a special borrowing authority issues nonguaranteed bonds to provide the capital to construct the facility, which is then leased for the bonding period for a rent which pays off the debt and generous interest. At the end of the lease, the authority or private group using it turns the debt-free facility over to the government. When legal borrowing capacities have been exhausted, such arrangements have been used to build civic centers and sports arenas. However, the private promoters which lease such facilities may go bankrupt, leaving the city with a municipal white elephant, such as a motor speedway, on its hands.

A final use of the city's credit involves industrial development bonds. These are usually a type of revenue or mortgage bond issued to build a plant site or factory to attract new industry to town. This will provide new jobs and will help the city's economy. The rent pays off the bonds, whereupon the facility may or may not be turned over to the private company.[7] Industrial development authorities' obligations do not ordinarily count against the city debt and are nonguaranteed. They are popular in economically depressed areas desperate for new industry, but city governments should be careful, since any industry willing to relocate solely because of tax advantages is likely to be economically marginal. A number of cities, especially in the South, where state governments have carefully planned and encouraged economic development, have benefited from the use of industrial development bonding. But many cities have found that the service demands of new industry were very costly, and in case the private company went bankrupt, the city's good credit name was tarnished, even though the bonds were not its legal obligation.

Municipal bonds are bought by those in upper income brackets because the interest is tax exempt. Both state and local obligations are sold in the municipal bond market, so-called because the cities were first to borrow. At the present time, although Congress periodically debates the topic, the interest paid on state and local debt obligations is exempt from the federal income tax because of the sovereignty of governments. This means, for example, that a person in the 40 percent income tax bracket can buy a municipal bond yielding 10 percent interest and receive a 14 percent return on his investment because it is tax free. In addition, many states having a state or local income tax make the bond interest earned from that jurisdiction exempt from their taxes. Thus a New York City bondholder does not pay city, state, or federal income tax on his municipal bond. No one knows precisely how much the rich benefit from this tax loophole, because most municipal bonds are issued in bearer form, not registered in the owner's name. While the federal revenue lost is considerable, according to calculations made by the U.S. Treasury, city and state officials have constantly testified in favor of retaining this exemption, contending that it allows local governments to borrow funds at reasonable rates of interest. Since their projects cannot compete in profitability with private corporations or offer the security of federal government obligations, municipal governments need the interest exemption in order to raise money in the capital market without crushing the taxpayers.

Controlling the Purse Strings: Budgeting

The budget is an essential tool for effective municipal financial management. Besides providing a cohesive plan for balancing revenues with expenditures, it is the city's means of describing in monetary terms the various services performed during each fiscal year.[8] The process of budgeting involves every aspect of municipal government for several reasons. It provides a means whereby all the actions of city government can be brought together and the priorities of the community can be listed.

At budget preparation time, the city governing body can evaluate the adequacy of municipal services and weigh the desirability of new or expanded programs together with the cost estimated to carry them out. This necessitates consideration of the long-range goals of the city and hence is a highly political process. Second, the budget focuses on the internal problems of running the city and its services for the coming year. It allows municipal administrators to recommend changes and improvements and to justify their programs of operation to the citizens' elected representatives who make the policy decisions. Finally, the budget serves as a tool for exercising control over expenditures through the fiscal year, usually through an allotment system. Most states have laws requiring municipalities to keep expenditures balanced within revenues, and no amount of cosmetic bookkeeping can keep the city from fiscal peril indefinitely if it lives beyond its means. The budget has been labeled *the* major policy document of the community, although it may be as informal as a set of figures in the mayor's or city clerk's head and in others an elaborate printed volume. A well-constructed budget and the publicity surrounding its adoption allow political consideration of the policies it proposes and furnish the public with an important guide in judging the work of their city officials.

There are several essential steps in the budget process, which begins well before the fiscal year and continues through into the next. The first stage is departmental estimates. Officials of each department plan their work for the coming fiscal year and estimate the cost of the program. The mayor, manager, or municipal governing body may have issued general financial guidelines to the departments, depending upon the city's economic situation. Second, collection of the separate agency requests into a preliminary total is made by the budget or finance officer. He also catalogs the fixed or uncontrollable expenditures: legal obligations such as retirement payments, the amount of city debt coming due which will have to be repaid, and others. Third, estimates of revenues for the coming year will be based upon previous collections and possible new sources. Besides a statement of anticipated taxes compiled by state revenue officials or the local finance officer, each department should calculate other income from fees or service charges. This is a most difficult task and each source should be itemized to take into account variables such as seasonal fluctuations, general economic growth, legislative tax changes and intergovernmental assistance policies. Fourth, preparation and recommendation of a budget must take into account any legal requirements that the budget be balanced—or that it meet city employees' wage demands, so that crucial workers are not lost to the private sector—and the political considerations of maintaining existing service levels and avoiding tax increases. When increases or cuts become necessary, there is a traditional set of priorities:

Spend	Cut
1. administrative salaries	5.
2. nonadministrative wages	4.
3. operating expenses, supplies and materials	3.
4. equipment	2.
5. maintenance	1.

The political fact of life is that supplies and equipment do not vote—city employees do. In an era of financial stringency it is not surprising that our cities are literally falling apart. The final step is adoption of the budget by the start of the new fiscal year, although subsequent ordinances may have to be passed if the financial situation changes unexpectedly. Public hearings, usually held, allow individual citizens and pressure groups to make their budgetary demands. The department heads or city employees may lobby directly for a bigger share and to gain publicity for their cause. The municipal governing body, after political consideration, may alter the budget, although in some cities it may only make reductions and not add new items against the recommendations of the chief executive. In strong-mayor cities, the mayor usually has the power of the item veto, which can be used to protect the integrity of his budgetary proposals, although the council may override by extraordinary vote on occasion.

There are several types of budgets. An executive budget is prepared by the city clerk, manager, or finance or budget officer and is presented by the mayor for legislative consideration. In many smaller towns, it is drawn up by the council as a whole or by a finance committee and is classified as a "legislative" budget. The municipal governing body plays an important role once the budget is enacted, because usually an extraordinary vote is needed to approve any changes. Expenditures are often divided into "operating" and "capital" budgets. The first includes regular day-to-day expenses, while the latter category is a long-term plan extending five to six years into the future for one-time major expenditures. The capital budget thus includes major public works, equipment, and purchases over a specified dollar amount or having a long use expectancy, and projects for which borrowing is necessary.

In format, budgets may be arranged by line item, giving the exact amount for each thing, or they may be arranged by program, showing the services to be rendered. Thus a line item budget might list "1 fire truck," "500 feet of 2 inch hose," and the wages of each fireman, while a program approach would list under the category "fire protection" the amounts for fire inspection, training, rescue work, answering alarms, and nonemergency work, with costs calculated for each function. Thus a line item budget, which is more traditional, gives an exact accounting for every expense, but tells little about how dollars are spent by purpose. Larger jurisdictions which would be lost in individual statistics favor program categories by function.

Municipal budgeting is usually incremental: past experience in revenue collection and expenditures is used as a guide to future fiscal policy. There are several reasons for this. First, past decisions are the most reliable tools for judging political repercussions and grappling with complex goals. Even the largest cities have small budget staffs for scrutiny, in part due to the reluctance of the operating departments. It is not unusual for a city with a $100 million budget to have a financial management staff of fewer than a half dozen, a scarcity of staff that would seem nothing short of reckless to the typical private company with sales of the same size. Second, a large proportion of the municipal budget is uncontrollable, despite the pledge of candidates for office to cut costs. Expenditures are fixed by essential levels of service; wage and salary scales constituting 50–75 percent of the budget are affected by inflation, local cost-sharing of state-required programs, and items enjoying so much support that it would be political suicide to cut them. Third, perhaps the most severe constraint is that of expected revenues. The stable nature of the property tax means last year's revenues will correlate highly with this year's receipts.

Review of the municipal budget thus tends to be limited.

- Many items are accepted as uncontrollable because of previous commitments or because they are considered essential programs.
- The focus is on the largest budget items and ways to minimize their increase.
- Decisions are based on concrete aspects of the program familiar to governing members, even if the item is only a small portion of the budget.[9]
- The view is on the short run rather than on long-range developments in each service area (taxpayers want to know what government has done for them lately).
- Attention concentrates on the dollars and cents of budget requests rather than on the program elements that the funds will buy.[10]

Thus budget execution becomes not only a means but a goal for better financial management. Fiscal control is ordinarily accomplished by asking each city department to submit a work program, often on a quarterly basis. Amounts from each account (general fund, street funds where certain revenues may be designated only for that purpose, and so forth) are then paid out in installments under an allotment system in accordance with the budget. Rather than maintain separate accounts which complicate recordkeeping, it has been advocated that all revenues be placed in the general fund, in terms of which spending priorities can be determined clearly. But most cities find it necessary to dedicate funds for a particular purpose in order to gain the political support necessary for their imposition.

A variety of accounting systems can be used to keep the city's books. On a cash basis, revenue is credited when it is actually received, and expenditures deducted when the disbursement is made. This is the simplest form, but it does not keep very good track of municipal finances. In accrual accounting, monies due the city are credited whether or not they have actually been received, and obligations are entered when the city commits itself, long before payment is made. A modified method to ensure conservative fiscal policy is to put revenues on a cash account and expenditures on an accrual basis.

Budgeting that measures the need and efficiency of civic operations is known as zero-based, or performance, budgeting. In its full development, this is known as "planning, programming, budgeting systems" (PPBS). Zero-based budgeting means that each spending demand is examined from the ground up and that each city department must fully justify its operations every year at budget time. It is designed to prune the bureaucratic deadwood of functions no longer needed, but few cities use this approach because of the time necessary for complete analysis when there is a deadline for budget adoption and because political scars tend to reopen in battles over the merit and spending priority of a particular program or policy. Performance budgeting tries more to evaluate the efficiency of municipal expenditures by measuring the per unit cost of service provided. A work unit is used to analyze costs: if each city employee works 2,000 hours annually, then the full-time equivalent number of workers is multiplied by 2,000 to calculate the number of work hours devoted to each activity. To find out how much each activity costs the city, divide total manhours by number of work units to obtain time spent on activity. Thus if 30 sanitation men made 365,000 trash pickups annually, then $60,000/365,000 = .16$ manhours per pickup at an assumed average employee wage of $8.00 per hour, or $1.28 each time the trash is collected. Such budgetary information can be important in setting equitable service charges. Similar ratios such as cost/cost, benefit/benefit, and cost/benefit can be compiled to calculate the performance between different-sized city agencies, expenditures, clientele, and functions. Such ratios neutralize disparities in measuring different branches of the activity and make possible comparison of the municipality with other cities as it performs its tasks.

In municipal government, productivity includes both economy and quality in service, not just the cost efficiency of private enterprise. But there are significant differences between the public and private sectors. Public officials do not have the management authority of private businessmen, and decisions which are not notably productive may be made for valid political reasons. External factors may have a greater impact on certain municipal services: the crime rate may be more affected by the proportion of juveniles in a community than by the quality of law enforcement. Citizen expectations play a large role when a municipal government is judged, and the results of many civic programs cannot be measured in profit-or-loss terms. While efficiency and effectiveness are usually linked, sometimes an increase in one decreases the other below a level that the public considers acceptable: reducing the number of police used as school crossing guards may mean a more efficient use of manpower elsewhere, but parents think a crossing light less effective for safety.

Finally, except in small towns where the clerk keeps all records, organization for financial administration is quite fragmented. Since fiscal management is seen as a tool for effective executive leadership, an integrated city finance department may be created under the mayor or manager, although a number of cities retain an independently elected city treasurer.

The department is likely to consist of several divisions. The budget division draws up the elaborate document we have discussed, which obviously entails fiscal planning. The collection division receives all tax money and revenues but usually deposits them at local financial institutions in time deposits and checking accounts. The accounting division maintains records of the amounts of money in each fund and may also keep the inventory of all public property and equipment. The purchasing agent compiles all buying needs, draws up the specifications for competitive bids, and is often able to save each department money by making volume purchases for the city as a whole.[11] The disbursing office, under the comptroller, performs many of the treasury functions: it sees that no department spends more than is authorized in the budget and that it has permission to make the expenditure by signing the payment vouchers (the city's checks). In smaller cities, the municipal governing body is likely to perform this task itself, with a considerable proportion of the meeting taken up with "billpayers."

As we have seen, the tax assessment process is separate, as is the auditing function. The auditor is an agent of the legislative branch and can either be an arm of the council in larger cities or an outside firm of certified public accountants hired to check the books, as in a private corporation. In a few jurisdictions, the auditor may be directly elected by the people, or else this may be a task of state government. A financial audit may go beyond records of bookkeeping to make recommendations on managerial efficiency. As municipal financial administration has become more complex, various financial tasks may be scattered throughout city government. It is frequently asserted that most cities could improve their fiscal management practices, and this has often led to the appointment of task forces composed of local businessmen who inspect on behalf of the citizenry. However, the guiding publications produced by the Municipal Finance Officers Association are highly professional and can assist cities in their financial planning.

Are Our Cities Broke?

Fiscal Crisis Linked
To Job Losses Here

Realization Gains That Economic Rise
Is Needed to Ameliorate City's Troubles

Newspaper headlines such as that shown above frequently proclaim that our cities are in financial trouble and that the economic base must be improved. For example, New York City lost 609,000 jobs between 1969 and 1977 as companies moved out of town, with the consequent loss in tax revenues. Newspaper headlines and campaign rhetoric aside, how can citizens determine when their city is in financial trouble? According to the federal Advisory Commission on Intergovernmental Relations, there are five symptoms of unhealthy financial condition.

- Current expenditures exceed receipts by more than 5 percent.
- The city has shown deficits in each of the preceding two years.
- Deficits appear in the general fund under cash-basis accounting.
- Short-term loans are still outstanding at the end of the year.
- Assessed real estate value (AV) shows a year-to-year decrease.

Voters are most likely to become aware of these danger signals only if they are constantly asked to approve bond issues. Nationally, the volume of municipal debt per city resident has risen greatly since World War II. Thus a quick indicator of a city's fiscal health is the portion of its budget devoted to debt service: less than 10 percent is normal, more than 15 percent warrants concern, and more than 20 percent means the city will find it very difficult to repay its obligations. When a municipality wishes to borrow money, the interest it must pay is ordinarily determined by an outside bond rating firm such as Moody or Standard and Poor. In determining the degree of risk, bond raters consider such factors as:

• The relative weight of the tax load on property owners. A debt load, excluding utilities, of less than 3 percent of the full value of taxable properties is very light, and 4–6 percent is good, but at more than 7 percent the taxpayers' burden becomes heavy.

• Property tax collection. If the jurisdiction collects 97 percent of its taxes on time, all is well, but if delinquency rises above 8 percent, revenue is seriously cut.

• Population of the community. A stable composition is reassuring, while sharp increases in recent years or an influx of low-income persons may necessitate more borrowing in the future.

• Economic background. A declining, volatile, or one-industry town is a riskier investment base, while a booming, diversified city or a mature suburb is more prosperous.

• The budget and debt retirement. Living up to the budget and maintaining a year-end cash balance are encouraging achievements, as are repaying debts on time and not greatly increasing borrowing. Chronic deficits requiring revenue anticipation notes are cause for concern.

Depending upon these conditions, and any legal or constitutional guarantees of debt repayment, bonds receive the following ratings:

Quality	Moody	Standard and Poor
Prime	Aaa	AAA
High	Aa	AA
	A1	—
Good	A	A
	Baa1	—
Medium	Baa	BBB

Such ratings significantly affect the interest charged, and nonrated bonds (NR) may be difficult for the city to sell. If a municipality's credit is questioned, there may not be a bid from the bond-underwriting syndicates (banks or brokerage firms which retail the bonds to investors) or a bid at an interest rate that the city cannot afford to pay.

Since the stock market collapse of the 1930s, only rarely does a local government default, or fail to pay its debts on time according to terms promised. In the thirty-five years since World War II, there have been fewer than thirty-five defaults, with New York and Cleveland the only big cities involved. But many cities have gone through budget crises, laying off employees, falling behind in the payment of bills or payrolls, and paying only interest, but not principal, on debts. If a city falls into serious fiscal difficulties, it may be forced to renegotiate the terms of its obligations and may come frequently under the financial supervision of the state, since the collapse of one jurisdiction will shake investor confidence in the rest. The insolvency of New York City in the 1970s forced the U.S. Congress to rewrite the federal bankruptcy act under which municipalities, like private companies, can be placed in receivership under the courts. The recession of the early 1980s caused a drop in the municipal bond buyers' index as investors became more cautious in lending and communities across the nation found it more expensive to borrow in the money market.

Such conditions invite some concluding observations about the resources and needs of our cities. While the wealth of our country is concentrated in urban areas, our municipalities find it hard to tap. Although the per capita revenue of local governments has risen greatly during this century, service demands also continue to increase, as people try to sustain their standard of living. The proportion of the governmental tax dollar going to local jurisdictions has increased, with one-third of expenditures made there. Yet numerous local governments compete for the tax dollar, especially in metropolitan areas where government is fragmented. It is difficult to relate costs and benefits when civic operations and their consequences spill over territorial boundaries. In order to finance public activities more equitably, cities have tried several approaches examined in chapter 3: areawide service in special districts; transfer of functions to the counties or state; regional financing so that urban taxpayers cannot flee the jurisdiction; and revenues allocated to local units to provide services or redistribution of wealth through state or federal policies. Yet the broader the financing base, the more desire for control by the local community. Our municipalities provide a structure for political accountability, which the public desires most of all at tax time.

Notes

1. The tax is levied as a flat rate and so necessarily takes a larger proportion of a poor person's income than of the rich man's.

2. Often the county commissioners or township supervisors, if not the city officials.

3. Which might be overassessed or underassessed because of local prejudice.

4. A number of urban reformers believe that many assessing jurisdictions in metropolitan areas are too small already, producing inadequate tax bases with poverty pockets and industrial and wealthy residential enclaves which do not contribute their fair share of overall value.

5. The rate can also be expressed in mills, from the Latin meaning one-thousandth of a dollar, or one-tenth of a cent. Thus a twenty-mill rate means two cents on the dollar, or $2 tax on each $100 of assessed valuation.

6. Robert L. Lineberry and Ira Sharkansky, *Urban Politics and Public Policy* (New York: Harper and Row, 1971), pp. 218–26, and the studies cited in John

C. Bollens and Henry J. Schmancht, *The Metropolis,* 3rd ed. (New York: Harper and Row, 1975), pp. 230–33.

7. During the time the bonds are outstanding, the property is legally owned by the government, and hence exempt from property tax.

8. The fiscal year, as distinguished from the calendar year, is usually tied to the receipt of major taxes and, depending upon the state, runs from July 1 to June 30 or from October 1 to September 30.

9. The spectacle of city fathers haggling over small details is a common one, ascribable to the human desire to look good by talking of things one knows about and/or the political strategy of setting a precedent for expenditure this year, which can be enlarged in subsequent budgets.

10. John P. Crecine, *Governmental Problem Solving: A Computer Simulation of Municipal Budgeting* (Skokie, Ill.: Rand McNally, 1969).

11. In a number of states, local governments may engage in joint purchasing arrangements or receive services under contract, often at considerable discounts.

For Further Reading

Advisory Commission on Intergovernmental Relations (1111 20th St., N.W., Washington, D.C. 20575) publishes topical reports of issues affecting municipal finance.

International City Management Association (12th and G Streets, N.W., Washington, D.C. 20036) has articles on municipal finance in *The Municipal Year Book*. See also *Management Policies in Local Government Finance*. Washington, D.C., 1981.

Lee, Robert D., and Johnson, Ronald W. *Public Budgeting Systems*. 2nd ed. Baltimore, Md.: University Park Press, 1977.

Municipal Finance Officers Association (180 N. Michigan Ave., Chicago, Ill. 60637) publishes its journal *Municipal Finance*. The association also prepared *Concepts and Practices in Local Government Finance*. Chicago, 1975.

U.S. Bureau of the Census. *Census of Governments, 1977.* vol. 4, no. 4. *Finances of Municipalities and Township Governments.* Washington, D.C.: U.S. Government Printing Office, 1979. These volumes of refined data appear after the Census of Government every five years.

7: Working at City Hall

Governmental employment in the United States—federal, state, and local—more than doubled from 1955 to 1975. Of the 15 million civilian governmental workers, more than 12 million are employed by state and local governments. Local government payrolls amount to more than $7 billion per month, and the city may be among the larger employers in a community. How this bureaucracy functions at city hall is the subject of this chapter.

Administrative Organization

In deciding how to arrange an organization to perform its tasks, planners have developed a number of management concepts. Channels for communication must exist to transfer orders downward, to receive feedback upward, and to join all parts of the organization laterally. If communications are blocked, rumor and speculation flourish, producing distorted information. "Span of control" indicates the number of employees who can be adequately supervised by each manager. The number will vary, depending upon the diversity of work performed and the degree of authority delegated. Job tasks are specialized, and workers can be grouped by the function performed, the location (by area), the type (process) of work, and the clientele served. Municipal administration must follow the due process required by the rule of law in our democratic system of government. The city may promulgate an administrative code or manual for uniform treatment of its employees and of citizens. Large measures of checks and balances are frequently found in city government structure, sometimes to the frustration of elected officials. Often the administrative precautions take the form of independent boards or commissions which exert policy guidance or even operational direction over certain city activities. There may be police commissioners, library trustees, hospital board members, public health superintendents, or museum directors who exercise varying degrees of budgetary authority and appointment powers over city departments. Members may be appointed by the city council (and hence may be independent from it or the chief executive) for long, overlapping terms. Legally, commissions may be bipartisan or nonpartisan in composition, but they frequently include representatives from the interest group or segment of the community concerned with that particular policy area. Politically such boards serve to insulate the legislature and the executive from certain types of pressure, since they are nonelective, and often devote many unpaid hours of expertise to solving community needs. At worst, they can become entrenched fiefdoms able to defy mayoral or council control. For this reason, the present tendency is to make all such lay citizen boards advisory only, providing useful input, and to mobilize community support for a policy, leaving executive authority in the hands of the mayor or city manager. The degree of executive authority often conflicts with the tradition of legislative supremacy found in American local government. Often city council members have not been content to stop at mere surveillance in their legislative oversight role but have sought, either personally or through council committees, to intervene in department operations. Conversely, "end runs," as the bureaucracy attempts to bypass the executive in order to reach the legislative body, may be attempted for the purpose of changing operating policies or supervisory practices or to increase pay. An insecure mayor or city manager may spend much time worrying about such efforts behind his back. It is more realistic to recognize the mutual attraction between the council, which needs political support, and the city bureaucracy, which lobbies for program support.[1]

As the city bureaucracy grows larger, it becomes more formally structured. Two major types of organizations are the functional model and the line-staff model (see figure 7.1). Administrators may periodically attempt reorganization efforts to obtain more control over the hierarchy or to increase their own power. Structural realignment, while often touted as a means to obtain greater efficiency or better management, is never politically neutral in its effects, and reorganization efforts succeed or fail for political reasons.

City Civil Servants

Personnel texts frequently begin by decrying the patronage system: its appointments through political favoritism, promotions by cronyism, padded payrolls, and other manifestations of corruption. Such a recital ignores the fact that two-thirds of all American incorporated municipalities have fewer than 2,500 inhabitants, and in such small communi-

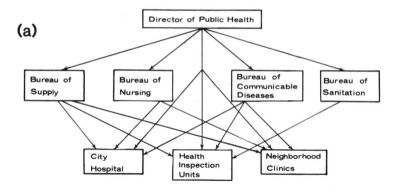

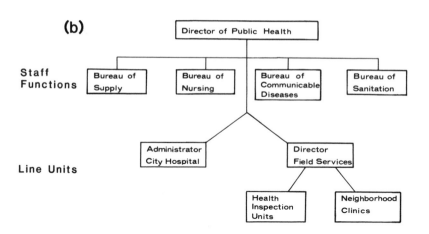

Figure 7.1. Organizational Models of the City Bureaucracy. (a) Functional model. Each bureau has direct authority to field units. This model is often used in smaller organizations with direct interaction. (b) Line-staff model. The chain of command and responsibility is clarified between staff, the secondary or auxiliary functions, and tasks that accomplish the primary line missions. A particular task could be classified as either line or staff, depending upon the unit's role.

ties, the few (even part-time) employees are jacks of all trades who obtained their jobs as hometown folks. Indeed, intimate familiarity with friends and neighbors is needed to attend to their diverse needs. How large a municipal work force is needed to make a formal personnel system feasible? The answer depends on the point at which job tasks become specialized enough to demand skills which can be recruited on a competitive basis. Many municipalities probably adhere to an informal personnel system, even though they could obtain better help through competitive practices, because informality facilitates political dividends.

A civil service or merit system recruits qualified applicants through open competition, promotes on the basis of fitness, and confers job security with removal only for just cause and not for partisan reasons.[2] A civil service system, however, does not guarantee a meritorious work force at city hall. The means used, position classification, is too often mistaken as the end, with the mythical separation of positions from the people who occupy them.

There are two major types of public personnel organizations currently in use. The independent civil service commission consists of three to five members selected on a bipartisan or nonpartisan basis for long, staggered terms by the municipal governing body or by some other indirect means. This commission draws up the job classification plan so that the qualifications for each position and the tests necessary to measure them can be determined. The commissioners, as part-time guardians of civic merit, usually hire a full-time chief examiner who administers the tests and sends the paperwork of the successful applicants to the hiring agency. The commissioners also perform as judges, hearing appeals by civil servants on grievances, proposed disciplinary measures, or dismissal for just cause. The second approach, a city personnel department, is considered a staff function, with a director who should be responsible to the chief executive, as in private industry. Organizing by public employees and the increase in state and federal regulations have emphasized the importance of personnel as a management function. Some cities have tried to merge the two systems by making the personnel director also serve as executive secretary/chief examiner to the civil service commission.

Position Classification. There are several basic steps in a civil service merit system. An initial phase, position classification, occurs before recruiting begins. Through job analyses, in which employees and their supervisors fill out questionnaires on their duties, and through observation by the personnel specialist, a list of the skills needed for each aspect of the job is compiled. Then minimum qualifications for each job and the appropriate testing measures can be set. Through factor comparison of the mental, physical, and skill requirements of each task, position classification can be related to pay classification. A major goal of the merit principle is "equal pay for equal work," but sometimes employees and their supervisors connive to inflate position descriptions to attain a higher pay classification. Table 7.1 shows how a salary schedule might look.

Table 7.1. A Sample Salary Schedule (in dollars)

Salary range	Steps with 5% intervals				
	1	2	3	4	5
20	500	525	551	579	608
21	525	551	579	608	638
22	551	579	608	638	670
23	579	608	638	670	704
24	608	638	670	704	739
25	638	670	704	739	776
26	670	704	739	776	815

Note: Monthly rate is shown; ranges can also be on biweekly basis or with more steps if the city wishes to reward longer service. Each position classification is assigned a salary range. Employees with satisfactory performance advance a step each year up to the top of their range. Among those interested in the city pay plan will be employees, their organizations, taxpayers' associations, civic groups, private employers who seek the same work force, city elected officials who must pass the budget, and sometimes the courts which ultimately resolve the labor dispute if wage negotiations break down.

Recruitment announcements of civil service positions are openly advertised at city hall, state employment service offices, and federal job information centers (see figure 7.2). This traditional posting of job vacancies may only reach a limited audience, so affirmative action programs to recruit women and minorities have used media advertising, mailing lists, work-study programs (internships) with nearby educational institutions, and displays or an open house. Referrals by current employees are frequently used, and several members of the same family may be employed by the city (although civil service regulations may forbid one relative to supervise another). The recruitment announcement lists the position to be filled, the minimum qualifications, and where to obtain an application form. The merit principle supposes an open competitive selection process; however, some promotional examinations may be closed or restricted to current employees, thus barring lateral entry by outsiders. Police and fire departments are most likely to be closed career systems having promotion from within. Also, some municipalities have residency requirements, meaning that successful applicants must live within the hiring jurisdiction. Residency requirements have decreased since the Great Depress-

CIVIL SERVICE CAREERS

06001-06201
1-16-76

The Personnel Board of Jefferson County, Alabama

ROOM 301 COURTHOUSE ANNEX
BIRMINGHAM, ALABAMA

Open Competitive

EXAMINATION FOR

POLICE OFFICER AND DEPUTY SHERIFF
(All Jurisdictions)

PURPOSE: To fill present and future vacancies with Jefferson County and the Cities of Bessemer, Birmingham, Fairfield, Fultondale, Gardendale, Homewood, Hueytown, Midfield, Mountain Brook, Pleasant Grove, Tarrant and Vestavia Hills.

STARTING SALARY $807*   *MAXIMUM SALARY* $1,029

CLOSING DATE   OPEN   *EXAMINATION DATE*   CONTINUOUS

FRINGE BENEFITS include group medical insurance, pension plan and credit union; Paid vacations, holidays, and sick leave; Job security and promotion by competitive examinations.

TIME, DATE AND PLACE

Applicants will be notified of the time, date and place to appear for the examinations.

ENTRANCE REQUIREMENTS

AGE: 21-33. Must not have passed 34th birthday on date of appointment.
EDUCATION: High school graduation or a bona fide G.E.D. certificate.
OTHER: Height, 5'2" to 6'10"; weight, 120 lbs. to 300 lbs. Applicants must pass a Class A physical examination prior to appointment, and height and weight must be found to be in proportion as determined by the examining physician.

DUTIES

Under supervision, performs general law enforcement work in protecting life and property; enforces criminal laws, traffic laws and local ordinances; performs related work as required.

EXAMINATION SUBJECTS AND WEIGHTS

Examinations will be administered which measure aptitude for police work and mental alertness (Minimum grade required, 70). Weighting for the various sections of the examinations will be explained when the test is administered.

*SALARIES: Pleasant Grove $832 - $1,059
             Jeff. Co. $823 - $1,050
             Mt. Brook $819 - $1,045

GENERAL INFORMATION CONCERNING CIVIL SERVICE EXAMINATIONS

THE JEFFERSON COUNTY PERSONNEL BOARD PROVIDES A PUBLIC PERSONNEL SYSTEM BASED ON MERIT PRINCIPLES. IT STRIVES FOR THE CONSTANT IMPROVEMENT OF THE PUBLIC SERVICE BY EMPLOYING AND DEVELOPING THE BEST QUALIFIED PEOPLE AVAILABLE, REGARDLESS OF THEIR RACE, COLOR, CREED, SEX, POLITICAL BELIEFS, OR NATIONAL ORIGIN.

FILING AN APPLICATION:
Applicants whose completed applications are not received by the date and time specified above may not be admitted to the examination.

AGE:
Applicants must not be less than the minimum age stated above on the date of examination, nor more than the maximum age stated above on the date of appointment.
2. All applicants born on or after January 1, 1915, must submit a birth certificate upon appointment to a permanent position.

FINGERPRINTS:
Male applicants will be fingerprinted when they obtain applications.

RESIDENCE:
The residence of applicants is not restricted, but applicants who live in Jefferson County shall be certified first.

EXAMINATION RESULTS:
1. Applicants will be notified of their results by mail within approximately two weeks of the date of examination. Those who pass will receive their grades and position on the eligible register. Those who fail will receive their grades.
2. Applicants who wish may review their grades within thirty days after the results are mailed. Test questions, however, are not subject to review by applicants.

MEDICAL EXAMINATION:
A medical examination by the Board's designated physician is required at time of employment.

APPOINTMENT:
As requisitions are received, they will be filled from the eligible register in accordance with Personnel Board rules.

CHARACTER INVESTIGATION:
Successful applicants are subject to a character and employment investigation prior to appointment.

PERSONNEL-21

Figure 7.2. A Recruitment Announcement for a Civil Service Position

ion of the 1930s, when it was felt that "city jobs should be kept for hometown folks." Defenders of residency requirements today argue that (a) the city should be able to summon its employees from nearby to deal with emergencies, (b) wage demands by unionizing workers will be moderated if they have to live within the jurisdiction and pay taxes like other citizens, and (c) employees who live within the city will do a better job because of their daily familiarity with civic problems.[3] While some cities advertise some positions nationally (usually for specialized department heads), most recruitment usually takes place within nearby areas.

Selection has traditionally been the written civil service examination designed to measure general aptitude to perform a job or practical achievement in a skill. But depending upon the position to be filled, there may be tests of physical agility, manual dexterity, or an "unassembled examination" where applicants are rated on their individual training (educational degrees, professional certification, or blue-collar trade rating) and experience without ever taking a test together. The civil service preparatory books produced by a number of commercial companies, covering widely found positions such as municipal policeman or bookkeeper, are often based on the New York City civil service exams, the most extensive given. Many smaller jurisdictions tend to use similar tests because it is expensive to compile and validate different tests for each town. Because general aptitude tests have tended to discriminate against members of minority groups with different cultural backgrounds, court decisions in the 1970s have required tests to be job-related: they must validly measure what is needed to do the job. Oral interviews may constitute a portion of the selection process to judge poise, appearance, and ability to think when asked a series of questions. The interviewing board frequently consists of a civil service or personnel representative, the head of the agency or unit with a vacancy, and an outside citizen or specialist concerned with the field. Each panelist ranks each applicant on a number of specified traits deemed desirable in the position. Public employee unions have tended to oppose oral interviews as too subjective and even susceptible to manipulation if favored candidates are dishonestly briefed on the questions likely to be asked. Whatever selection processes are used, the candidates are then ranked from 1 to N according to their scores, usually with a cutoff of 70 percent.

Certification from the Eligibility List. The civil service commission "certifies" the top-ranked names (or "eligibles") from the list and sends them to the hiring unit, which fills the position. Many jurisdictions use the "rule of the three," meaning that the top three names are sent, while others use the rule of five or even ten. New York City under Mayor Beame (who rose through the civil service ranks) used the "rule of one," meaning that the top person on the list must be hired or promoted. Such "absolute merit" may be rejected, since this gives the hiring agency no discretion, and only one-tenth of a point may separate the leading scores. Some jurisdictions allow a veterans preference of 5 bonus points (or 10 if disabled) to those honorably discharged, while a few cities give absolute preference in exceptional circumstances (e.g., a policeman is killed in the line of duty: if his widow—or widowed mother—is able to pass a civil service test for a position, that jurisdiction will hire her first, regardless of ranking). Another controversial practice is selective certification. Due to past discriminatory practices, certain minority groups have been excluded or severely underrepresented in some city work forces. For example, a minimum height/ weight requirement for police officers of five feet eight inches and 160 pounds would exclude most women and certain ethnic groups. In such cases, the courts have ordered waivers to the average height or weight of the excluded groups, requiring that candidates with passing scores be selectively certified to the hiring agency until such time as the excluded group is proportional in the work force to the population served. This does not mean that such candidates are unqualified—all of them have passed the selection process above the 70 percent or other cutoff score—but it has meant on occasion that some cities would continuously recruit for women or certain minorities, hire each of them along with one white male under the court order, and still have vacant positions to fill (such as understrength public safety forces). In the normal course of events, the civil service position is filled from the hiring roster until the eligibles' scores drop near the cutoff, at which time a new recruitment announcement is made, and a new list of eligibles compiled. Persons on the previous list who were not hired may have to apply and go through the selection process again, or they may have their old scores transferred to the new register, depending upon the jurisdiction.

During a **probationary period,** commonly six months in most cities, a newly hired employee can be discharged for simply not fitting in on the job; after that he or she acquires civil service tenure and can be dismissed only after a hearing procedure with the burden of proof on the city. (The U.S. Supreme Court in *Elrod, Sheriff* v. *Burns,* 427 U.S. 347 [1976], held that even non–civil service employees who do not make policy cannot be discharged simply for partisan reasons when the opposition party gains power.) Such terminations are infrequent (accounting for less than 5 percent of all terminations) and are usually for misconduct on the job rather than for routine inefficiency. However, tenured city servants can lose their jobs as a result of financial exigency; New York City cut its payrolls during the 1970s. Such reductions in force (sometimes called RIFs) occur with accelerated early retirements and laying off of civil servants with the least seniority (thus often reducing those newly hired under affirmative action programs).

Retirement systems and earlier retirement ages have been a major attraction of civil service employment but also a major financial burden upon cities. Many cities have their own retirement system or participate in a state employees' retirement plan. However, lack of actuarial planning, the impact of inflation, and cost-of-living escalator clauses recently negotiated have led at least one study[4] to conclude that many local government pension plans are seriously underfunded. The total compensation paid employees includes not only salaries but fringe benefits (vacations, leave, insurance, medical services, and retirement) whose cost may become fully apparent only with the passage of time (see table 7.2). Elected officials may have found it politically expedient to agree to employee demands, but the city will be financially committed long after they have passed from office. Since 1954 state and local government officials have been eligible to participate in the federal social security program and since 1978 have covered by federal unemployment insurance. However, in the 1976 case *National League of Cities* v. *Usery, Secretary of Labor,*[5] the U.S. Supreme Court ruled 5–4 that state and local government employees are not covered by the federal Wages and Standards Act in setting the minimum wage or overtime provisions. While the ruling was attacked by public employee unions, the civil service goal of parity with private sector pay and prevailing labor market conditions dictates that municipalities will have to maintain competitive pay scales.

Table 7.2. Total Labor Cost of New York City Employees (in dollars)

Average base salary of all city employees, March 31, 1976	16,091
Cost of living adjustment, longevity pay, and paid holidays (exclusive of overtime)	220
Fringe benefits: health insurance, welfare funds, and uniform allowance	1,116
Retirement benefits: pension, social security, and annuity funds	5,576
Leave benefits, paid vacation	3,524
Total cost to city	26,527

Note: A New York City panel urged a cut in fringe benefits, but New York City's employees are not the most highly paid in the country. Many municipalities are faced with growing costs of employee compensation.

Source: Lee Dembart, "Panel Urges Cut in Fringe Benefits," *New York Times,* June 3, 1976, p. 32.

Has municipal civil service served the people? As with any system, it can be manipulated to produce certain outcomes. A large number of positions may be exempt or excluded from civil service coverage. Or large numbers of city workers may be classified as temporary and hence exempt, although their appointments may be renewed year after year. Civil service job security may appear to the public as a sinecure for inefficiency. Hence there have been recent attempts to enhance government performance, but there is no bottom line by which public programs are measured in terms of profit or loss: "First, public managers are faced with a variety of organizational constraints uncommon in the private sector, such as restrictive legal authority and civil service rules. Second, public managers operate in a political environment. Decisions may be made by local elected officials for logical political reasons which may not be consistent with maximum productivity. Third, citizen expectations play a major role in the provision of local government services."[6] The diversity of public opinion ensures that citizens will not agree on the results of city programs. On the other hand, city employees are likely to resent implementation of individual performance appraisals unless there are incentives, monetary or other, to reward superior service.

Municipal Unionism

In 1919, Boston police officers struck, and public reaction was summarized in the telegram sent by Gov. Calvin Coolidge to American Federation of Labor president Samuel Gompers: "There is no right to strike against the public safety by anybody, anywhere, any time." The striking policemen were fired, and nonrecognition of public employee groups was the rule for nearly fifty years. But in the past decade, hardly a month goes by without a strike by sanitation workers, firemen, teachers, hospital attendants, or other dissatisfied workers. This new militancy in city hall reflects the organization of public employees by unions or associations and represents a major issue in municipal administration.[7]

City employee associations existed as social groups long before the advent of collective bargaining and hence were scorned as management-dominated "company unions." Public employee unions which explicitly seek to represent their members have had the greatest success at city hall, with their membership now exceeding that of the associations. These can be independent groups (including associations now seeking representation rights) or locals affiliated with a national union.

The major unions organizing city workers today are: the American Federation of State, County and Municipal Employees of the American Federation of Labor–Congress of Industrial Organizations (AFL–

CIO). AFSCME, 900,000 strong, consists only of government employees, but they may be in any field. The International Association of Firefighters, AFL–CIO, and the Fraternal Order of Police limit their membership to their respective branches of public safety. The Service Employees International Union, AFL–CIO, and the International Brotherhood of Teamsters have most of their members in private industry but seek to represent almost all types of local government employees. At present, some type of employee organization exists in three-fourths of the nation's municipalities and represents two-thirds of the personnel employed by city hall.

However, in a particular city, several employee groups may be in competition for members and bargaining rights. The second largest cause of public sector labor disputes during the 1960s was striking for recognition—virtually unknown in private industry where laws provide procedures for representation. Public employees are likely both to see the benefits of having an organization represent them and to attract union or association interest in jurisdictions of about 50,000 population.[8] The general strength of organized labor in the area and the existence of state legislation protecting the right of government employees to organize and bargain collectively are also influential.

Nonrecognition of employee groups is no longer a realistic alternative. Federal courts ruled in *Atkins* v. *City of Charlotte, N.C.* that local laws forbidding city employees to join a union are unconstitutional violations of freedom of association under the First and Fourteenth Amendments.[9] Since most federal labor relations acts do not apply to state and local government employees, many state legislatures originally ignored the subject or dealt with it piecemeal after labor disputes had occurred.

The result for a particular city may be that representation procedures for certain employees may be specified by law or unwritten local political tradition, while recognition of other groups is granted at the option of the city administration. Fragmented local government and the eagerness of employee organizations to gain adherents (members of a Fraternal Order of Police lodge may work in several different cities) has meant difficulty in determining bargaining units. Ideally, employees choose at a certification election the group which is to be given exclusive recognition as their bargaining agent. But many public employees may not wish to join a union, and an open shop arrangement is encouraged by many governmental employers. The union shop, where employees are required to join a union or else pay a representation fee equivalent to dues (the agency shop) negotiated in a contract, may conflict with civil service protections. Governmental supervisory levels are not as distinct, with first-line supervisors often enrolled in employee groups, meaning that municipal management cannot work alone during a strike. Thus in a single city department, employees may be represented by several bargaining agents, or none at all, if the city administration has resisted recognition. Determination of bargaining units in some big cities has been according to politicians' best interests politically: elected officials are not private bosses; they serve all the people and particularly the organized ones. As a result, balkanized bargaining units may negotiate a crazy quilt of compensation agreements, causing more labor strife. Since union leaders may be in competition for members and representation, they are more militant, because they cannot afford to lose a demand. One result is "me tooism," with "the same, plus a better deal" negotiated by different groups of employees.

Negotiations, Agreements, and Disputes

There are two negotiating relationships used, "meet and confer" and "collective bargaining." Under the first, when an agency has organized employees, the law determines how the group will be recognized; consultations on wages, benefits, and working conditions take place. But the employer has the power to make the final decision. This provision recognizes government's sovereign role and responsibility to the public (beyond that of a private employer). However, "meet and confer" is attacked by organized labor as one-sided. Collective bargaining, on the other hand, permits both labor and management to negotiate as equals and to arrive at a mutually acceptable agreement. The first state laws passed in 1959 allowing collective bargaining, and more than thirty-five states now permit it among at least some of their public employees. Half a dozen states now legally allow a limited right to strike to some categories of municipal employees.

The democratic system of checks and balances makes the public employer an amorphous entity for bargaining purposes. Management authority may be diffused among a mayor, a city manager, a personnel director, the council, independent boards or commissions, and sometimes the state legislature. The negotiator for a municipality ("management" in private industry) may not have authority to discuss basic terms and conditions of employment (which are written into law or civil service regulations), leading the union to bargain at several levels of government, including an "end run" to the legislature. If they don't like what the city has to offer, public employees create a powerful interest group which can lobby the council or legislature. As one union leader happily said, "We can elect our employers."[10]

The part-time council or average mayor does not have the time for lengthy negotiations with experienced union representatives; the initial city tactic of "divide and rule," reluctantly recognizing employee organizations one at a time, has instead resulted in a continuing series of

demands by the different groups. Since ethnic groups have traditionally sought public employment, bargaining may have its racial aspects.
Because of the public's right to know about government, labor negotiations lead both sides on a rhetorical quest for favorable community
opinion. An astute city administration will carefully prepare its bargaining position, will decide who (personnel specialist, city council, or
assistant to the mayor) will negotiate on its behalf, and will deal with
employee representatives on a day-to-day basis.

Given the shortness of municipal experience in bargaining, growing
pains are not surprising. Should the parties "meet and confer," concluding nonbinding "memoranda of understanding," or will collective
bargaining with formal contracts prevail? For public employee labor
organizations, the written contract is the symbol of legitimacy and
equality with the municipal employer. Newly organized employee
groups will seek recognition and union security provisions first and will
then expand the subjects of negotiation.[11] But in the public sector the
scope of bargaining may be limited by state law. Thus, instead of means
for negotiating grievance procedures, civil service rules may provide
avenues for appeal, or the political tides may carve some unusual
grievance channels. The trade-offs reached in an agreement may be
determined by political costs, not simply economic ones.

Since three-fourths of a municipal budget is likely to go for personnel costs, labor agreements should be concluded before the budget is
submitted to the legislative body. Otherwise supplementary appropriations or new revenue measures have to be enacted after the start of a
fiscal year. The city often faces a timing dilemma: it desires a longer
contract for labor stability but cannot legally obligate money beyond
the annual budgetary period. Also, a new agreement should be considered not simply on the basis of its direct costs but also as to whether it
alters benefit levels among different groups of city employees. While
municipal union pressure may not result in great salary advances,[12]
every year limited demands are met, so that costs spiral over a decade.
Cities may avoid filling vacancies, freeze new promotions, delay purchasing equipment, postpone repairs and routine maintenance, and
cut back on services to squeeze the money out to meet personnel costs.
A liberalized pension plan can affect the quality of services offered if
large numbers of skilled employees decide to retire early. Such personnel benefits, gained at the expense of necessary capital improvements
and maintenance, are reflected in the physical deterioration and run-
down facilities of some cities.

If labor and management representatives reach an impasse, three
procedures may be tried to reach a settlement: fact finding, mediation,
and binding arbitration. If there is a dispute over the information
presented by each side, an impartial fact-finding tribunal may be cre-

ated to investigate the issues and charges made by each party. Besides a citizen's committee, sometimes a governor, a state legislative committee, or a grand jury may perform this role in municipal labor disputes. The fact-finding group may present its conclusions with recommendations, although this may start the parties on end runs around the tribunal to the legislature, other budgetary authority, or the public.

Public sector mediation, in which an impartial mediator (or panelists chosen by each side, who then agree on a third member) seeks to reconcile differences,[13] is quite different from that process in private enterprise. First, factors such as tax structure, legislative controls on the budget, state aid formulas, and civil service rules tend to control rather than a free labor market, business competition, or profit levels. Second, many disputed issues fall into the realm of public policy, such as equal pay for police and firemen or the size of school classes. Union political assistance in increasing the government's ability to pay—often asked by the city administration—is a unique aspect of public sector bargaining not present in labor relations in private industry.

Most public employee leaders oppose compulsory arbitration, where a binding settlement is imposed by outside authority, except in essential services where strikes are barred. Reliance on this impasse procedure may stultify the collective bargaining process because both sides may reckon that an arbitration award—which frequently splits the differences in dispute—will be more advantageous than a negotiated settlement. A technique for reducing extreme positions on each side is "final offer," or "last best offer," arbitration. In this process, the arbitrator must pick the final offer which appears most reasonable as proposed by management or by labor, so that one side gets all or nothing. Fear that the opposite side will gain too much tends to moderate each party's demands and hence to bring their final positions together.

Newspaper headlines tell how a comparatively small number of organized, strategically placed employees can hamstring a city by a strike, by withholding of full services, or by other work stoppages called "job actions" (such as police "blue flu" or the fire department's "red rash" sickness). The demonstrated success of such walkouts has meant that municipal employees have found the power to strike more relevant than legal prohibitions against it. The percentage of local government work stoppages has been increasing, while the number of workers involved in all strikes as a percentage of total employment has remained fairly stable. Data indicate that public employee strikes usually last only a few days, the mean duration of all local government strikes being about nine days, and the median four days.[14] The reasons why strikes persist may be that fines against unions amount to only a few dollars per day per worker, and management finds that the strike cuts salary expenses while city revenues keep coming in.

Strikes in the city often affect more than one function because the organization calling the action increasingly represents workers in several departments, and union strategy may also call for reinforcement from members working in the private sector (such as refusal to cross picket lines around city facilities) and increasing pressure for settlement by withdrawing from at least one essential service. However, the demand for government services is relatively inelastic, a fact which, combined with the immediate impact of their public nature, makes "essentiality" an inadequate gauge of the permissibility of employee strikes. When the government is the employer, the public views it as having the power to settle immediately. Are elected officials politically able to identify the point at which the length of the strike determines the magnitude of danger, tolerate the disruption, and describe the distinction for a disgruntled public? Contingency planning and partial municipal operations are only administrative efforts to reduce the city's vulnerability to strikes. Those who deny the right of public employees to strike say that as a matter of public duty (vital services must not be interrupted), a strike against the people must be dealt with severely. But suppose strike leaders are arrested for contempt of court after ignoring an order to return to work: will negotiation progress from a jail cell? Strike penalties may be so harsh that they cannot be applied without creating politically unacceptable levels of revulsion in the community. A diversity of legal sanctions is indicated for the array of job actions. Two observers have cautioned: "Nothing has so confused, befogged, and frustrated the modernization of public employment relations as the tendency to view the problem as a question of law rather than as an issue of public policy."[15] The public must be made aware of the costs of agreement to decrease the political pressures for a precipitous settlement.

Thus, public employees seek to advance their interests on a number of fronts: at the bargaining table, in the city council and the state legislature, in the electoral arena, and in the courts. While labor relations have an economic foundation in industry, they have a political base in government, since resolution involves many factors. The city is vulnerable to a strike because the costs of settlement can be hidden more easily by political leaders, fearful of losing office, from a disgruntled, amorphous public, which rarely votes for officials who remain firm in the face of an inconveniencing strike. Citizens inconvenienced by a strike either may not vote to approve taxes to pay for a wage settlement or may vote against incumbent officials for showing "lack of leadership" in "letting a strike take place." Although editorial writers and politicians opposed to labor demands may accuse employee groups of driving the city toward bankruptcy, they know very well that local government is not going to go out of business: a temporary taxpayers' revolt or the defeat of elected officials is most likely. For these reasons it appears that labor relations will continue as a major challenge in municipal administration seeking creative solutions.

Government as an Employer of Last Resort

Concern about high unemployment has led Congress to appropriate money for public service employment (PSE) designed to hire those unable to find work in private enterprise.[16] Federal funding for such public service jobs is scattered among a variety of domestic programs. These include antirecession aid to help state and local governments maintain basic services during periods of high unemployment and various public works and community development programs (grants in aid to state and local governments for quickly starting construction projects). The titles frequently change (see the federal *Catalogue of Domestic Assistance*, a thick index published annually), but the process remains essentially the same. The president and the Congress identify a problem area (such as the long-term hard-core unemployed, the underemployed seeking full-time work, youth seeking summer jobs, ex-offenders, or poorly educated minorities) and authorizes funding the category. The cabinet agencies then devise an eligibility formula, and the grantsmen at city hall consult the *Catalogue of Domestic Assistance*. Civic need may automatically trigger "countercyclical" federal aid (for a ghetto area within the city with high unemployment, for example), or municipalities may, along with counties and states, apply to become prime sponsors of programs for the unemployed. Large cities, particularly, are likely to lobby through state legislative and congressional delegations for funding formulas which will favor them.

When municipalities enter the job market as employers of last resort, many difficult questions are raised. How long will public service employment last? Congress, or, in some cases, state legislatures, must periodically decide whether to continue the appropriation, since programs often pass as emergency employment measures. How is hiring priority established among needy applicants? Can civil service merit rules be applied to those without qualifications, or will local politicians use these as a new source of patronage? Can funds be used to rehire already trained city employees laid off because of city financial exigency? For those without prior work experience, will government employment be "leaf-raking, make-work" jobs, or will it give skills which will enable the trainee to leave the public payroll and enter private enterprise as a tax-paying citizen? The search for answers continues to be politically important for the president, Congress, and state governments, as well as at city hall.

Decision-Making

The decisions made at city hall are the essence of local politics. An examination of the decisional processes at city hall is in order before the following two chapters on the major municipal functions of public safety and services. All those who work for the city participate in decision-making to some degree as they go about their duties. Indeed, the implementation of any policy will depend on each employee: anything that officials proclaim at city hall can be nullified by the actions seen by the public. City workers have discretion in enforcing regulations and can delay or frustrate policies they are opposed to. Career advancement may depend on keeping out of trouble, and this may stifle innovation.

The procedures used by officials to make decisions are not fixed; they vary over time among different communities. Decisional impacts can be both "areal," affecting the entire city, and "segmental,"[17] affecting only certain individuals or portions of the town. The outcome of some decisions can be measured, while other indications are intangible or psychological benefits. Politicians recognize the importance of such intangible benefits by the attention they pay to the style of decision-making (such as reaching a consensus), as well as the substance. One of the most difficult problems in decision-making is how to deal with spillover effects of unanticipated policy consequences. For example, improving a city street may change not only traffic flow but also downtown shopping patterns, with unanticipated economic effects upon retail merchants. All decision-making takes place under conditions of uncertainty, as figure 7.3 shows.

City governments try to reduce decision-related risks by spreading out the process (through public hearing procedures, for example), although this frequently results in charges of bureaucratic delays. As choices are made, more and more alternatives are eliminated, resulting in a more permanently fixed course of action. These are known as "sunk costs": costs consisting not only of the previous resources, time, and effort expended on the earlier choices but also of the options passed over (hence "opportunity costs"). Policy is therefore frequently copied from nearby cities: if a neighboring jurisdiction had a similar problem, what solution did it find?

Are all decisions compromises? Are they not simply satisficing courses of action under the circumstances?[18] The barriers to rational choice include lack of information, prejudice, and ignorance. To solve these may be easier than to reconcile value conflicts between the participants in a decision.

No decision can be effective unless it is implemented. Administrators are constantly engaged in building coalitions of support for their poli-

Figure 7.3. Will There Be New City Taxes? A Decision Tree. Each alternative adds branches to the tree. The sum of the probable outcomes is always equal to unity (1). Using decision analysis forecasting, we can compute the probability of the four possible outcomes by multiplying the respective conditional probabilities:

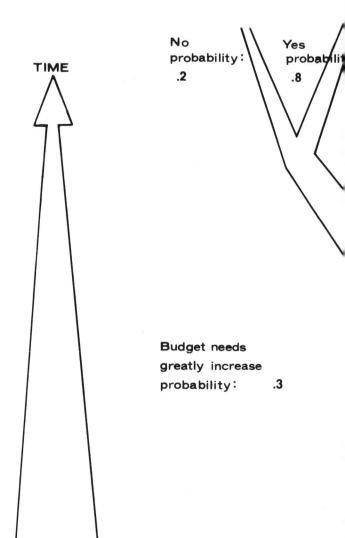

TIME

No
probability:
.2

Yes
probabili
.8

Budget needs
greatly increase
probability: .3

New tax because of greatly increased budget   .24
No new tax with greatly increased budget   .06
New tax with only moderately increased budget   .07
No new tax with only moderately increased budget   .63
  Total   1.00

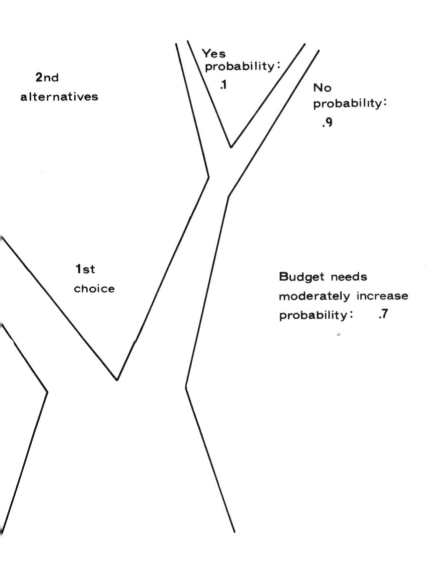

cies. With many publics to serve, no city government can expect a constant climate of goodwill. But its decisions need not unnecessarily antagonize the public (or even its own employees) by arbitrary action. The more people feel they have been involved in a decision, the more easily they will accept it, or at least the more their opposition will be based on substantive rather than procedural grounds. In observing decision-making at city hall, the importance of timing or appropriateness appears a paramount consideration. While the ultimate wisdom of a public policy cannot be forecast with absolute certainty, the sensible decisions are regarded as being ones acceptable to the public.

Notes

1. The heads of the largest city departments (usually the police chief, the fire chief, and the public works or street superintendent) can form a powerful triumvirate to resist the executive authority of a mayor or city manager if they succeed in cultivating council support.

2. Abstention from overt, partisan political activity has been the traditional price for civil service job protection.

3. In 1976, the U.S. Supreme Court in *McCarthy* v. *Philadelphia Civil Service Commission*, 424 U.S. 645, upheld residency requirements, noting that they did not violate the right to due process or equal protection.

4. Louis M. Kohlmeier, *Conflict of Interest: State and Local Pension Fund Asset Management* (New York: Twentieth Century Fund, 1976).

5. 426 U.S. 833 (1976).

6. Steve Carter, "Trends in Local Government Productivity," in *The Municipal Year Book, 1975* (Washington, D.C.: International City Management Association, 1975), p. 180.

7. This section draws upon the author's review essay "Municipal Unionism," *Public Administration Review*, vol. 34, no. 3 (May–June 1974), pp. 274–79.

8. Jack Stieber, *Public Employee Unionism* (Washington, D.C.: Brookings Institution, 1973), p. 230.

9. 296 F. Supp. 1068 (1969).

10. Stieber, *Public Employee Unionism*, p. 199.

11. The city, as employer, may reserve certain management prerogatives, or its rights to act as manager.

12. David Stanley, *Managing Local Government under Union Pressure* (Washington, D.C.: Brookings Institution, 1972), p. 74.

13. Mediators and arbitrators may be supplied by the private American Arbitration Association, Federal Mediation and Conciliation Service, and a few states have created a state public employees labor relations board to hear disputes.

14. Stieber, *Public Employee Unionism*, pp. 165–67.

15. Sterling Spero and John Capozzola, *The Urban Community and Its Unionized Bureaucracies* (New York: Dunellen, 1973), p. 312.

16. For a case study of 1971 legislation, see Howard W. Hallman, *Emergency*

Employment: A Study in Federalism (University: University of Alabama Press, 1977).

17. Lewis A. Froman, Jr., "An Analysis of Public Policy in Cities," *Journal of Politics,* vol. 29 (February 1967), pp. 94–108.

18. This descriptive phrase was coined by Charles Lindblom in his article "The Science of Muddling Through," *Public Administration Review,* vol. 19 (spring 1959), pp. 79–88.

For Further Reading

Crouch, Winston W., ed. *Local Government Personnel Administration.* Washington, D.C.: International City Management Association, 1976.

Gustely, Richard D. *Municipal Public Employment and Public Expenditure.* Lexington, Mass.: Lexington Books, 1974.

International City Management Association. *Developing the Municipal Organization.* Washington, D.C., 1974.

———. *Managing the Modern City.* Chicago, 1971.

International Personnel Management Association publishes a bimonthly journal, *Public Personnel Management,* and the Public Employee Relations Library on personnel subjects.

Rapp, Brian W., and Patitucci, Frank M. *Managing Local Government for Improved Performance.* Boulder, Col.: Westview Press, 1977.

Rich, Wilbur C., ed. "Mini-Symposium: The Municipal Civil Service under Pressure." *Public Administration Review,* vol. 37, no. 5 (September/October 1977), pp. 505–19.

Spero, Sterling, and Capozzola, John. *The Urban Community and Its Unionized Bureaucracies.* New York: Dunellen, 1973.

Stanley, David, with Cooper, Carole. *Managing Local Government under Union Pressure.* Washington, D.C.: Brookings Institution, 1972.

Stieber, Jack. *Public Employee Unionism.* Washington, D.C.: Brookings Institution, 1973.

Thompson, Frank. *Personnel Policy in the City.* Berkeley and Los Angeles: University of California Press, 1975.

U.S. Conference of Mayors, Labor-Management Relations Service, publishes the *LMRS Newsletter* and other publications.

Wellington, Harry, and Winter, Ralph. *The Unions and the Cities.* Washington, D.C.: Brookings Institution, 1972.

Zagoria, Sam, ed. *Public Workers and Public Unions.* Englewood Cliffs, N.J.: Prentice-Hall, 1972.

8: Public Safety

Among the functions traditionally associated with municipal government, public safety is a task found in even the smallest communities. Public safety activities by American cities began in colonial days with the night watch making the rounds calling: "Two o'clock and all's well." New York City in 1659 bought 250 leather buckets and a supply of hooks and ladders with revenue raised from a chimney tax. Such precautions were necessary because lamps, cooking fires, and flammable wood construction meant that many towns burned to the ground. Law enforcement functions were added much later, during the nineteenth century, in part to prevent fighting between rival volunteer fire companies which were paid by private insurance underwriters.[1]

Fire-Fighting Tasks

Our first local fire departments were volunteer organizations: Ben Franklin formed one in Philadelphia during the 1730s. Volunteer fire companies still exist in many smaller communities. The town buys a fire truck, often with state assistance or from military surplus. Sometimes there is one full-time paid chief or engineer to maintain the equipment. When a fire is reported, a whistle or siren can be heard all over town, and the volunteers gather. There may be a rotating force, with a certain number on call every day. If the municipality can afford it, volunteers may have a telephone link or citizen's band radio which tells them the location of the fire, so that they can go directly there rather than gather at the firehouse first. The articles of organization for Ben Franklin's group contained an agreement to meet together once a month for an evening. The social affairs often held to raise money for volunteer fire organizations are an important political activity in many small communities.

Most municipalities now have full-time, paid professional fire departments. American cities have some of the finest fire-fighting equipment in the world, but our losses are also the highest: 12,000 Americans lose their lives to fires and $4 billion in property go up in smoke in an average year. Most urban fires are man-made, due to carelessness, ignorance, or risk taking. Public education is thus the most effective form of fire prevention. Fires may also involve crimes such as arson or extreme negligence. Fire investigation begins as soon as the flames are extinguished. A third task is fire inspection to enforce fire safety standards and spot potential hazards. Fire inspectors are frequently present at large public gatherings. Periodic inspections familiarize fire fighters with the area of their district, hydrant locations, and the layout of buildings. Inspectors look at incinerators, heating plants, fire doors, extinguishers, and sprinklers, and the storage of combustible materials.

Fire engines roll out only a few times a day at most, but when they are needed, everything must be in working order. While many citizens are aware of equipment being maintained only when they see hydrants opened to flush out the mains, communications and alarm devices are also checked. Fire fighting is hazardous, and training should go on constantly. Finally, fire fighters perform many other civic duties, such as operating firehouses as polling places, rescuing animals, and registering bicycles. They may repair Christmas toys to be given needy children and put on the Fourth of July fireworks show.

Problems in Municipal Fire Administration

Placement of Firehouses and Equipment. Unlike other types of insurance which determine premiums by losses, fire insurance rates depend upon the availability and quality of fire-fighting equipment. This is because fire spreads uncontrolled the longer it is uncontained. Fire insurance rates are of concern to every city business and homeowner. It is not unusual to see the fire chief, flanked by a group of major merchants, appear before the municipal governing body to plead for additional fire defense forces, water lines and hydrants, and alarm systems. The city leaders are usually receptive to the argument that this investment will improve the city's fire rating by the underwriters (insurance carriers writing policies in the area). However, the city may also require a private investment in fire protection, such as expensive sprinkler systems, fire (proof) walls, and alarm systems in major buildings.[2] Because of geographical distance to minimize response time, the city is restricted in the location of firehouses, meaning that it may be expensive to purchase a suitable site with adequate street access for the fire engines. Personnel must be properly distributed around the clock, and reserve forces must be shifted around the city when fires are actually in progress.

The basic engine company consists of the pumper (capacity described as "1,200 gallons per minute"), carrying hoses, portable pumps, small extinguishers, a few ladders, and a variety of tools. The ladder truck has extendable aerial ladders, powerful pumps for spraying high-pressure water into upper heights of buildings, and searchlights. The stationhouse may contain auxiliary equipment such as an ambulance with a resuscitator for rescue work[3] (including fire fighters who have inhaled smoke), a tanker truck to carry water to areas where there are no mains or other supply, and other standby, obsolescent apparatus, since anything in reserve that will pump water is better than nothing should several fires break out at once. But too often the equipment does not meet the city's changing needs. Only after a fire disaster will the department's requests for new equipment be heeded: the elected officials are less inclined to buy protection which is expensive to maintain for uncertain future contingencies. For example, a fire helicopter for rescues from high-rise buildings[4] is likely to be bought only in conjunction with law enforcement use unless a local "towering inferno" is fresh in civic memory.

Recent years have seen the application of space technology to fire fighting with heat-resistant clothing, helmet communication, and breathing devices. High-pressure plastics are replacing canvas hoses which needed to be hung up in a drying tower of the firehouse before reuse. The introduction of "rapid water," a chemical additive which reduces friction and allows more to be pumped at higher pressure, and nozzles designed for easy handling, should significantly enhance fire-fighting capabilities.

Police-Fire Pay Parity. Traditionally, city police and fire fighters have been paid the same wages. Recently, the police have pressed for higher salaries, justified, they claim, because they are shot at and have constant patrol duties rather than "just sitting around the firehouse." Yet statistically it has been more hazardous to be a fire fighter.[5] Not only do more fire fighters die in the line of duty each year than police, but they die earlier than the general population, often as a result of heart disorders from the stresses of the job. Such statistics have an important effect on demands made by public safety employees for special consideration (such as early retirement and insurance plans) beyond that given other city workers.

Organization of the City Fire Department. Public safety forces are organized along paramilitary lines. The typical rank structure involves a hoseman (some large cities have fire cadet programs) and an engineer (or fire lieutenant), who drives the fire truck and operates the pumps. He is responsible for the equipment. Finally, a captain heads each firehouse. In a large city, there may be districts headed by a battalion chief. The fire department is headed by a chief (engineer) who invariably is a professional fire fighter who came up through the ranks.[6] Fire fighters often work a twenty-four-hour shift and sleep overnight at the stationhouse.

Other important components of a big-city fire department not seen by the public are the fire alarm system and the dispatcher and a system of prevention. The dispatcher receives the call from telephones, the public fire boxes, and private alarm systems in major buildings (including schools) and decides which equipment responds. This is skilled work because time is crucial, and several fires in progress may require special equipment. Unfortunately, as many as 25 percent of all calls are false alarms, not only dangerous to public safety should a real fire break out, but adding to city operating costs. Some cities are improving their alarm systems by switching to radio[7] and two-way-communication street-call boxes. Unless the caller answers, the fire trucks will not respond; moreover, the type of fire or accident can be explained, allowing the proper police or fire equipment to be sent.

Personnel sometimes regard fire prevention as exile because of its low visibility. The head of the detail may even be a fire fighter disabled in the line of duty—that is, the position may be treated as "light duty" rather than as a grave responsibility for a specially trained person. Sometimes personnel are assigned on a rotating basis because the typical fire fighter does not want to be permanently involved in preventive work. Yet routine prevention familiarizes firemen with their town, and if a municipality gives proper attention to fire prevention, raising its importance in the public consciousness, the city is likely to have fewer fires and suffer less loss.

The Role of the Police

The major tasks given to the police in our society have been identified as:

1. Prevention of criminality, including reducing the causes of crime.
2. Repression of crime through patrolling the community and reducing the opportunity to commit illegal acts.
3. Apprehension of offenders, which also discourages others from illicit activities.
4. Recovery of property, reducing the incentives for a life of crime.
5. Regulation of noncriminal conduct to enforce the public safety and warn against deviant actions.
6. Performance of miscellaneous services.[8]

In carrying out these missions, how do the police actually spend their time? James Q. Wilson in a sample of city radio calls found that while the common public image of police is that of law enforcer, the service role is far more common:

> Service, 38 percent. Responding to accidents, illnesses, ambulance calls, animal problems, assist an individual or drunk person, escort vehicle, fire, power line or tree down, missing person, lost or damaged property.
> Maintenance of order, 30 percent. "Keeping the peace" such as gang disturbance, investigate a fight or assault, family dispute, feuding of neighbors.
> Information gathering, 22 percent. Get a report, book and check.
> Law enforcement, 10 percent. Investigate a vehicle, open window or door, prowler, burglary in progress, make an arrest.[9]

Maintenance of order is the most controversial role, since it involves breaches of public serenity. These are disputes in which the fault is not self-evident and is possibly shared equally among the parties involved. This ambiguity allows maximum discretion on the part of the peace officer, who usually resolves the dispute informally. Such intervention in a situation can be extremely hazardous. The Federal Bureau of Investigation reports that one-fifth of the police killed on duty are responding to a complaint of family strife. Somebody calls the police, but all the emotion is focused on the outside officer. Many cities are instituting training in family intervention so that the police can use psychology to defuse the situation.

The police represent to citizens the most visible symbol of the city's authority. But the public's image can be highly subjective. To a child taught to approach police for assistance, the officer is a friend in need. But to a ghetto kid, "The Man" is remembered as hassling a buddy, arresting an older relative, breaking down a neighbor's door, or generally acting as an unfriendly representative of an oppressive society. As adults, we applaud the police for catching offenders but are highly resentful when we are caught doing something wrong ourselves.

Such public ambivalence is reflected in the attitudes that the police hold themselves. What kinds of people go into law enforcement? "Working class background, high school education or less, average intelligence, cautious personality" was the description of the modern police recruit given by Arthur Niederhoffer in *Behind the Shield*.[10] Some individuals may seek ego gratification through the feeling of power they derive from wearing the badge and a gun. As agents for social control, the police are likely to be politically conservative. Exposed to the seamy side of society on the job, police are also likely to become cynical about human nature. What do these personality traits mean for police administration?

Screening. In many small towns, police are hired without experience at the minimum wage. In a not unusual episode, a veteran discharged from military service needed a job and, since the chief was a friend of his father's, was hired as a policeman. After buying his uniform, he was taken over to the city jail so that he could acquit himself in dealing with prisoners, and he was walking his first beat that evening. A routine fingerprint check by state authorities even turned up a few wanted or former felons employed as policemen in small towns. The practice is illegal; still, the municipal officials were apparently satisfied with the men's performance following the philosophy "It takes a thief to catch a thief!" Some police departments are now using polygraphs and screening to weed out obviously unfit personalities, although such measures may be resented.

Training. Most states now require a certain number of hours of basic police training (including firearms practice) within a certain period after employment. Municipalities with small forces may find it difficult to release officers to attend a state training academy. A few states are beginning to provide salary incentives for officers to improve their law enforcement education.

Equipment. While on duty the police may act forcefully, with the choice of weapon only between a stick (baton) and a gun, because the city has bought no lesser measures (such as an incapacitating spray) to allow flexibility. The municipality must adopt a policy on the use of warning shots and the types of weapons or ammunition to be used.[11] Some cities require police officers to wear their service revolvers off duty for greater everyday protection (in effect a doubling of plain-clothes force). Nevertheless, many complaints about police action come from middle- or upper-class people unused to being detained. While upholding the law equally for all, the police are expected to treat an intoxicated pillar of the community with more consideration (driving him home) than they do a common drunk (he is taken to jail to sober up).

How Municipal Police Departments Operate

Most local police forces are very small—with fewer than ten officers.[12] In the small towns, there may be no twenty-four-hour patrol service. The fragmentation of law enforcement authority means that certain services may be provided by the state police, county sheriffs, or a municipal police department. Figure 8.1 shows that the national average is about 2.5 police employees per 1,000 population served, with larger cities having more officers.

Police departments of any size are usually structured on paramilitary lines with a personal rank structure and geographic coverage.

"Patrol officer" is the entering rank.

"Detective" may be an officer with specialized investigative duties or the next higher rank.

"Sergeant" is the first line supervisor.

"Lieutenant" heads a work shift or "watch."

"Captain" is in charge of a precinct stationhouse.

"Major/inspector" heads a functional division, or this may be a captain's responsibility if there is only one city police station.

"Assistant chiefs or chief" may or may not hold civil service tenure.

AVERAGE NUMBER OF POLICE DEPARTMENT EMPLOYEES, AND RANGE IN NUMBER OF EMPLOYEES, PER 1,000 INHABITANTS

BY POPULATION GROUPS, 1979

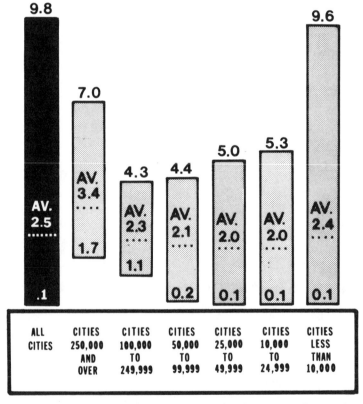

Figure 8.1. Police Employee Data. *Source:* Federal Bureau of Investigation, *Uniform Crime Reports, 1979* (Washington, D.C.: U.S. Government Printing Office, 1980), p. 233.

A professional chief of police may serve under an elected commissioner or public safety director appointed by the mayor, city manager, or council. Who controls the appointment of the police chief varies by city. In cases where there has been past police corruption, the state legislature or governor may appoint the chief local law enforcement officials.[13] Choosing the chief may be the mayor's prerogative, while in other municipalities an effort to take this sensitive position out of politics has resulted in creation of a multimember police commission serving staggered terms with varying degrees of authority. Political preferences for a chief who knows the community or legal barriers (such as civil service residency requirements) work against the appointment of an outsider as police chief, although a number have developed a national professional reputation and have moved between large cities, perhaps brought in to clean up a department.

Larger police departments are usually divided into six specialized units. The patrol division is likely to be the largest, with about half the police personnel assigned to it. The city is divided into geographical "beats," and patrol officers are responsible for law enforcement in the areas assigned to them. Police personnel are ordinarily assigned to three eight-hour shifts for round the clock coverage, although some cities have officers work four ten-hour periods per week, which allows an overlapping of police on duty during high-crime (usually evening) time.

A traffic division may be established separately from the patrol function if vehicle congestion, traffic accidents, school safety, parking control, or miles of freeway within the city warrant it. An investigations force consisting of detectives trained to search for clues and to follow up leads to solve major crimes can be set up along with a criminalistics laboratory. (In small towns or fragmented metropolitan jurisdictions, these tasks may be performed by state police.) Also, a vice control unit consisting of plainclothes personnel may be separately established to enforce social norms and may also gather intelligence on organized crime which is often involved in prostitution, gambling, and narcotics activities.

A juvenile unit consisting of both male and female officers may handle delinquency or dependency (e.g., child abuse) cases, since many crimes are committed by youthful offenders. Staff services include internal management and inspections, case records and evidence storage, communications, and vehicle maintenance.

Jail management may be shared with another jurisdiction, or may be an added task of the desk officer on duty. Municipal jails are mainly holding facilities—almost all are overcrowded, and separation of prisoners other than by sex is rare. There has been little public sympathy for efforts to improve prison conditions confronting juveniles, although youthful offenders, mental patients, and addicts may be thrown in large cell tanks with hardened criminals. If the municipal jail is used as more than a holding facility for prisoners awaiting trial, common sense dictates that those serving minor sentences should be exposed to the appropriate type of rehabilitative treatment lest they commit more serious offenses after release. Local churches and service organizations, which may criticize jail conditions, should become involved in correctional programs so the city jail is not a community shame, degrading prisoners and injuring police enforcing discipline. At least one million Americans spend some time in jail annually, and few benefit from the experience.

Public Issues in Law Enforcement

There are several areas in which the police are likely to be a major issue in city politics. First, why do police become "political"? Unlike firemen performing an emergency service, the police role involves discretion in regulating human activity. Because our laws cannot anticipate every circumstance or behavior pattern, individual officers must decide the appropriate action in each situation. These are relative criteria, depending upon the officer's judgment and shaped by popular attitudes (the essence of politics). Selective enforcement also results from the need for priorities: limited police resources will be devoted to illegal activities which the community considers serious crimes. The response of police will depend on whether protection of persons or property is considered more important (e.g., will police shoot at looters?). Police become political participants when they seek policy changes or material benefits, like any other interest groups.

While employee activism was discouraged for many years after the breaking of the Boston police strike in 1919, police are increasingly organizing today and are securing union representation for collective negotiations. Even without contract settlements, the police are likely to lobby their demands before the municipal governing body or, if satisfaction is not forthcoming, before the state legislature. In many cities, public safety employees have placed city charter amendments or direct initiatives on the ballot regarding benefits or in opposition to proposed policies (such as creation of civilian review boards). They may seek to have their wage scale tied to other law enforcement agencies or create pension systems. Police organizations may endorse candidates or give campaign money, and members may register voters or present their association's views door to door during time off duty. Public concern with the politics of law and order has led to the election of former policemen to the city council or mayor's office (Mayor Tom Bradley of Los Angeles was one example). The public safety employees are likely to be the largest portion of city workers, so that they constitute an important voting bloc, even if overt political activity is forbidden by local civil service rules.

A second issue in community law enforcement is likely to be the visibility and type of police patrol. Nearly 90 percent of the patrols are motorized; fewer patrols walk the beat. While giving the officer a wider operating range in all weather, isolation in a vehicle cuts off interaction with the residents in a neighborhood. Contrary to police dramas featuring the patrolman and his faithful partner, most assignments are to one-man cars. Giving every officer a vehicle almost doubles the number of squad cars on patrol, increasing police visibility.[14] Larger cities usually double up police in troublesome areas or during higher-risk evening hours. Unmarked cars and other vehicles may be used for undercover work or occasionally in residential suburbs desiring a low enforcement profile. Two-wheel motorcycles are usually restricted to traffic control (where they can go between clogged lanes) and escort duty, since they expose the operator to inclement weather and the higher probability of injury.[15] Rather than acquire expensive high-speed motorcycles (which cannot be used as roadblocks anyway), many cities are buying small motor scooters for parking control and to go into confined areas. Few cities retain horse patrols unless they have extensive park areas, although they are useful in crowd control, allowing the mounted officer to ride a barrier into place with good visibility. Canine patrols have proven effective, although negative publicity surrounding their use against human protestors has led most jurisdictions to restrict their use to high-risk situations for officers and to situations requiring detection of explosives or narcotics. Some wealthier cities have a police helicopter which can carry injured persons, observe traffic jams, and act as a burglary deterrent at night, spotting with a powerful searchlight for reported prowlers.

A third issue has been the assignment of policewomen to patrol duties. Slightly more than 10 percent of all police employees are female, although most are civilians used as file clerks, communications dispatchers, and meter maids. The need for women to be jail matrons and to take on juvenile assignments and undercover work has required them to assume "sworn officer" status possessing full arrest powers and weapons. But many departments have been reluctant to put these trained policewomen on patrol assignments by themselves, often pairing them with male officers (which in turn has led to protests from patrolmen's wives).

Personnel, Hiring, and Public Relations

Municipalities are increasingly hiring civilians so that the maximum number of uniformed officers can go out in the field. With more costly state training standards, pressure by uniformed services for higher wage scales, and peace officer insurance and pension obligations, civilian employees are an economic bargain. Police departments are also under pressure to be representative, although physical standards, educational levels, and the greater probability of being arrested for minor offenses as a youth can disqualify motivated minority applicants. Minimum height and weight requirements have barred not only women but certain ethnic groups. A number of court cases have reduced physical standards to the averages possessed by women, Hispanics, and Asians. Most cities having a large proportion of minorities rarely have a police force of the same composition.[16] If a pattern of previous discrimination can be proven, the courts have been willing to order the hiring of qualified minority or female applicants for every white male until the police force in composition generally reflects the population served.[17] While quotas are highly controversial (the merit principle was examined in chapter 7), police employment is highly symbolic because of its role in social control, and it has traditionally been regarded as an occupational stepping-stone for ethnic groups.[18] If police restrict the sorts of individuals whom they hire in a city of changing social composition, there may be controversy over the use of auxiliary reserve officers who are ordinary citizens (often of the dominant political and social group) who act as policemen part time. Municipalities often utilize reserves in emergencies or for crowd control at large public events, although extent of training and arms varies widely by jurisdiction. The role of private security guards also deserves community attention. Usually these watchmen have no public arrest power like that of a peace officer, merely a responsibility to their private employer on his property. Businesses unhappy with the level of public law enforcement may hire private security forces and control their training (if any) and armament. While some cities do not mind this security supplement, others have experienced problems and require private guards to register and to undergo a background investigation.

Relations between the police and the public are not merely a matter of image. They are the view of police held by the public and by the police themselves, acting as agents for social control in an era of change. Citizens want effective crime control but do not want to live in a police state. The discipline expected of police and their work in a threatening environment breeds a high in-group loyalty which external control (political accountability) is likely to erode. Morale problems often arise under such conditions. There are three major ingredients for hostility between the police and the public. The first is police brutality. While there have been police riots when units got out of control, investigations[19] have found that only a tiny portion of complaints involved excessive force but that many charges come when citizens unused to discourtesy encounter rude or discriminatory treatment. Second, citizens, especially ghetto residents, may believe that they are receiving inadequate police protection. The poor are most victimized by crime, and they may think that the police are either unresponsive or overreacting against them. Thus the public may feel that grievance mechanisms are inadequate. There may be demands by segments of the community for "civilian review boards" which can be a major political issue at city hall. Most citizens' complaints against policemen have been handled internally by the departments, in which high in-group loyalty and hostility to outsiders have meant perfunctory treatment. Most police forces have strenuously resisted departmental discipline by outside civilian review boards, and such adversary proceedings between a citizen complainant and defendant officer have been defeated in voter referenda in most cities.

A most serious situation develops when there is widespread corruption in the police department. Graft among city police has been around

---

POLICE CAUTIONED ON HOLIDAY GRAFT

'Passive Corruption' Target

Warning against the temptations of graft during the holiday season, Police Commissioner . . . said yesterday that corruption in the Police Department was at its "lowest level yet" but that he was still not satisfied.

Speaking to . . . his highest ranking officers, the Commissioner . . . said that this week he had received a two-month study by the department showing no organized corruption now existed among policemen. But, he said, there is still a "high potential" for individual graft taking.

The Commissioner said also that many commanders had reported finding a "passive type" of corruption among their men, such as taking gratuities and free meals. Such corruption, he said, is generated by the public and condoned by society to some degree.

[He] . . . pointed out in the annual holiday message against corruption that giving gifts to policemen was against the law, "no matter how innocently motivated," adding that any officer found to have solicited or received gratuities would be disciplined.

He asked that the public report any police corruption during the holiday season by telephoning . . . or writing. . . .

Names have been deleted from this excerpt from a newspaper article to avoid identifying the city involved.

a long time. A seamy section of nineteenth-century New York was known as the Tenderloin because a police captain assigned to command the precinct in return for looking the other way, allegedly exclaimed: "My family can afford a piece of tenderloin." Corruption spreads because an honest officer will find that even if he is not personally bribed, there is no point in his attempting to enforce laws that it is not the policy of the department to administer. He will not secure convictions or be promoted, so the officer becomes frustrated in his job and cynical. Certain activities (victimless crimes such as drunkenness, obscenity, and gambling) run counter to the law but are indulged by community mores or at least tolerated in certain parts of town. Protection money may be paid by criminal syndicates to police for ignoring illegal and highly profitable racketeering activity. Where the city has been corrupted by organized crime, reforms have included a specialized vice squad reporting directly to the prosecuting attorney. Media exposure (see box) of police graft shakes public confidence in law enforcement and is often made in the course of city political campaigns to embarrass the incumbent administration. A serious charge should not be made lightly, and if the evidence is strong, citizens should consider bringing in a reputable professional police chief from outside rather than simply electing opposition candidates (organized crime frequently contributes to both sides). Unless corruption is corrected from inside, police morale will be low and the city may even lose local control of law enforcement—either to criminal elements or else to an outraged state government. The cop on the take is the most effective repudiation of the concept of equal justice for all.

Other types of disruption of the body politic are major civil disorders, campus riots, or urban political assassinations. Most local police are ill equipped to handle major disturbances, requiring assistance from the state police or the national guard. Some basic precautions are listed below.

• City administrators should make every effort to establish solid lines of communications with all segments of the community.

• The police should maintain good working relationships with neighboring law enforcement agencies and should be acquainted with procedures for calling in outside assistance.

• The mayor and governing body should be familiar with emergency powers available to municipalities, such as setting a curfew and/ or closing commercial establishments selling firearms, ammunition, gasoline, explosives, and alcoholic beverages.

• Such proclamations, checked in advance to be sure they meet legal requirements, can be prepared, ready for passage as emergency ordinances in needed situations.

• The city's chief executive and police chief should carefully prepare plans of action to be followed and should ensure that police officers have the proper equipment and are trained in its use. Such precautions by municipal authorities will reduce the damage and injuries when the order to disperse is given to the mob.

The equipment used by local police becomes more than a matter of operational effectiveness if community concern is aroused. The detective fiction of two-way wrist radios and remote control television cameras for surveillance has become reality with miniaturized electronics. Electronic eavesdropping, legally regulated by the courts, may be practiced by local law enforcement agencies with public tolerance or the cooperation of local telephone officials. Does drug enforcement or organized crime justify whatever means are necessary to attack these evils? Are paid informants or police toleration of petty criminals necessary to gather information on criminal activities? Are decoys and undercover purchases of evidence necessary to reduce street crime, or are they illegal entrapments? Depending on community attitudes, police may be taken out of uniform and dressed in civilian blazers or, at the opposite extreme, equipped with hard helmets and military-style gear. Purchase of police equipment is a major expenditure, and local businessmen may resist changes in supplier. For instance, the decision to rent patrol cars on a fleet basis, so that the city merely provides an attachable roof bar with siren, flashing lights, loudspeaker and spotlight, radio, and police decals, is likely to bring the local automobile dealers to city hall to debate performance specifications and maintenance contracts. Ideally, equipment should increase the flexibility of police response and reduce officer injury. While such hardware is expensive, it can often be bought with state and federal funds. Still, although it may reduce personnel costs,[20] no equipment is more effective than the police officer using it.

Administratively, police and fire forces may be under a combined department of public safety. In a few small cities, with population under 10,000, fire and police functions have been integrated organizationally into a single unit. A patrol vehicle carries both police and basic fire-fighting equipment, and public safety employees are trained in and perform both functions. Such police/fire integration is found in smaller communities wishing to employ their limited personnel full time and can increase the pool of trained manpower available in emergencies.

Are our police effective? There are no formulas which yield the best police protection in terms of force sizes. Community toleration of crime, the financial support available for law enforcement, the persuasiveness of the police chief, and the concern felt by the politicians are all influential in determining police/population ratios. Nor is city police performance easily measured. There are many factors affecting crime rates, such as the town's location; its density and size; its population composition, since offenders are concentrated by age, race, and sex; educational and religious characteristics; economic status; and the stability and mores of the community. All of these, and seasonal climate variations which aggravate certain types of crime, are quite beyond control of the police. Statistically, the number of crimes reported, compared with the small number of offenders convicted, shows that crime does pay. Perhaps that is why the public feels that there is an increasing amount of it in our society. But an increase in the crime rate in a given community is not necessarily due to the inefficiency of the municipal police, although it may become a city issue evoking near-hysterical fear in political campaigns. The only national basis for comparison is offered by the *Uniform Crime Reports* issued annually by the Federal Bureau of Investigation and based upon possibly incomplete reporting by local police agencies. A surge in a jurisdiction's crime rate may be due to better police reporting or detection of offenses. Surveys have shown that many crimes go unreported because the police are considered to be ineffective or private vengeance is preferred.

Citizens should ask themselves which types of crime are reported to be increasing and whether governmental authority can be a deterrent or whether private precautions (against embezzlement or worthless checks, for instance) are necessary. Moreover, vigorous city law enforcement activity will not reduce the incidence of crime (such as acts committed in passion), and even crimes against property may simply be perpetrated in surrounding, more vulnerable local jurisdictions. A basis for evaluation of police efficiency is crime clearance rates, that is, the percentage of investigated offenses which resulted in the arrest of suspects found guilty by the courts. A high proportion of "unsolved" major crimes is a cause for community concern about public safety.

Notes

1. On the facade of old buildings one may still find the insurance plaque; seeing it, rival fire companies fought over the limited water available to save the premises.

2. If the city fathers are willing to enact strict fire codes requiring private measures to protect against fire, the municipal fire-fighting costs will be less, but such measures are expensive and hence politically unpopular.

3. If more than first aid medical service is provided, the city is likely to encounter opposition from private ambulance operators.

4. Uses might include carrying injured persons, water rescues, or delivery of fire fighters to inaccessible terrain.

5. Fire fighting is the most hazardous U.S. labor occupation, with a death rate higher than that associated with any other job and a frequency of injuries greater than that in police work.

6. As opposed to many police chiefs, who may not have a technical life career in law enforcement.

7. Even underground communications, impervious to fires, can be disrupted by other civic disasters, such as floods.

8. International City Management Association, *Municipal Police Administration*, 7th ed. (Chicago, 1971), p. 3.

9. James Q. Wilson, *Varieties of Police Behavior* (Cambridge, Mass.: Harvard University Press, 1968), p. 18.

10. Arthur Niederhoffer, *Behind the Shield* (Garden City, N.Y.: Doubleday, 1967), p. 38.

11. For example, automatic, high-velocity firearms cause more injury, and some officers buy hollow-pointed bullets for their stopping power; such bullets are forbidden in international warfare.

12. Half of all American municipalities have population under 1,000, so that they have either no police force at all or only one or two officers.

13. States are increasingly involved in certifying "sworn officers" possessing arrest powers by setting minimum training standards. Courts have upheld the principle that general police power is vested in state government, giving it the right to determine the size of the local force and its financial support, including police salaries and pension obligations and restrictions on the rule-making authority of a city police administrator.

14. This is an important consideration for small forces. Cars will be reduced in number only if a city cannot afford capital investment in several vehicles or if it must economize on gasoline operating costs.

15. An officer disabled in a motorcycle accident will cost the city far more than the saving achieved by not enclosing him in a car.

16. If a small town is dominated by one race, it is likely to have a police force of similar composition, especially if that ethnic group controls city hall.

17. E.g., the city of Chicago in 1976.

18. The Irish cop is legend, and Jews and Italians have also entered police ranks at later periods.

19. E.g., the President's Commission on Law Enforcement and the Administration of Justice.

20. For example, a speed-measuring device can mean that the traffic officer has the ticket written by the time the motorist reaches his vantage point, so that there is no subsequent argument.

For Further Reading

Federal Bureau of Investigation, *Uniform Crime Reports*. Washington, D.C.: U.S. Government Printing Office. (Published annually)

International Association of the Chiefs of Police. *The Police Yearbook*. (Published annually)

International City Management Association. *Local Government Police Management*. Washington, D.C., 1977.

——. *Municipal Fire Administration*. 7th ed. Chicago, 1967.

ICMA's *Municipal Year Book* also contains sections on police and fire services.

National Commission on Fire Prevention and Control. *America Burning*. Washington, D.C., 1973.

9: Municipal Social Services

Many of the social services which affect the quality of life in a community are not under municipal control.

> Local government traditionally has not been involved in funding human services, although some local governments have administered general assistance welfare programs. The federal government and, to a lesser extent, state governments have provided the real impetus for city and county government in social service delivery systems.[1]

In most parts of the country, however, counties play a much larger role than do municipalities in the direct delivery of human services, especially in health and welfare. Service responsibilities typically are divided among state, county, and municipal governments, plus various private voluntary associations. Nevertheless, the city is the location where complex human problems are focused and is the arena where programs meet people in need. This chapter considers the administrative points of contact—resulting in either friction or cooperation—between city hall and other organizations which provide education, health, housing, and welfare services.

The City and the Schools

In most states public education is undertaken by independent special districts with separately elected school boards having their own taxing powers. In some states, the county or the city governing body appoints school board members, who then have policy-making autonomy during their terms of office. In other jurisdictions, the city or county governments may even be obligated to raise portions of the revenue needed to finance the budget set by the school board. Such financial obligations may make the city and schools rivals for available tax sources. They may even have competing bond issues on the same election ballot!

The idea behind making school districts semiautonomous entities operating in a municipality is to remove education from politics. Yet the public expects schools to solve many of the problems facing urban society: teaching job skills to reduce unemployment, promoting health education on the dangers of drug abuse, creating recreation and athletic entertainment for the community, resolving racial conflict by integration, reducing hunger through lunch programs, instilling safe driving habits, and preventing juvenile delinquency by keeping teenagers in the classroom during the day—to name a few. The culture of poverty which loses payroll and tax bases for a city similarly creates educational problems. Even in wealthy communities, the competition for resources has been indicated by city employees striking, following the teachers' example. With education taking the largest single portion of the local tax dollar, schools cannot avoid the politics of allocation. Even where a substantial proportion of children are enrolled in parochial schools, city governments may be under pressure to provide services to pupils (providing that this does not infringe the constitutional separation of church and state).

Administratively, the school board usually coordinates with municipal government in the following six major areas:

Location of schools. Are there city sidewalks, crosswalks, and traffic signals placed along city streets where cars and children meet? What police assignments are needed during school hours to deal with traffic problems? Are schools located along transportation routes, and do students ride city buses?

Recreational facilities. Are playgrounds, swimming pools, athletic fields, and other facilities such as auditoriums used by the community during nonschool hours? Do the city, the schools, or both divide the costs of recreation programs?

Crime and vandalism. Educators have traditionally been reluctant to let police mount undercover operations in the schools. Yet with crimes, even shootouts between warring gangs, on the school grounds, security forces have been hired by school boards, and the city police are called in to make investigations. During vacations there may be costly vandalism of school property. Guns, narcotics, and stolen property may be traded on the school grounds for later resale on the streets. With a "closed campus" policy, nearby merchants may complain of loss of school pupil business during lunch time; however, free egress has in some neighborhoods resulted in increases of shoplifting and daytime burglary. Juvenile delinquency points to the need for closer cooperation between schools and government to provide effective youth services.

De facto segregation and busing. School segregation was held illegal by the U.S. Supreme Court in 1954,[2] but has persisted as a result of housing patterns. Popular desire for the neighborhood school, which is easily accessible to children, has meant that enrollment reflects the prevailing ethnic makeup of the area. Residential patterns, in turn, are influenced by the city's zoning laws and building codes, as discussed in the next chapter. When courts have ordered pupils bused to schools outside their neighborhood, intervention by local law enforcement agencies has sometimes been necessary to maintain order.

Educational programs for city health problems. A high incidence of venereal disease or drug abuse indicates the need for sex education or drug information programs. Some segments of the community may strenuously oppose such proposed topics in the curriculum, and such controversies have bitterly polarized some towns.

Community control of the schools. Decentralization of a few large metropolitan school systems into neighborhood units has been tried with mixed results, most notably in New York City.[3] If decentralization creates conflict, city politicians are often drawn into the melee, initially as peacemakers, but eventually because of the implication for decentralizing city services (see chapter 4).

Community Health and Sanitation

Originally public health consisted of quarantine measures to isolate those with infectious diseases and the abatement of nuisances constituting hazards to public health. Services offered by health units at the local level now include several other functions.

Preventive Medicine and Public Health Education. Because of the advent of inoculations and acceptable standards of public cleanliness, quarantine notices are now seen rarely. Unfortunately, many children do not receive necessary immunizations unless schools require proof for enrollment. Except for the common cold, venereal diseases are the most prevalent communicable diseases in the city today and are being combated by a campaign that has involved signs on city buses and other public dissemination of information about VD.

Sanitation Services. The collection and disposal of rubbish has been expanded to the entire field of environmental sanitation. This ranges from city inspection of food processors to legal standards for pure air and water as well as ordinances to control noise. The public is probably aware only of health inspection at eating places, where a placard of approval must be displayed. Findings of unsanitary conditions bring warnings and publicity, and repeated violators can lose their license and be closed by the city.

Statistics. Collection and analysis of vital statistics gives a profile of the community. Evaluation of possible hazards from various types of pollution increasingly depends upon such long-term data. Accurate reporting requires the cooperation of private physicians and nurses.

Drug Abuse Programs. Alcohol and drug abuse is a suburban as well as an inner city problem reflected in many traffic accidents, overdoses, and drug-related suicides. Whether the community response should be law enforcement or treatment poses an administrative dilemma. The rising rate of addiction strains the resources of local law enforcement. Major undercover investigations and substantial amounts of money may be budgeted for buys from pushers, although this practice merely touches the symptoms. Cities often contract with private treatment organizations because government means prosecution to those for whom help is sought. Some cities have sponsored information hot lines, counseling, rap groups, and referrals to a detoxification center. But most voters are unsympathetic to storefront clinics or residential facilities for addicts located in their neighborhood. Effective community-based treatment programs require coordination between law enforcement personnel, health officials, and school counselors.

Child Welfare. Common issues in child welfare are family planning, unwed parenthood, maternal and child health services in baby clinics, nutrition programs, and dependent (neglected or abandoned) or abused children. Individual programs in these areas are undertaken by family service agencies, the Salvation Army, the Young Men's/Young Women's Christian Associations, and other service organizations funded by churches, the Community Chest or United Way, and local governments. While municipalities have long run detention centers or group homes for delinquent youths, runaway children and teenagers need other treatment. As the proportion of working mothers rises, municipalities have increasingly been called upon to offer day care services directly or to fund their delivery.[4]

Mental Health. Outpatient counseling tries to reach those in need. Both mental health and retardation programs are increasingly being run on a community treatment basis. Living facilities and sheltered workshops for the retarded or handicapped are sometimes opposed by residents, who may support such efforts in theory but not in their neighborhood. Mental health centers may be administered by private or public nonprofit organizations under local government auspices, offering counseling programs, rape treatment, and crisis intervention or suicide prevention teams.

Operation of Hospitals. A municipal hospital was established as early as 1736 in New York and still operates under the name Bellevue. Even with federal and state governments paying for care of the poor under medicaid, hospital operations tend to run a chronic deficit. Because federal categorical grants for hospital construction have diminished, hospital special districts are now less feasible, prompting regional (and cost-sharing) health systems agencies. Many rural communities face an acute health practitioner shortage, with local governments pleading with the federal government to assign them doctors from the public health service or nearby military bases. The development of electronic telemetry equipment allows cities to train police and firemen as emergency medical technicians, enabling them to follow the directions of doctors monitoring a patient's condition while still at the scene of the emergency.

The service area of municipal health departments may vary. City health departments may serve a single jurisdiction or one or more counties as well. Or other county, regional, or state health units may serve the city. Administratively, the health department is headed by a medical doctor as public health officer, or the physicians in private practice may collectively serve part time as the board of health.

Public Housing

The Federal Housing Act of 1937 permitted creation of public housing authorities with generous federal financing if state and local governments approved construction.[5] Housing projects may be owned and operated by the local housing authority or units may be leased from private contractors. Rents are scaled to family income, while municipal services are provided at minimal cost. An influx of poor families was frequently resisted by long-time neighborhood residents, so that public housing was defeated in some communities by referendum. Elsewhere, a concentration of large public projects proved unmanageable; some were later demolished.[6] During the past decade, federal housing policy has shifted from such projects to subsidies enabling poor families to rent or buy existing housing.

Despite an improvement in American living standards, urban housing problems remain. Inflation pushed the average cost of new home construction in the 1980s to more than $60,000, beyond the means of many families. The "trickle down" theory that poorer families will eventually move into homes vacated by those buying new houses did not work because new home construction never met the goal sought by the Federal Housing Act of 1949, which promised "a decent home and a suitable living environment for every American family."

Municipal government is constantly concerned with housing. Most of its services and many of its regulations are designed to provide optimum residential living. Yet government activity is minimal in shaping the housing market, compared with private investment. Even the Federal Housing Administration (FHA) and Veterans Administration (VA) programs merely guarantee the loans made by private lending institutions. For many central cities, federal mortgage insurance financed middle-class flight to the suburbs in the popular desire to own a single-family dwelling. The result in many cities is spreading urban decay and abandonment of property.

Abandoned Housing. Increased overhead (maintenance and fuel costs), higher property taxes, and charges for city services have made household operation economically unfeasible for some owners. Unable to collect rent from indigent tenants and faced with city citations to make expensive repairs, the owner simply abandons responsibility and stops paying taxes. The building becomes prey to vandals, who rip out salable fixtures, as well as a haven for undesirables. The few remaining terrified tenants leave. Eventually, the property reverts either to the federal government, if a VA- or FHA-guaranteed mortgage is foreclosed, or to the city or county, for nonpayment of taxes. Because the property is off the tax rolls, neither government has appropriations to make repairs, and the structure is eventually demolished or falls prey to arson. As a result, government has become the biggest slumlord in our cities.[7]

Such blighted areas are "redlined" by commercial lenders, who refuse to make loans for rehabilitation or other purposes. The cancellation of insurance policies makes it impossible to run a business.[8] Under pressure, a few states have urged banks and insurance companies to participate in a common loan or policy pool in such high-risk areas, but for obvious reasons no private enterprise likes to be told where and how to run its business. Some unscrupulous speculators have acquired run-down properties simply to collect on government loan guarantees or fire insurance proceeds, since arson is difficult to prove.[9]

With thousands of vacant properties, governments have tried urban homesteading measures that permit people to acquire title by paying as little as one dollar and promising to rehabilitate and live in the building within a certain period.[10] After initial enthusiasm, many homesteaders find that they have acquired a vacant shell needing thousands of dollars to make it habitable. Homesteading has been most successfully accomplished by middle-class professionals who can afford conventional loans. But such a program can affect only a small proportion of the total abandoned properties. A new variation is "sweat equity"— low-income people do the repair themselves in vocational job training programs and pay back the cost of materials later. The lesson of public housing programs over the last forty years appears to be that government can help most the people who desire and are able to help themselves. Paradoxically, by increasing their income, people may become ineligible for public housing programs.

The Costs and Politics of Welfare

The city has always beckoned the rural poor and has been an avenue upward for many ethnic groups. In a wage-earning economy, poverty is tied to employment. National unemployment figures matter little to a particular city: a vigorous employment situation means more people will come looking for jobs. Conversely, cutbacks in production, even the loss of a government contract, by a large employer can suddenly change the economic outlook for an entire community. If the jurisdiction contains a large proportion of depressed ethnic groups or youth, the local unemployment rate can soar upward to 40 percent because those segments of the population have the fewest job skills. Since the largest number of people on public assistance are too young or too old to work, the demographic composition of the city is a determining factor of its welfare caseload.

Welfare relief responsibilities have increasingly been assumed by the federal and state governments. Depending upon the individual state laws, cities may be required to contribute toward the costs of public assistance or its administration. The extent of municipal obligation, stemming from the heritage of local poor relief, is frequently a subject of political controversy. Eligibility requirements are set by state or federal agencies, but it is local employees—caseworkers, teachers, police—and private charities who identify people in need.

Thus the major welfare responsibility of municipalities is the identification of those who need help and, to a lesser extent, the function of service delivery. A pathetic illustration, which happens every winter, can serve as an example. City police are summoned to a home or dilapidated apartment, where they find an elderly person or couple dead from exposure due to lack of heat and malnourishment. Everyone disclaims responsibility. The utility company, which shut off gas or electrical service for nonpayment of the bill, points out that many warnings were delivered—which are often found in the post box, since the late occupants were either too infirm, insolvent, or senile to pay. The neighbors say that the deceased were seen recently and appeared to be all right; therefore the social caseworkers were never aware of their existence. The tragedy may be the subject of a newspaper editorial and a sermon topic, but precisely the same thing happens the following winter.

City employees in the course of their duties as policemen, firemen, garbage collectors, and meter readers are most likely to be the first officials to encounter those in dire circumstances. It is a matter of civic policy whether the destitute (runaway children, alcoholics, shopping bag ladies) are left to sleep wrapped in newspapers under park benches or viaducts or are housed for the night in the city jail on a charge of vagrancy. A compassionate city administration will coordinate with private charities and state relief agencies the services available to which those in need of assistance can be referred. This information should be presented to every city employee in the course of training sessions.

While state and federal eligibility rules have replaced the old political machines in determining individual assistance, battles still rage at city hall over their location. Where should public housing projects be placed? Where should community development grants be spent? Where should day care facilities for children or senior citizens be established? Where should office space be rented to house welfare programs if public buildings are not available? The allocational conflicts in the Community Action Agencies set up to direct the War on Poverty in the 1960s ultimately became so severe that most municipal governments exercised their option to take control.[11]

As an example, consider some of the bureaucracies dealing with unemployment: the state employment service, work incentive welfare programs, the state vocational rehabilitation agency, public school courses in adult vocational education, and the jurisdictions hiring under federal funds. Yet cities, in their role as a governmental "employer of last resort" under the federal Comprehensive Employment and Training Act of 1973, appear no more likely to solve the hard-core unemployment problem. While CETA gave temporary jobs, most municipalities could not afford to create permanent positions for those so trained, and indeed in some cities, CETA funds were used to rehire laid-off municipal employees rather than the poor. The response by some community activists has been organization of the poor into "welfare rights" groups seeking to mobilize a clientele-based constituency. While noisy demonstrations have been conducted at city hall, which often resulted in the cooptation of the activists by giving them jobs in the welfare bureaucracy,[12] the vast majority of recipients remain politically apathetic.

Developing a Municipal Matrix for Social Services

The role of the city in the planning and delivery of human services will vary, depending on its size, population composition, the presence of voluntary associations, governmental tradition, experience in dealing with social problems, and municipal financial capacity. In some communities, private charities, religious, or nonprofit organizations provide a wide variety of services. Here municipalities serve as a conduit for federal or state funding of those who provide local service. Some social service programs have been transferred to higher (county, state, or even federal) levels of government because of state mandate, the interests of greater economy or eliminating duplication, the lack of local qualified personnel, or municipal fiscal incapacity. Given municipal budgetary constraints, it may often be more effective for a city to obtain funds or to contract for social services from other sources rather than to operate programs directly.

One observer has concluded: "Most human services activities of local governments have grown up in an irregular, ad hoc fashion, as responses to crisis centered on a particular problem, or to a mandate handed down from a higher level of government, or to the actions of a demanding group of citizens."[13] Developing an effective social services policy at city hall requires the following strategies:

Local needs assessment. Social problems have varying impacts and are perceived differently in different communities. Available records should be scrutinized, surveys taken to fill in data gaps, and public hearings held. Group advocacy should not be resented as pressure tactics but should rather be considered part of the process of identifying need.

Planning objectives. Comprehensive planning will involve all interested groups and often several governmental agencies or jurisdictions. Community committees and task forces on special problems can both investigate and conciliate. Citizen participation is vital to determine community priorities, and such advisory groups can serve as an excellent feedback device to monitor program performance very well.

Choosing the approach. Municipalities have a wide range of policy options ranging among various mechanisms.

1. Advocacy. The city recruits and trains volunteers for community programs.

2. Information and referral. Compilation of a directory of services available and hot-line assistance through the city hall switchboard.

3. Coordination among agencies. The city assumes a lead role facilitating the efforts of public and private organizations.

4. Staff support. The city assists other service providers by supplying office space and transportation and arranging bulk purchasing.

5. Regulation. A municipality decides site location through zoning, inspects premises for health/safety violations, and may license personnel.

6. Technical assistance. The city acts as a human services capacity builder for other organizations through advice and lending of trained personnel.

7. Demonstration programs. The city initiates or funds a pilot project which can then be taken over by another public agency or community service organization.

8. Contracting services. The city negotiates a formal agreement with another jurisdiction or private organization to provide the service.

9. Direct operation of services. Some state and local governments have offices together ("colocation") with some private relief agencies in a common facility (community center) to coordinate services.

Implementation and Evaluation. Are the target clientele's problems being solved, or do they keep reappearing through the bureaucratic revolving door? Access is being emphasized, given the growing legal pressures for equity in the provision of services.[14] The city must coordinate goals among private and public service providers and must consider the cost-effectiveness of each program.[15] Establishing such accountability is difficult because "the foremost political consideration is that services integration always involves a struggle for power."[16]

Public concern about welfare fraud and rising program costs too often has resulted in bureaucratization, overprofessionalization, and overregulation. Multiproblem clients face obscure, ever-changing regulations and eligibility requirements. Dispersed responsibility for programs is compounded by a variety of organizational arrangements which blur accountability. The result often is termed the bureaucratic "run around" for assistance, or the "revolving door." Federal or state programs may not adequately meet community needs, or there may be a lack of program continuity as outside funding legislation is amended. Human services administrators need to cultivate local officials and the media if their programs are to enjoy long-lasting political acceptance.

Notes

1. Alvin N. Taylor, "Relations with Other Agencies Delivering Human Services," in *Managing Human Services,* ed. Wayne F. Anderson, Bernard J. Friedan, and Michael J. Murphey (Washington, D.C.: International City Management Association, 1977), p. 40.

2. *Brown* v. *Board of Education of Topeka, Kansas,* 347 U.S. 483 (1954).

3. "City to Take over Three School Regions in Fiscal Trouble," *New York Times,* October 29, 1978, p. 1.

4. Cynthia J. DiTallo, Carol Jackson, and Hugh B. Price, "Day Care: Municipal Roles and Responsibilities," in *Managing Human Services,* ed. Anderson, Friedan, and Murphey, pp. 365–80.

5. The housing authority, appointed by the city or county governing body (although some members may be elected by tenants), issues bonds to finance construction, which are backed by a federal guarantee. Such borrowing does not therefore count against the city's debt limit and can, it is hoped, be repaid from rental income.

6. The most notorious example was the Pruitt-Igoe project in St. Louis, designed in the 1950s to house 12,000 for $36 million and demolished twenty years later at even greater cost.

7. The President's Housing Message to Congress, 1974. See also: Joseph P. Fried, "Worsening of Slum Housing Abandonment Is Feared," *New York Times,* February 26, 1974, p. 1; William E. Farrell, "Housing Agency Assailed as a Top Slumlord of U.S.," *New York Times,* December 10, 1975, p. 1; Arnold H. Lubasch, "Officials Debate Financial Ability of City to Play 'Biggest Landlord,'" *New York Times,* February 13, 1979, p. B-6.

8. See "Fed Outlines Rules to Block Redlining," *New York Times,* June 10, 1976, p. 1, and "Insurance Redlining Rises," *New York Times,* January 24, 1979, p. B-1.

9. "Arson at an Epidemic Rate, with 300% Rise in Three Years," *New York Times,* February 27, 1979, p. A-12.

10. The Council of State Governments, *Urban Homesteading* (Lexington, Ky., 1975); "Urban Homesteading Test Faltering in U.S. Cities," *New York Times,* May 30, 1975, p. 1.

11. See how the goal of "maximum feasible participation" by the poor became, in the words of Daniel Patrick Moynihan, one of its architects, *Maximum Feasible Misunderstanding* (New York: Free Press, 1969).

12. For an amusing account of how to intimidate welfare bureaucrats, see Tom Wolfe, *Radical Chic and Mau-Mauing the Flak Catchers* (New York: Farrar, Straus and Giroux, 1970).

13. Michael J. Murphey, "Organizational Approaches for Human Services Programs," in *Managing Human Services,* ed. Anderson, Friedan, and Murphey, p. 193.

14. Sidney I. Gardner, "The Changing Role of Local Governments," in *Managing Human Services,* ed. Anderson, Friedan, and Murphey, pp. 67–68.

15. For a case study, see Jeffrey L. Pressman and Aaron B. Wildavsky, *Implementation: How Great Expectations in Washington Are Dashed in Oakland; Or, Why It's Amazing That Federal Programs Work at All* (Berkeley and Los Angeles: University of California Press, 1973).

16. Robert Agranoff, "Services Integration" in *Managing Human Services,* ed. Anderson, Friedan, and Murphey, p. 555.

For Further Reading

Blair, George S. *Government at the Grass Roots.* 3rd ed. Pacific Palisades, Calif.: Palisades Publishers, 1981.

Council of State Governments. *Urban Homesteading.* Lexington, Ky., 1975.

Friedan, Bernard J., and Kaplan, Marshall. *The Politics of Neglect: Urban Aid from Model Cities to Revenue Sharing.* Cambridge, Mass.: M.I.T. Press, 1975.

International City Management Association. *Community Health Services* and *Managing Human Services.* Washington, D.C.: International City Management Association, 1977. (These additions to the municipal management "green book" series contain numerous selections and bibliographies.)

Krosney, Herbert. *Beyond Welfare: Poverty in the Supercity.* New York: Holt, Rinehart, and Winston, 1966.

Moynihan, Daniel P. *Maximum Feasible Misunderstanding.* New York: Free Press, 1969.

Pressman, Jeffrey L., and Wildavsky, Aaron B. *Implementation: How Great Expectations in Washington Are Dashed in Oakland; Or, Why It's Amazing that Federal Programs Work at All.* Berkeley and Los Angeles: University of California Press, 1973.

Rosenthal, Alan, ed. *Governing Education.* Garden City, N.Y.: Doubleday, 1969.

Wolfe, Tom. *Radical Chic and Mau-Mauing the Flak Catchers.* New York: Farrar, Straus and Giroux, 1970.

10: Shaping the City

The daily decisions made at city hall about the location of facilities and land use can affect the quality of many lives for years to come. Even inefficiency in street cleaning or snow removal can have political repercussions. Public opinion frequently judges a city administration by its performance of such routine services.

Public Works and Public Utilities

Public works are performed by government itself and are usually undertaken to develop physical facilities or capital improvements. Public utilities are services undertaken by the governmental entity or by a regulated utility company. These are often a more concrete force in shaping a city than zoning because growth builds first on the availability of public services.

Public works can be done by city crews, while new construction is usually contracted out to private firms. Who gets the city's business can be highly controversial. It is not unusual for empire-building bureaucrats to compete with local businesses to have cities do things directly rather than contracting with outsiders to do the task. Each method has its advantages and liabilities. Contracting allows work to be done by experienced outsiders, perhaps using specialized equipment which the city cannot readily afford and would use only a few times a year. We may take the example of sidewalks; examine the pavement and you will often find the stamp of a private contractor or the mark "city inspected." The risk is that the sidewalk may be crumbling after a few years. A city inspector may have been bribed to look the other way while the contractor added a few shovelfuls of sand instead of cement to the mix to save on costs.[1] City crews perform the routine maintenance afterward, which may be boring and also may not improve their construction skills. Organized labor's position on contracting out is ambivalent. In earlier days when city employees were forbidden to join unions, organized labor urged that work be contracted to unionized firms. Now that city employees may be members of locals, labor leaders often encourage the work to be done in organized city departments or on a pro rata share with union shops.

When city business was contracted in the days of corrupt political machines, it went to favored businessmen who kicked a portion of the

---

Public Works for Private Profit

The location of public facilities is of interest to land speculators who try to obtain options on property that may then be sold to the city at an inflated price. In this excerpt, Boss George Washington Plunkitt describes the technique, still tried today despite conflict of interest laws.

Honest Graft and Dishonest Graft

Everybody is talkin' these days about Tammany men growin' rich on graft, but nobody thinks of drawin' the distinction between honest graft and dishonest graft. There's all the difference in the world between the two. Yes, many of our men have grown rich in politics. I have myself. I've made a big fortune out of the game, and I'm gettin' richer every day, but I've not gone in for dishonest graft—blackmailin' gamblers, saloonkeepers, disorderly people, etc.—and neither has any of the men who have made big fortunes in politics.

There's an honest graft, and I'm an example of how it works. I might sum up the whole thing by sayin': "I seen my opportunities and I took 'em."

Just let me explain by examples. My party's in power in the city, and it's goin' to undertake a lot of public improvements. Well, I'm tipped off, say, that they're going to lay out a new park at a certain place.

I see my opportunity and I take it. I go to that place and I buy up all the land I can in the neighborhood. Then the board of this or that makes its plan public, and there is a rush to get my land, which nobody cared particular for before.

Ain't it perfectly honest to charge a good price and make a profit on my investment and foresight? Of course, it is. Well, that's honest graft.

From *Plunkitt of Tammany Hall: A Series of Very Plain Talks on Very Practical Politics*, delivered by ex-senator George Washington Plunkitt, the Tammany Philosopher, from his rostrum—the New York County Court House bootblack stand, recorded by William L. Riordon (New York: McClure, Phillips, 1905), pp. 3–12.

proceeds back to the political leaders (see box). Such overcharging of the city treasury through excessive prices and graft led most states or local reformers (usually by city charter amendment) to pass competitive bid laws. City business to be contracted out must be openly solicited in an announcement giving the specifications required. Competitors must then submit sealed bids. The contract is awarded at a public meeting to the lowest responsible bidder meeting the specifications. Such a meritorious procedure has undoubtedly reduced municipal corruption but in some jurisdictions can be manipulated.[2] Most competitive bid laws apply only to purchases over a specified amount, since petty items do not warrant the paperwork and time involved in bidding. An initially strict bid law applying to all purchases over $500 can be amended after political pressure to a more lenient $2,000. Purchases can then be divided up over a period so as to fall below the figure over which bidding is required.[3] Second, some state laws give local bidders a 3 to 5 percent preference on the theory that they are local taxpayers and employers deserving of the city's business. This gives local bidders the same percentage edge over outside competitors who may be the lowest bidders. Third, bid specifications may be so vague as to leave discretion to the politicians when choosing the successful award or else so narrowly drawn that only the favored manufacturer's product qualifies. Performance specifications can be arranged so that only one brand has the necessary combination. Or a service clause may be a condition which only a local supplier can afford to offer at low bid. Fourth, bidders may frequently be required to post a performance bond, a stipulation which discourages new firms (such as minority-owned businesses) which do not have an established reputation. While this requirement protects the city against nonperformance by the low bidder, the bond can be set unrealistically high.

The most serious potential manipulation over which the city has little control is collusion among the bidders.[4] Several local suppliers may decide that competitive bidding is bad for profits (or even survival of their businesses) and may illegally conspire to fix prices or award certain proportions of municipal business among themselves. Prearranging their supposedly sealed bids, awards are made in rotation to the lowest bidders. Even an alert city purchasing agent may not be able to detect such a ring unless the conspirators become too greedy and their collusion is too obvious.[5]

Even without chicanery, visitors to city hall at bid openings may be puzzled that the lowest tender submitted is not always successful. The reason is that the lowest unit cost is not the ultimate cost: if the city already has several tractors of a certain make, the lowest bid for a new brand may not be a bargain because different oil filters, tires, and other expendable items may have to be stocked to service it. Perhaps the best economies of scale are obtained where state bid laws allow municipalities and other local governments to pool their requests with the state to obtain bulk discounts on hundreds of typewriters or fleets of police cars purchased at one time. However, such joint purchasing may be slower, with bids for each item taken only twice per year, or different specifications may be necessary to meet local needs.

Public utility services may be operated by the municipal government, a special district,[6] or an "investor-owned utility," a private company operating under state regulation.[7] State governments entered the regulatory field largely because of municipal gaslight era scandals in which perpetual franchises were corruptly granted to the business friends of the political machine in power. While water, electric, gas, and telephone systems technologically (as "natural" monopolies) need to be regulated on a state or even national basis (see box), a number of local services may be controlled at city hall. Fierce controversies with accompanying charges of favoritism have erupted over the awarding of franchises for cable or community antenna television, taxicabs, ambulance, and wrecker service within a municipal jurisdiction. One or several competing companies may be authorized to provide these services for a specified number of years. The city may charge a flat fee or require payment of a percentage of the profits as a "licensing" cost (also providing another source of revenue).

Municipal governments cooperate with private utility companies in granting easements along city streets and scheduling digging activities. City ordinances may require utilities to be put underground in shared conduits. On occasion, city police have used utility servicemen's cover in "stake-outs" to monitor criminal activities and even for illegal (without court order) electronic surveillance.[8]

The public utility services most likely to be directly operated by city governments are water, electricity, natural gas, airports, and sewage.[9]

Water. Municipalities originally took over water supply for reasons having to do with health and fire fighting. Until the twentieth century, American cities regularly were swept by typhoid or cholera epidemics and disastrous fires. Today, water is circulated through filter beds and sedimentation tanks to remove foreign matter, chemically treated to soften minerals, and chlorinated to kill bacteria. Then the potable water must be distributed at constant pressure, necessitating further pumps or tanks which may be difficult to camouflage in residential neighborhoods, causing citizens to complain.

Older cities like New York and Washington, D.C., have sought water from outlying areas for over a century yet still have shortages. Cities such as Los Angeles have built reservoirs and hundreds of miles of canals to import water. Denver tunneled under the Continental Divide in the Rockies to obtain its supply. Even smaller expanding municipali-

ties often have to purchase inadequate water systems (private companies) in order to gain legal water rights[10] and then have to construct
new facilities. A municipal annexation program can create substantial
service overlap with special districts or private water companies. Water
availability is worth millions of dollars in property values for residential

PHONE CALLS SIMPLIFIED
FOR A TOWN IN ILLINOIS

BLUFF SPRINGS, Ill.,
March 30, 1974—After 34
years, it is finally possible for
a resident of this town of 55
population to make a telephone call across the street
without calling long distance.

The change was instituted
by the Illinois Commerce
Commission, which held six
months of hearings.

Since 1940, Bluff Springs
has had two telephone companies, Illinois Bell and Cass
County Telephone. They
split the town in half, with
residents on the east side of
Bluff Springs' single street
served by Illinois Bell and
those on the other, by Cass
County.

The Commerce Commis-
sion gave permission for the
town to be served exclusively
by Illinois Bell.

Most utility services are natural monopolies which can be most logically
provided by one supplier. Competition would be impractical and uneco-
nomical. Government must therefore regulate the determination of
rates, usually on the basis of a reasonable return (fair profit), set after
lengthy public hearings. A franchise granted for a number of years
describes the privileges and conditions (service levels to be provided and
rate structure) under which a utility is to be operated in that jurisdiction.
The United States Supreme Court in *City of Lafayette* v. *Louisiana Power
and Light Co.* 435 U.S. 389 (1978) held 5 to 4 that cities operating
municipal utilities are subject to federal antitrust laws.

or industrial uses, putting municipal governing bodies under tremendous economic pressure when deciding the placement of water lines. Main size, water pressure, and location of hydrants are important components of fire-fighting capability affecting the city's fire insurance classification and thus the amount of premiums paid by every policyholder in the community.

During the 1950s many communities were embroiled in controversy over artificial fluoridation of water to reduce tooth decay.[11] Critics contended the additives were ineffective at best and un-American at worst. Eventually the hysteria died down (some areas of the country contain enough natural fluorides to permanently stain teeth). As a result of the episode, Americans did become more concerned about the elements in their public water supply. Increasingly sophisticated analyzing devices detected contaminants (especially chemical pollutants) in varying concentrations whose long-term hazards are only now being discovered.

A most important public policy is that of water pricing. Even municipalities in areas of heavy rainfall are encountering periodic flooding and/or water shortages. The basic financing choice is between general taxation or user fees; usually a combination of the two is selected. Shared benefits such as reservoirs for water supply and flood control are usually financed from general revenues. Water users may be charged scaled rates (typically lower rates for larger consumers) plus installation fees or special assessments for connection. Few cities can afford the luxury of unmetered water. Individuals or companies may feel that their share is too expensive and may lobby at city hall to have the cost reduced and eventually paid in part by other revenues, that is, by the larger public.

Electricity. Municipalities near falling water have often undertaken hydroelectric generation as a sideline of water supply operations. In some areas with a heritage of municipal socialism, cities buy electricity wholesale from private utilities, special districts, state or federal power projects and in turn retail it to residents. A few cities have built or bought out conventional generating plants and manufacture their own electricity, but usually as a supplement to an earlier hydroelectric capacity. In an era of spiraling utility rates, advocates of municipal power systems contend that eminent domain powers for construction and exemption from state and federal taxes allow a city to retail power at cheaper rates, and often make a profit for the city rather than for a private company.[12] Critics point out that virtually all good hydroelectric sites have already been utilized and that it is beyond the financial capacity of most cities to construct new generating plants (nuclear or conventional) or to buy existing ones. However, public utilities are reluctant to relinquish the profitable retailing systems that they already operate.

Natural Gas. Municipalities originally entered the manufactured gas business during the gaslight era for safety and street illumination reasons. Nearly half the municipal gas systems are located in five states (Alabama, Georgia, Louisiana, Tennessee, and Texas), often on or adjacent to a pipeline from a natural gas-producing field.

Airports. Many municipal airports originated as training fields constructed during the world wars and declared surplus by the military after the conflict. Local governments were given first chance to acquire these bases (and many did), although sometimes they were used to develop an industrial park or public housing. The airport can be run as a department of city government, although usually an airport authority was set up to create a separate bonding capacity to finance extended improvements.

Sewage. Two-thirds of American municipalities run their own water systems,[13] and 60 percent collect and treat sewage. Although some portions of a growing city may depend on private wells and septic tanks, residential density eventually results in falling and often contaminated water levels. An outbreak of infectious hepatitis has sometimes been necessary to persuade residents who invested several thousand dollars in their own well or septic tank to pay the costs of sewer mains. Besides insisting on a pipe capacity in excess of present needs but adequate to meet projected requirements, the city must decide whether to construct separate sanitary and storm drains. Combining them is certainly cheaper, but in case of flooding they can overflow, aggravating the health hazard. Even in moderate runoff, the sewage treatment plant cannot accommodate the volume of rainwater. Combined sewers are more prone to blockage if gutters carry leaves and sticks into them. Cities having industry with toxic byproducts may have to invest in a third type, an industrial outfall sewer. Otherwise chemicals (even those discarded following experiments in school laboratories) can destroy normal biological breakdown treatment. The magnitude of waste for disposal presents real problems for metropolitan areas: New York City operates a fleet of sewage boats which round the clock dump twelve miles offshore and have created an ecological "dead zone" in the sea. Industrial outfall sewers into the ocean, abandoned mines, and other dumping places are under increasing scrutiny by environmentalists.

Pollution Regulation

Under federal water quality control acts,[14] municipalities can be sued in federal court for being polluters. The fact that cities can sue upstream polluters, and can also be sued themselves, has largely eliminated dangerous situations: rivers running through Cleveland and

Detroit were so contaminated that they caught on fire, and St. Louis dumped its sewage untreated into the Mississippi, from which Memphis draws its water downstream.[15] Under the stimulus of federal legal action, states have adopted water quality standards specifying that their cities can no longer remove solids as primary treatment and dump the remaining liquid into the nearest lake, stream, or ocean to finish decomposing. Most municipalities have secondary treatment distinguishable at the sewer farm by the effluent being sprayed into the air to hasten oxidation and biological breakdown (the odor associated with this process may lead to complaints at city hall). Under progressively stricter pollution control standards, by the 1980s most cities will have to install tertiary treatment, which means that the water discharged cannot be contaminating. Purifying sewage enough to drink is very expensive, and neighboring jurisdictions are banding together (with substantial federal grants) to build treatment plants and industrial outfall sewers.

Disposal of household garbage and other refuse, called solid waste, was cited by municipal officials as their number one problem in a survey conducted by the National League of Cities.[16] Thus San Francisco, surrounded by other municipalities, added to its area by filling in the tidelands until it became obvious that the rate of dumping would make its famous bay disappear by the year 2000. After the city tried sea disposal, the tide washed garbage back through the Golden Gate. The city finally shipped its refuse by rail 200 miles north to fill in a canyon despite ranchers' protests.

While perhaps their problems are not of the same magnitude as that of San Francisco, many communities are faced with equally perplexing and expensive difficulties.[17] Open burning or dump piles have not only engendered rodent infestation and complaints about odors but have also resulted in lawsuits under state environmental standards. Since garbage must be cooked before it can be used as animal feed or for fertilizer, commercial sale of solid waste is usually unprofitable. Cities attempting complete incineration found it too expensive because of spiraling energy rates.[18] Sanitary landfills, where refuse is buried in ravines, bogs, or excavated trenches and then covered, are unstable to build on as they settle and may have long-range polluting effects on groundwater. In desperation, some cities with limited disposal sites have contoured, covered, and seeded refuse piles as an expensive parkland. Despite some noble experiments in recycling glass and metals and burning organic materials, the political fact of life is that most voters do not care to separate wet trash. In the early 1960s Sam Yorty became mayor of Los Angeles partly because he campaigned to liberate housewives from separating the cans for pickup by a metal salvage firm which had a contract with the city. In some municipalities where the city handles residential garbage and private collection firms handle trash from businesses, there is enough of one type of refuse (glass, metal, or cardboard) to make commercial salvaging economically feasible.

Air pollution control has been preempted by federal automobile emission standards and state regional air basin monitoring. To enforce air quality standards, a number of cities are suing polluters and are testifying at state hearings against granting any variances (exceptions) to the regulations.

Municipal governments enforce pollution regulation in two major ways. Under its general police power to protect public health, the city may enact ordinances against water contamination, insect or rodent breeding grounds, or excessive noise violations, to mention a few, and offenses can be prosecuted as misdemeanors. Second, the municipality may proceed to abate nuisances by a court suit in equity. A nuisance is typically defined in legal language as "anything that worketh hurt, inconvenience, or damage to another (which might be otherwise lawful) as would affect an ordinary, reasonable man."[19] A nuisance is a recurring condition injurious to the health, morals, comfort, or welfare of a community. It may be a public nuisance (which affects all who come within its sphere of operation) or a private one (limited in its injurious effects to one or a few people). The city may sue in the first situation and may encourage litigation by the affected people in the second.

Transportation

The costs to the city for present modes of transportation are seen in vehicle congestion even when it is not rush hour: nearly half the nation's driving is done on the 15 percent of the highways and streets in urban areas. There are other costs for city government. As much as a third of a city's land surface is devoted to freeways, streets, and parking lots, with an even higher proportion in central business districts.[20] Routine traffic patrol and accident investigation are the most time-consuming activities of city police. Street paving, repair, cleaning (possibly snow removal), and illumination take considerable portions of the municipal budget. An improper road gradient, although imperceptible to the motorist, can affect drainage and preclude subsequent installation of gravity flow sewers, with dire results for those living along the street.

The decisions as to where street and major highway routes will be located produce exceedingly permanent effects and can change the economic and social life of the city. Federally financed interstate freeways have cut wide swaths through cities, cordoning off certain areas. People want convenient access to expressways but do not want to live near interchanges and noisy traffic which vibrates twenty-four hours a day with heavy trucks. Building a highway is expensive, and trenching below ground level and landscaping to reduce noise add considerably to the cost, especially in arid areas which require sprinklers for shrubbery. Municipal governments frequently lobby state and federal highway planners to influence routing and landscaping decisions.

At the local level, traffic engineering comprises a substantial activity for the public works department. Smaller towns may employ civil engineering firms as technical consultants. This is likely to be a long-term relationship lasting twenty or thirty years, since planning decisions on siting and gradients for streets and sewer mains must be made long before construction is actually done. Such plans are the product of the engineering consultant, and the city wishing to change these recommmendations has the choice of breaching professional ethics by turning drawings and specifications over to a competing firm or else incurring reengineering costs. Moreover, a municipality must coordinate street plans with adjacent jurisdictions so that four-lane highways do not shrink to two lanes at the city limits.

Street configurations result from consideration of competing uses. Shall maintenance costs be minimized by limiting heavy traffic to designated truck routes through town, or does this restrict commercial activity? Shall traffic flow be maximized by restricting parking, or do merchants insist upon on-street parking? Shall high-volume diagonal parking which cuts available street area to one lane in each direction be used, or parallel parking, which might allow an additional lane? Which configuration has a lower accident rate? Two issues which provoke conflicts at city hall are one-way routes and parking meters. It is not uncommon for policies to be reversed with a change of officials after an election campaign dominated by these issues. Increasing traffic volume can be channeled with less congestion by prohibiting lefthand turns and introducing one-way streets. Such limitations may be bitterly resisted by adjacent retail merchants or property owners because old driving habits are upset and shopping patterns altered. The optimum routing scheme based on scientific traffic flow measurements is frequently compromised at city hall in response to pressure and pleas for exceptions which, considered singly, appear reasonable. Only a portion of the original plan may be adopted, which in practice turns out to be unworkable (one-way streets suddenly become two-way) or does not produce the level of benefits initially projected.

Parking meters were introduced as a user fee and are a steady revenue producer because they can be altered for coins of larger denomination. By putting fine collection boxes on every few meters, enforcement compliance is achieved largely without court appearances. The growth of shopping centers with free parking has often brought agitation from central business district merchants for meter removal as the panacea to revive downtown retail trade. Since long-established downtown merchants are likely to have considerable political clout, city street conversion into pedestrian malls and similar improvements represents a municipal subsidy to keep them competitive. The cost of parking decks is prohibitive unless the city's parking garage cost can be counted toward federal urban renewal matching requirements.

Many larger cities are in the transportation business, either directly or through a public mass transit authority. All subways and the few remaining streetcar (or light rail) lines are under public ownership for construction reasons, since eminent domain authority is used to obtain rights-of-way. The network of interurban electric streetcars which developed during the first third of this century has been replaced by the private automobile. Some cities now use the overhead wires originally powering streetcars for electric buses which can maneuver in and out of traffic. Fewer than 3 percent of municipalities operate other kinds of transportation systems, usually bus lines; originally franchised to private operators, many bus lines are now losing money because of increased costs of fuel and unionized drivers. To keep fares low, the city is forced to subsidize them (either directly or by guaranteeing school pupil riders) and eventually to take them over outright. The breaking point usually comes when the private operator asks for a revision of the franchise for higher fares (which are politically unacceptable), often to replace obsolete vehicles. Unable to raise rates to obtain capital, the private operator abandons the franchise, leaving the city the choice of losing bus service or operating it publicly. Since the elderly and those who cannot afford a private auto may depend on public transportation to reach their jobs,[21] the city may enter business, especially if a large federal grant can be obtained from the department of transportation to purchase a new fleet of buses. This may be opposed by competing taxicab operators, who argue that, given the diffused origin and random destination of most trips, cabs should handle the traffic rather than bus lines, which would require a public subsidy. Since shopping, errands, and recreational driving constitute a large proportion of use, and given the noneconomic psychological preferences for private cars,[22] it seems unlikely that city buses will noticeably relieve congestion on the streets. Some municipalities have experimented with minibuses circling downtown areas and providing more frequent service, but these are expensive to operate, with fewer revenue-producing seats. The flat rate fares typically charged mean that the city must usually obligate funds for an operating subsidy from taxes on property, business, or gasoline.

Transportation administration remains a most vexing problem for the city, as illustrated by the common pothole. Every year alternating freezings and thawings weaken the roadbed, causing ruts or holes to appear. Disgruntled citizens complain, not realizing that lasting repairs cannot be made until the water has evaporated or has been removed and the crevice filled with chert and paved. A premature patching will not last and will bring further criticism of the work done by city crews. In urban transportation policy as well a durable solution to problems is being sought.

Planning and Land Use

Besides deciding placement of public works and utilities, most municipalities attempt to control the use of land by the private sector.

Legal Powers and Court Cases. The city's authority to regulate land use derives from its general police power to protect public health, from abating hazards to promoting a healthful environment. In the landmark test case, *Village of Euclid (Ohio)* v. *Ambler Realty Co.* in 1926, the U.S. Supreme Court ruled 5 to 4 that a municipality's welfare, safety, and health powers allow it to pass restrictive zoning ordinances prohibiting certain types of usage.[23] For nearly half a century after upholding the principle of zoning, the U.S. Supreme Court declined to hear appeals on the subject. In 1974, in *Belle Terre* v. *Boraas*,[24] the Court upheld, 7 to 2, a Long Island village ordinance which permitted only single-family dwellings and banned occupancy by more than two unrelated people.[25] Since this zoning law prohibited apartments, boarding lodgings, and fraternity houses, a group of college students sued, contending that their constitutional rights of privacy and freedom of association were being violated. The majority opinion, written by Justice William O. Douglas held: "The police power is not confined to the elimination of filth, stench, and unhealthy places. It is ample to lay out zones where family values, . . . and the blessings of quiet seclusion and clean air make the area a sanctuary for people."[26] In *City of Eastlake (Ohio)* v. *Forest City Enterprises, Inc.*,[27] the Court held 6 to 3 that city voters, by popular referendum, have the right to decide zoning in their communities. The Court's recent receptiveness toward such cases has prompted a number of zoning appeals, which appear to be broadening administrative authority. The Court has ruled 5 to 4 that it is constitutional for cities to use zoning laws to restrict the proliferation of adult movie theaters, bookstores, bars, and similar establishments.[28] Upholding a Detroit ordinance which required 1,000 feet between such sexually oriented businesses as well as that they be located away from residences, the majority ruled: "The city's interest in attempting to preserve the quality of urban life is one that must be accorded high respect. Moreover, the city must be allowed a reasonable opportunity to experiment with solutions to admittedly serious problems."[29]

Tools for Municipal Planning. A master plan shows the present land uses and projected needs of the city. It is a design for optimum land usage, given the population and economic requirements of the community. Zoning ordinances are adopted which classify the permissible land uses in accordance with the master plan. Besides zoning, existing structures may be regulated by city building codes which require safe conditions. (Code enforcement is discussed in a following section on urban renewal.) Further, various subdivision controls[30] may be placed on new development in accordance with the master plan. When necessary, through its power of eminent domain, a city may condemn private land for a wide variety of public purposes. In such legal action, the government requires the property owner to sell his land at a fair market price to make way for some public project. This action can be challenged in court.

The specifics of a planning bureaucracy depend upon the size of the city. The physical appearance of too many American municipalities suggests no coherence at all in designing the community. Is planning an expensive delusion at city hall? One observer has concluded: "Hundreds of communities have gone through the years with both civic leadership and the people assuming that zoning—and not very adequate zoning at that—constitutes city planning."[31] Most municipalities cannot afford the services of a resident professional, certified by the American Planning Association, until it reaches about 50,000 population, by which time it is too late. Most smaller jurisdictions use planning technicians (paraprofessionals usually with training in drafting) in the city engineer's office or public works department, with a planning consulting firm hired to do a master plan and other major planning contracts. Day-to-day administration is handled by a part-time planning commission composed of local citizens, with possibly a separate board of zoning appeals. The advantages of this typical arrangement are economy, with routine tasks being performed by the engineering, building, and other city departments but with the prestige of an outside expert planning consultant. The disadvantage is that expert advice is intermittent, and not on the day-to-day decisions which shape the city. A few nationally known consultant firms are notorious for preparing plans which are essentially the same: only the data of the contracting municipality is plugged in, the recommendations remain the same and may be inappropriate for the local community. Conversely, if a firm of local architects is employed, their municipal planning advice may be biased by their private clients. A compromise tried by some smaller jurisdictions is to share the services of a resident planner with the county or an adjoining municipality.

The Politics of Planning. Government regulation in effect limits the availability of land for designated purposes. The common law "Use your property in any way that does not injure your neighbors" has now been restricted in response to political and other pressures.[32] City planning and zoning decisions have tremendous economic consequences as reflected in the composition of many planning commissions.[33] Unless there are strictly enforced state or local conflict-of-interest laws,[34] realtors, contractors, developers, and retired persons whose income may come from dealings in real estate will frequently seek representation for themselves or members of their families on governmental planning bodies. Even if they abstain from voting on matters in which they have a direct personal interest, they benefit from direct knowledge of the way in which a town is growing or by knowing that building permits are being issued and variances (exceptions) granted.[35] A typical reaction to indictments charging bribery is: "Zoning is the single biggest corruptor of the nation's local governments."[36] Even without chicanery, tremendous economic pressures affect planning decisions. Suppose a new industry is considering settling in town. The city council, which is usually the body of last appeal in zoning matters, is anxious to have new industry to create jobs and increase the tax base. The council is supported enthusiastically by the civic development association, composed of merchants who anticipate an increased payroll. Any pleas for restraint by groups concerned with city beautification are appreciated, but progress is progress. The best the planning commission can do is to work out a compromise, generally through zoning. One has only to observe the master plan drawn up by many cities to recognize that it adapts itself to the status quo; the plan is riddled with deviations established by influence, circumstance, and the other contingencies of the situation.

A city planning commission can research and estimate the effects of a situation but too often cannot influence the course of events. Many planning bodies have minimal professional staff whose expertise is heeded in varying degrees by the city council. However, if technological advance, the prospect for profit from land speculation, and the desire to beat a neighboring rival city are strong enough, an industry, shopping mall, or other large development will be induced by almost any means[37] to locate in town, the orderly visions of the planners notwithstanding.

The political difficulty with planning is that it assumes that there is a general good,[38] a single public interest which can be identified and then achieved through rational action—that is, planning.

The Master Plan and Zoning

After World War II, many American communities went through a master planning craze. This resulted in a beautifully drawn and colored chart prepared by a prestigious planning consultant firm. Thirty years later, the promise has not been fulfilled. Many municipal master plans tended to reflect the status quo rather than an improved design for the future. Many city fathers, having invested several thousand dollars of the taxpayers' money in a master plan compiled in 1948, have never seen the necessity to revise it, since it was designed to endure until the year 2000. Thirty years, however, may have made the projections upon which it was based hopelessly inadequate.

On zoning depends the public control of land and the various structures upon it (see figure 10.1). It may be comprehensive or limited to certain sections of the municipality.[39] It usually applies only to privately held property: other governmental entities are exempt (e.g., a county can build a water tower to serve its system in a residential section of a city). Thus private pressures and actions by other governments make administering a zoning ordinance a formidable task. Two problems are prevalent.

Prior Nonconforming Uses. Legally, the original owner can usually continue to use his property as he did before adoption of the plan, although the plan would otherwise forbid such an undertaking in that section of town.

Spot Zoning. This refers to small parcels of property which are zoned differently from the surrounding area. This occurs because of the liberal granting of variances, based on personal pleas—such as the widow who wants to run a beauty salon in her home in a residential area where business is ordinarily forbidden. Besides such hardship cases, there can be real economic incentives for a desirable location in a residential neighborhood to be zoned commercial—the owner can sell his lot for a profit, while loss in community value is spread among many people. Unless neighbors are aware of the application for a variance and vigorously object, it is often granted. Such political accommodation, however, vitiates planning based on single (and presumably best) use. The zoning map in some communities portrays a mosaic of the political pressures exerted by land profiteers.

Municipalities have long restricted such nuisances as livery stables or slaughterhouses, have forced into isolated areas dangerous structures such as petroleum storage tanks, and have insisted on safe building practices such as filling in swamps and forbidding wooden structures in congested areas (such a measure was taken in Philadelphia as early as 1795). But the question remains open as to whether other activities should be restricted by zoning laws.[40] Community controversy has raged over sign ordinances[41] and other aesthetic zoning restrictions which are largely questions of taste. Should a city be allowed to compel its residents to build in a certain architectural style? One southern California city, proud of its Spanish mission heritage, did so, even to requiring tile roofs. The courts allowed it on the basis of fire safety; homeowners wishing to deviate found that the only roofing alternatives with as much fire resistance as tile were expensive slate imported from New England or lead sheeting similar to that used on medieval cathedrals!

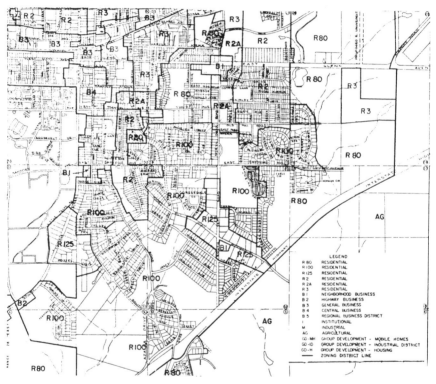

Figure 10.1 Typical Zoning Classifications. Land use is usually designated into basic categories with gradations of strictness: residential (single-family homes; multiple dwellings); commercial (enforced through the granting of business licenses); industrial (light and heavy). A higher use (e.g., residential) can be allowed in a lower use area (commercial or industrial), but not vice versa. Each has lot size, building heights, and setback (from the property line) requirements. There may also be transitional zones (vacant land or parking lots) and public use categories (government buildings, parks, cemeteries, schools, and other public facilities). *Source:* City of Auburn, Alabama.

A more insidious use of municipal power is "fiscal zoning" to exclude those considered economically (and usually socially) undesirable. Thurgood Marshall, the first black U.S. Supreme Court justice, declared, in a vigorous dissent to the *Belle Terre* v. *Boraas* case, "The village has, in effect, acted to fence out those individuals whose choice of lifestyles differs from that of its current residents."[42] Modifying its view in 1977, the U.S. Supreme Court, by a 5 to 4 vote, struck down a zoning ordinance which limited the single-family dwelling essentially to parents and their own children.[43] Such exclusionary zoning ordinarily takes the form of requiring large-sized lots and a minimum square footage of construction that only the rich can afford to erect. At the present time, state courts appear to be considering lot requirements over one acre to be excessive. However, a lot of one acre can push land and construction costs well above $100,000. The result is illustrated by Hewlett Bay Park, whose per capita income of $22,554 in 1972 made it the wealthiest municipality in New York State:

> This Hewlett lead over any other community can be partly explained by the one-acre zoning which precludes all but the wealthiest of professionals and businessmen.
> The least expensive home is worth at least $125,000, according to the Mayor, with some worth more than $500,000. Nobody pays less than $6,000 a year in town, village, and school taxes.
> The per capita figure is not dragged down by hordes of children: no baby has been born in this community in seven years.[44]

This Long Island village does its best to keep problems outside by allowing no commercial buildings in its 249-acre jurisdiction.

Zoning and Growth Limitation. From coast to coast, American communities are finding that they cannot expand indefinitely. Eventually they face limitations on space and in the public services that they can supply. To preserve their desirable ambience, many jurisdictions are seeking to limit residential density by zoning restrictions on apartment houses and trailer homes and placing moratoriums on new building permits and utility connections. These are being challenged by a coalition of old political antagonists, civil rights groups, and real estate interests, who maintain that such controls discriminate against low-income people and infringe constitutional guarantees of equal protection and the right to travel. These suits have produced a legal labyrinth of state court opinions. In 1976, the U.S. Supreme Court in *Construction Industry Association of Sonoma County* v. *City of Petaluma (California)*[45] upheld a growth restriction plan which limited multiple-unit housing construction to 500 units a year for five years. It appears that growth controls which are patently exclusionary of low-income groups or simply seek to preserve the status quo are vulnerable legally but that a well-thought-out, long-range phased plan or temporary freeze on building permits and sewer connections due to strain on present facilities, will be upheld by the courts as justifying a compelling governmental interest in adopting such restrictions.

Urban Renewal

In the past twenty-five years many American cities have spent millions of local dollars and billions in federal money for improvement efforts. The term "redevelopment" is often supplanted by "urban renewal," which indicates the magnitude of the task. While proponents of urban renewal make great promises, administratively there are some remarkably difficult problems. In order to succeed, planned renewal must, above all, be utilitarian by:

- Increasing the city's economic efficiency
- Enlarging the tax base, hoping it will pay for the project's costs
- Rehousing people living in the area—at least some of them
- Helping unsnarl the traffic and produce more open space

Urban renewal involves conservation, rehabilitation, and redevelopment.

Conservation. Cities are constantly changing with new construction. A building which is well designed, situated, constructed, and maintained will not become a problem to the city, which maintains a legal and administrative interest in every structure from its conception to demolition. The municipality's interest in design is generally limited to engineering, health, safety, and similar mundane elements. While some cities may restrict alterations in designated historic areas, this is more in the interest of preservation of original appearance than of beauty.[46] In the location of a building, the city should be careful that it will not overburden such public facilities as traffic, parking, schools, sewers, and water. During construction, the city ensures through a system of permits and inspections that the building, electrical, and plumbing codes are followed. Compliance is ordinarily obtained by the utility companies, which are not allowed to turn on service for occupancy until city inspectors have approved the new work.

After a building is completed, the city must be vigilant to see that it is properly maintained. Maintenance depends upon vigorous code enforcement, investigation of complaints, and periodic surveys—all of which present administrative problems. While a half dozen regional building codes exist (various climatic conditions will determine necessary roof slant, for example), these are suggested models, and each city must adopt its own specific regulations. Codes, like the buildings they regulate, grow old and can specify construction materials and techniques which have been supplanted. Thus, a municipal electrical code enacted twenty-five years ago may require metal conduits rather than the more recently developed sheathed plastic cables, which are considerably cheaper. However, if one local hardware store stocks the conduit pipe, copper plumbing fixtures, or other mandatory items, there will be considerable market pressure not to change the code. Also, city inspectors tend to be older men who have retired from the hard physical labor of the building trades in hopes of a civil service pension. They naturally wish to help their former brothers in the carpenter's union to drill the conduit holes, the sheetmetal workers to bend the pipe, and the electricians to pull the wires through it; they may, in short, prefer not to have the home hobbyist simply staple flexible electric cable to the wall studs. The city has a legitimate safety concern in installation, but many municipal codes protect local economic interests and make mass-produced, prefabricated housing impossible. The rigidity of municipal building codes encourages do-it-yourself weekend improvements which are usually uninspected and too often unsafe.

Investigation of illegal alterations means that neighbors have to be outraged enough (usually because they feel the economic value of their property is being impaired) to complain at city hall that their neighbor's new garage is being built too close to the property line or that a basement is being converted into an apartment in a single-family dwelling zone. Vigorous city followup of violations is necessary because people may be quite unaware of nonconforming practices (for example, if a gas water heater needs to be replaced, it may no longer be permissible to have it in the bathroom). Legal prosecution in a case of noncompliance with building codes is usually rare for homeowners and sporadic in the case of commercial structures, usually occurring as a result of fire safety inspections. (In a few cities, inspections may be used as a tool to close unwanted businesses or as harassment to extort political "contributions.") The conscientious municipality will conduct periodic surveys of buildings, but code enforcement tends to be desultory and selective, avoiding the worst areas. A city inspector as a practical matter cannot evict a poor family from an unsanitary tenement or the elderly from an unsafe single room occupancy hotel, simply because they have no better place to go.

Rehabilitation. Few cities have such consistent inspection programs (they are criticized as government snooping on private property), so that existing housing can be stricken with obsolescence—conservation is unheard of, renovation only a dream. Homeownership is the major lifetime investment of most Americans. By the time a thirty-year mortgage is paid off, many people are on a fixed income or are unable to do painting and repairs. New construction is too expensive for them to buy, and they are sentimentally attached to the home where they raised their family. Run-down neighborhoods frequently consist of the elderly (or are owned by old people who have gone to live with their children or are institutionalized) and low-income families who are renting. Thus, as a neighborhood deteriorates, people move in even as living conditions worsen. This paradox occurs because the run-down housing stock comes within their price range. City governments can do very little to stop this flood of population into slum districts.[47]

Redevelopment. Total land clearance and redevelopment is one solution taken in most cities. It is not the only answer, but this option is so heavily subsidized that renewal has been called "the federal bulldozer."[48] All states, under federal incentive, have statutes authorizing urban renewal and redevelopment by municipalities and/or special authorities.

To be eligible for federal assistance, a city must submit a workable program consisting of a plan for the designated area, analyses of present neighborhood conditions, building-housing-health-fire codes for future enforcement, and an organization responsible for urban renewal (often a separate authority for bonding purposes, but appointed by the city governing body). After land has been acquired by purchase or condemnation, substandard buildings removed or demolished, the site prepared, and the necessary public improvements installed, the cost of the project is totaled. The land is then resold to private developers and the proceeds deducted from the total figure. This gives the net project cost. The federal government supports two-thirds of any loss, and the municipality (or local bonding authority) pays the remainder. The city's one-third liability does not have to be paid in cash; the public improvements (streets, sidewalks, lights, sewers, and so forth) installed in the renewal area will qualify as contributions to the local share. Furthermore, the federal government pays the entire cost of relocating residents of the cleared area, so that the actual municipal share usually is only 25 percent. For an urban renewal plan to succeed, private investment must be attracted, which may mean seeking the participation of several large chain retail establishments or local department stores to anchor the project.[49] Indeed, it is the incentive of urban renewal that mobilizes private capital: with federal backing there is little risk.

What has been learned from a quarter century of experience in redevelopment projects? First, central business district renewal predominates. The city has too much prior investment in its center to allow decay. Major downtown businesses usually support renewal, since they face obsolescence and competition from new shopping centers or industrial parks on the urban periphery. Therefore, problems with eminent domain are less prevalent in commercial districts (homeowners will not complain that they are being dispossessed), because renewal is not going to change the complexion of the area. Second, redevelopment costs are going to be much more expensive than envisaged in the original plan, as inflation takes its course during the ten years or more of the project. A number of American municipalities, for example, have vacant fields downtown; by 1978, when the land acquired in 1968 had been cleared and prepared for resale, the cost caused potential buyers to lose interest. Third, many of the small businesses originally located in the renewal area never reopen. Small businessmen who operate in a slum district either have been there for many years as the area deteriorated and will use their renewal condemnation money to retire or are marginal enterprises which were located there because rents were cheap. They may also have had the poor as customers (pawnshops, used furniture and clothing stores, bars or poolrooms are examples). If so, they may find that floor footage rents in a redeveloped mall are too high, their type of business is not considered to enhance the image of the city's new pedestrian shopping arcade, and most of their customers have relocated. Fourth, redevelopment has had the tendency to reduce urban housing and on occasion has been identified as a form of Negro removal.[50] Land clearance often disperses low-income people to other available housing that they can afford, which can create crowded conditions elsewhere in the city.

By the time redevelopment is completed, the costs can be so high that it is possible for commercial activity alone to recoup the outlay. In recent years, the federal government has recognized this drawback, providing relocation assistance, and requiring the workable program to specify a mixture of residential/commercial uses for redeveloped areas. The hard economic facts are, however, that cities will not embark upon renewal projects unless they have commitments from large private investors. Banks, financial institutions, and insurance companies will not lend money to private developers unless they can show a reasonable prospect of profitable commercial activity and the sale of condominiums or other residential housing in the area to be redeveloped. In redevelopment acreage which has failed to attract private investors, in desperation some municipalities have used the site for public facilities—city hall, police station and/or jail, library, civic auditorium, stadium, public housing projects for the poor and elderly. State and federal governments have also been persuaded to locate offices and other facilities on unsold parcels. Although the vacant land is put to beneficial use, it is expensive renewal for the municipality because governmental ownership exempts it from property tax rolls.

While erosion of downtown retail trade and population flight from the center of the city have brought serious problems, service and office employment often becomes the largest generator of jobs. Downtown areas remain the major transportation hub and may be the most important single contributor of property and sales taxes to the city. Realization of community plans is contingent more upon private enterprise than upon any government regulatory action.

The City Tomorrow

Although we are beset by urban problems, "far too little attention has been devoted to the public administration process in our cities."[51] This book has endeavored to present a succinct survey of the administrative dynamics of managing municipal government. The continuing challenge of this career has been graphically described by the distinguished planner and experienced administrator, Roger Starr:

> By eight, or ten, or eleven o'clock in the evening the last speaker says he is certain that having heard what the people want, the elected officials will [or will not] proceed along the lines they previously indicated. . . . Two groups slowly rise to their feet and with a last cajoling, threatening, fearful, unhappy glance at the officials, wander out of the hearing room. . . .
>
> At that hour of the night no one official with the power to decide, can once again review the arguments and counterarguments . . . in which he has been left to soak. The burden is in the case he is carrying, crammed with the responsibility for making a decision which may be right, may be wrong, may be neither or both, that will offend, please, anger, placate, irritate. Newspaper editorials, telephone calls, casual words from old friends over a highball, a bland assumption on the part of someone who gave $4,000 to the last campaign, an emotional plea from an old woman he didn't know—all weigh on him, all make him hate to face the need to make a decision. . . . Walking down the steps to the car, the thought does not please him. He hates fights; he hates being unpopular; he hates the interior squirming, the sense of guilt, that corrodes him when he speaks to reassure the old woman that what she fears will never be done, knowing that he may be very well forced to order it. Of course he can hope that one group will settle for gaining . . . a little less than it has said it requires, and perhaps more likely, that another group already blessed, may give a little more than it wishes in order to maintain peace, to keep the city going. That, as he disappears into the car, dropping the briefcase on the seat beside him, almost showing strain not to look at it, is finally what he has on his side. The city hall, with its clock and empty flagpole, looms above him, lit by reflected light on the darkened city. The city exists, its institutions are alive.[52]

Notes

1. John A. Gardiner and David J. Olson, eds., *The Theft of the City: Readings on Corruption in Urban America* (Bloomington: Indiana University Press, 1974). See especially "Corruption in the Construction Industry," pp. 229–36, 238.

2. For examples see George Amick, *The American Way of Graft* (Princeton, N.J.: Center for the Analysis of Public Issues, 1976), pp. 16–17.

3. For examples see the case study of "Wincanton," in John A. Gardiner, *The Politics of Corruption: Organized Crime in an American City* (New York: Russell Sage Foundation, 1970), pp. 9, 30.

4. Amick, *American Way of Graft*, pp. 40–44, and Gardiner, *The Politics of Corruption*, p. 30.

5. Amick, *American Way of Graft*, pp. 16–17.

6. See chapter 3.

7. If the utility service operates only within the city, it may be subject just to municipal regulation, depending on state law.

8. Surveillance techniques can be far more sophisticated than telephone wiretapping.

9. Less common municipal utilities are public markets and scales. The annual *Municipal Year Book* lists the utilities operated by each reporting municipality.

10. The law frequently determines appropriation of water by previous riparian (stream) usage and extraction (pumping) of groundwater.

11. Since either enough fluoride had to be added to all water to be effective or none added at all, compromise was not possible; both sides either won or lost completely. Such a situation is called a "zero sum" game and has the highest political stakes.

12. The profitable records of municipal power departments in Los Angeles and Seattle are often cited.

13. Others are served by the county, special districts, or private water companies.

14. The Water Pollution Control Act Amendments passed by Congress in 1972 set the goal of "zero discharge."

15. See Peter Schrag, *Out of Place in America* (New York: Random House, 1969), reprinted in *The Politics of Neglect*, ed. Roy L. Meek and John A. Straayer (Boston: Houghton Mifflin, 1971), pp. 167–75; and Walter A. Rosenbaum, *The Politics of Environmental Concern* (New York: Praeger, 1973), p. 124.

16. *America's Mayors and Councilmen: Their Problems and Frustrations* (Washington, D.C.: National League of Cities, 1974).

17. The U.S. Supreme Court in *City of Philadelphia* v. *New Jersey*, 437 U.S. 617 (1978), held 7 to 2 that states cannot ban dumping of wastes from neighboring governments inside their jurisdictions.

18. Jane Rockman, "Trash Power: A Worthy Notion That Doesn't Yet Pay," *New York Times*, November 11, 1979, p. F–6; Frances Cerra, "Garbage-to-Fuel

Recycling in U.S. Moves Slowly, Mired in Problems," *New York Times,* August 19, 1980, p. 1.

19. *Code of Alabama,* recompiled 1958, Title 7, Sec. 1081.

20. A study of downtown Los Angeles concluded that two-thirds of the land was devoted to the automobile. George M. Smerk, *Urban Transportation: The Federal Role* (Bloomington: Indiana University Press, 1965), p. 70.

21. The McCone Commission investigating causes of the 1965 Watts riots found that unemployment had been aggravated by discontinuance of bus service, causing some residents working elsewhere in Los Angeles to lose their jobs. Some municipalities have given senior citizens free passes or reduced bus fares during nonpeak hours.

22. Inculcated by advertising to which we are subjected from birth.

23. 272 U.S. 365 (1926).

24. 416 U.S. 1 (1974).

25. This would allow unmarried couples to live together but not communes.

26. 416 U.S. 9.

27. 426 U.S. 668 (1976).

28. *Young, Mayor of Detroit* v. *American Mini Theatres, Inc.,* 427 U.S. 50 (1976).

29. Ibid., at seventy-one.

30. Municipalities may also require subdividers to install paved streets, curbs, gutters, sidewalks, sewers, or streetlights and dedicate (or reserve for later public purchase) land for schools, parks, and utility easements. While such improvements save the city money, they increase the price of lots and the initial costs to developers, who may strenuously oppose such controls. Unless the subdivider has submitted an approved plat, the local government might not record the lots.

31. William O. Winter, *The Urban Polity* (New York: Dodd, Mead, 1969), p. 439.

32. Francine Rabinovitz in *City Politics and Planning* (New York: Atherton Press, 1969) classifies the ways in which planners see their roles: as neutral technicians, brokers specifying alternatives and negotiating solutions, or advocates who mobilize community support for their plans.

33. Houston, Texas, is the only major American city not having a zoning ordinance. With a free market, Houston's eclectic land use reflects the economic forces of supply and demand.

34. Since most planning bodies are part time and unsalaried, they may not be included in disclosure legislation. Members are often chosen in an effort to coopt any opposition to the planning effort and to "sell" it to the public.

35. See Gardiner, *The Politics of Corruption,* pp. 29–31.

36. "Zoning Scandal Upsets Miamians," *New York Times,* May 13, 1975, p. 64.

37. Including "giveaway" tax abatements. See Amick, *American Way of Graft,* pp. 96–97.

38. A point debated by political philosophers from Plato to the present.

39. A few municipalities have "defensively incorporated" in recent years in order to avoid the land use regulation that is increasingly being adopted by counties. Subdivision deed restrictions are private contractual agreements designed to protect residential property values in the absence of public zoning. But enforcement against violators depends on neighbors' filing of civil suit in court.

40. Even pornographic businesses, as mentioned above.

41. Originally upheld by the courts because massive billboards restricted the healthful circulation of air. In *Metromedia* v. *City of San Diego* (No. 80-195, decided July 2, 1981), the U.S. Supreme Court upheld an ordinance prohibiting commercial advertising billboards as a proper exercise of the city's authority to regulate land use and promote traffic safety. Signs on commercial premises and outdoor advertising carrying political or noncommercial messages were not included in this ruling.

42. 416 U.S. 16-17 (1974).

43. *Moore* v. *City of East Cleveland* (Ohio), 431 U.S. 494 (1977). The ordinance allowed a head of household and spouse, their unmarried children, only one grandparent, and minor children of only one of the children. A grandmother who lived with a son and grandson had been convicted when a second grandchild came to live with her (and his uncle) after his mother died when he was an infant.

44. George Vecsey, "Hewlett Bay Park," *New York Times,* July 18, 1975.

45. 424 U.S. 934 (1976) cert. denied; 522 F.2d 897. See also *Agins* v. *City of Tiburon* (Calif.), No. 79-602, decided June 10, 1980.

46. As noted in the preceding section, aesthetic zoning is a matter of taste.

47. The previous chapter examined public housing and the failure of the "trickle down" theory, creating an imporous housing perimeter. Rehabilitation is cheaper and faster than demolition and new construction, but renovated structures may be too costly for the residents.

48. Martin Anderson, *The Federal Bulldozer* (Cambridge, Mass.: M.I.T. Press, 1964).

49. Once these large investors have purchased property or signed long-term leases, the rentals necessary to recoup costs can be calculated for smaller businesses to take up the remaining acreage or indoor square footage.

50. Theodore J. Lowi, *The End of Liberalism* (New York: Norton, 1969). See chapter 9, "Housing Policy in Iron City: Have a Plan When You Plan."

51. John H. Baker, *Urban Politics in America* (New York: Scribners, 1971).

52. Roger Starr, *The Living End: The City and Its Critics* (New York: Coward, McCann, 1966), p. 284. Reprinted by permission of the Julian Bach Literary Agency, Inc. Copyright © 1966 by Roger Starr.

For Further Reading

The literature on the topics considered in this chapter is voluminous. All of the following works contain further sources of information.

Allensworth, Don T. *The Political Realities of Urban Planning.* New York: Praeger, 1974.

Altshuler, Alan A. *The City Planning Process: A Political Analysis.* Ithaca, N.Y.: Cornell University Press, 1965.

Amick, George. *The American Way of Graft.* Princeton, N.J.: Center for Analysis of Public Issues, 1976.

Bergman, Edward M. *Eliminating Exclusionary Zoning.* Cambridge, Mass.: Ballinger, 1974.

Catanese, Anthony J. *Planners and Local Politics: Impossible Dreams.* Beverly Hills, Calif.: Sage, 1974.

Crain, Robert L., Katz, Elihu, and Rosenthal, Donald B. *The Politics of Community Conflict: The Fluoridation Decision.* Indianapolis: Bobbs-Merrill, 1969.

Danielson, Michael N. *The Politics of Exclusion: Suburban Barriers to an Open Society.* New York: Columbia University Press, 1976.

Gardiner, John A. *The Politics of Corruption.* New York: Russell Sage Foundation, 1970.

————.*The Theft of the City: Readings on Corruption in Urban America.* Bloomington: Indiana University Press, 1974.

Gordon, Diana R. *City Limits: Barriers to Change in Urban Government.* New York: Charterhouse, 1973.

Greer, Scott. *Urban Renewal and American Cities.* Indianapolis: Bobbs-Merrill, 1965.

Lowi, Theodore J. *The End of Liberalism.* New York: Norton, 1969.

National (Douglas) Commission on Urban Problems. *Building the American City.* Washington, D.C.: U.S. Government Printing Office, 1968.

Nelson, Robert H. *Zoning and Property Rights.* Cambridge, Mass.: M.I.T. Press, 1977.

Rabinovitz, Francine F. *City Politics and Planning.* New York: Atherton Press, 1969.

Siegan, Bernard. "Non-Zoning in Houston," *Journal of Law and Economics,* vol. 13 (April 1970), pp. 71–147.

Smerk, George M. *Urban Transportation: The Federal Role.* Bloomington: Indiana University Press, 1965.

Starr, Roger. *The Living End: The City and Its Critics.* New York: Coward, McCann, 1966.

Wallwork, Kenneth L. *Derelict Land: Origins and Prospects of a Land Use Problem.* North Pomfret, Vt.: David and Charles, 1975.

Weaver, Clifford L., and Babcock, Richard F. *City Zoning: The Once and Future Frontier.* Chicago: American Planning Association Planners Press, 1980.

Wilson, James Q., ed. *Urban Renewal: The Record and the Controversy.* Cambridge, Mass.: M.I.T. Press, 1966.

Winter, William O. *The Urban Polity.* New York: Dodd, Mead, 1969.

Index

WITHDRAWN